Dave Jessup
A Speedway Journey

To 'J' 'D'
My Very Best Wishes

Peter Lush

London League Publications Ltd

Dave Jessup
A Speedway Journey
© Peter Lush.
Foreword © Philip Rising

The moral right of Peter Lush to be identified as the author has been asserted.

Front & back cover design @ Stephen McCarthy.

All photographs are from private collections unless otherwise credited to the photographer or provider of the photo. No copyright has been intentionally breached; please contact London League Publications Ltd if you believe there has been a breach of copyright. Photos credited to JSC are from the John Somerville Collection.

Front cover photo: Dave with the Overseas Final Trophy in 1982 (JSC) and riding for England. (JSC)
Back cover: Dave riding for England in the 1980 World Team Cup qualifying round at King's Lynn. (JSC)

This book is copyright under the Berne Convention. All rights are reserved. It is sold subject to the condition that it shall not, by way of trade or otherwise, be lent, resold, hired out or otherwise circulated without the publisher's prior consent in any form of binding or cover other than that in which it is published and without a similar condition being imposed on the subsequent purchaser.

A CIP catalogue record for this book is available from the British Library.

Published in October 2020 by London League Publications Ltd, PO Box 65784, London NW2 9NS

ISBN: 978-1-909885-24-0

Cover design by Stephen McCarthy Graphic Design
46, Clarence Road, London N15 5BB

Editing and layout by Peter Lush

Printed and bound in Great Britain by Ashford Colour Press Ltd, Gosport, Hants PO13 0FW

> Peter Lush would like to dedicate his work on this book to the memory of John Chaplin, the doyen of speedway historians.
>
> Dave Jessup would like to dedicate his work on this book to Vicky, his wife and partner for over 50 years.

Foreword

Any debate on the subject of who is the best speedway rider never to have won the World Championship would inevitably, and correctly, include Dave Jessup as a prime candidate.

Dave was among a crop of outstanding English riders including Peter Collins and Michael Lee, both of whom did reach the highest rung on the speedway ladder who emerged, largely from a flourishing grasstrack scene, during a golden era for the sport in Great Britain.

Although FIM gold in the individual championship eluded Dave, he was runner-up to Michael Lee in 1980, won the World Pairs with Peter Collins that same year and helped Great Britain win the World Team Cup on six occasions. An impressive resume for any rider at any time.

But Dave's global achievements were the mere tip of a substantial iceberg, his record in domestic speedway also underlines his credentials to be considered among Britain's elite brigade. No doubt his full list of speedway achievements will be highlighted elsewhere in this book so suffice to mention here that he has the British, Commonwealth and Overseas championship titles in his extensive locker.

Ipswich born, Dave rode for a whole host of British clubs, most notably Leicester, Reading, King's Lynn and Wimbledon, and after hanging up his leathers assumed the role of Great Britain team-manager from 1998 to 2000. He missed out on becoming the first (and only) Brit to win a World Team Cup gold medal as both a rider and manager when Mark Loram was excluded in a title race-off with Sweden's Tony Rickardsson.

The multi-talented Jessup also was team manager at King's Lynn, ran his own speedway spares business and was machine examiner at Arena-Essex and Rye House.

Dave may well have embarked on an alternative professional sporting career, one as far detached from speedway as it can get ... his talent on a golf course saw him achieve a scratch handicap and enjoy considerable achievements and success in pro-celebrity tournaments across Europe. His prowess at golf saw him chosen in his later years to represent England in Amateur Seniors (over 55) internationals where, as in speedway, he clocked some notable achievements and victories.

And I can speak from personal experience, despite my handicap being way above that of DJ, he was a delight to play with and to marvel at his undoubted talent.

If you ever have the opportunity to meet and have a chat with the affable Mr Jessup, ask him about his beloved, highly polished Porsche, his pride and joy. That will undoubtedly get his and your juices flowing. The name of David John Jessup is indelibly etched both in speedway record books, and justifiably so, but also figures strongly on the chronicles of golf's amateur circuit.

Philip Rising
Managing Editor, *Speedway Star*

Introduction

The idea for this book came after I had completed my book on Freddie Williams, the third title London League Publications Ltd had published about or linked to the Wembley Lions. I wanted to do another biography about a rider who rode for Wembley. I thought about doing one of the legends of the post-war era, and that may still happen, but I also considered writing about one of the riders I watched as a young supporter in 1970 and 1971.

Dave Jessup was the obvious candidate. He rode for Wembley in both seasons, and went on to become one of the most successful British riders in the 1970s and 1980s. I tracked him down by writing to the secretary of his golf club, we met and he agreed to do the book.

Some people say that a biographer should not meet the subject of their work. I disagree. To be able to sit down with someone, usually after they have retired from the sport where they made their name, and reflect on their career, is a privilege and – to me – the ultimate primary source. Yes, you have to check everything they say, stories change over time and memories fade, but it is still their memories, opinions and views that you are being given.

This book is very much an 'authorised' biography. It gives Dave a platform to put forward his point of view on his career, while also drawing on reports – mainly from the *Speedway Star* – and other books, yearbooks and contemporary material, and occasionally adding my own views or interpretation of events.

The speedway part of this book was relatively straightforward to write. Although I would not describe myself as a primarily a speedway historian compared to some other writers, my work on the Wembley Lions gave me a good background to write this book. It was also an advantage that I had watched speedway for some parts of Dave's career, and had some memories from that time, along with large piles of copies of the *Speedway Star*, books and programmes. What I do not claim is any expertise on motorbikes and the technical side of speedway. I've left that to Dave to explain!

The golf section of the book was more difficult for me, because I don't really follow the sport. I had written about David Williams's career as a professional golfer and golf official, and that of his daughter, Lucy, in the biography of his father, Freddie Williams. Again, I have relied on Dave's knowledge and memories for the coverage of his golf career.

There is an old saying, 'never meet your heroes'. So far in speedway I don't agree. Bert Harkins was a delight to work with, and he and his wife Edith have become friends – and he has got me involved as a volunteer with the WSRA. I never met Freddie Williams, but enjoyed meeting his brother Ian, his wife Jen and various members of Freddie's family.

Another person I interviewed for that book was Brian Crutcher. There are many similarities between Brian and Dave Jessup. Both started in speedway at a young age, both rode for Wembley and were very successful without winning the World Championship. Brian retired from speedway at the age of 25, but both turned to golf when their speedway careers were finished and were successful in business. I enjoyed spending a day with Brian and his wife Margaret, and have also had a good time talking to Dave and Vicky about Dave's sporting career and their life together.

I hope everyone enjoys reading the book as much as I did writing it, and that it keeps the name of the Wembley Lions alive for a little bit longer.

Peter Lush
September 2020

About the author

Peter Lush grew up in London, where he still lives, a bus ride from Wembley Stadium. He first watched speedway at Wembley in the early summer of 1970, when a talented young prospect called Dave Jessup had just been signed by the Lions from Eastbourne. He had never heard of the sport before a friend took him there on a Saturday night. He was a football fan, and watched cricket in the summer. But he soon became a 'regular' at the speedway meetings, and a Wembley Lions supporter, which he still is! When the Wembley Lions closed in 1971, not wanting to support one of their London rivals, he became an Ipswich Witches fan. He watched them on-and-off until he drifted away from the sport in the mid-1980s. He rediscovered speedway about 20 years later and started watching again on television. He finally decided to go to a live meeting at Rye House, only to find it was rained off when he got there. He now watches regularly on television, goes to the Cardiff Grand Prix each year and two or three other meetings. He has a great interest in the sport's history, and reads *Backtrack* and *Classic Speedway* regularly. He wrote, with John Chaplin, *When the Lions Roared – The story of the famous Wembley Speedway team* and then the biography of Freddie Williams, which was published in 2019. He contributed to the *British Speedway Memories* book produced by Retro Speedway, writing mainly about the Wembley Lions.

He started watching rugby league at Fulham in October 1980 with Dave Farrar. In 1995, with Michael O'Hare, they wrote *Touch and Go – A history of professional rugby league in London*, and Peter and Dave set up London League Publications Ltd. The company has now published around 100 books, mainly on rugby league. Peter often has to work on book development and design, but has written or edited 16 books on rugby league, football, speedway and cricket. He was also joint editor of the national rugby league magazine *Our Game*, and has written for various magazines, journals and newspapers on the game and other sports. In real life he spent most of his career in the social housing and voluntary and community sectors. He is also a magistrate and sits as a member of Employment Tribunals.

Previous books by Peter Lush

Touch and Go – A history of professional rugby league in London (with Dave Farrar and Michael O'Hare)
I wouldn't start from here – A travelling supporters' guide to British Rugby League grounds (with Dave Farrar)
From Arundel to Zimbabwe – A cricket followers guide to British and International cricket grounds (with Robin Osmond and Dave Farrar)
Tries in the Valleys – A history of rugby league in Wales (editor with Dave Farrar)
From Fulham to Wembley – 20 years of rugby league in London (editor with Dave Farrar)
The Rugby League Grounds Guide (with Dave Farrar)
Trevor Foster – The life of a rugby league legend (with Simon Foster and Robert Gate)
Rugby's Berlin Wall – League and Union from 1895 to today (with Graham Williams and David Hinchliffe)
Rugby League Review 2007 (editor with Dave Farrar)
Rugby League Review Number 2 (editor with Dave Farrar)
Peter Fox – The Players' Coach (with Graham Williams)
Hendon Football Club – the first 100 years (with David Ballheimer)
Big Jim – Jim Mills - A Rugby Giant (with Maurice Bamford)
Rugby Football – A United Game (historical novel)
Tries and Conversions – South African Rugby League Players (with Hendrik Snyders)
When the Lions Roared – The story of the famous Wembley Speedway team (with John Chaplin)
Freddie Williams – Double World Speedway Champion

Thank You

Thanks to Dave for agreeing to the project, taking part in interviews and meetings, reading drafts and providing photos; Vicky for her help, support and hospitality; Matt Jackson for statistical records; John Somerville for providing photos; Philip Rising for writing the foreword and reading the final draft of the speedway chapters (any mistakes are down to the author!); Steve McCarthy for designing the cover, the staff at Ashford Colour Press for printing the book and the staff at the British Library for their help in supplying materials for the research.

Dave would like to thank everyone who supported him in his speedway and golf careers.

The Speedway press: To save space and to make the text easier to read, the *Speedway Star* (or *Star & News*) is referred to as the *Star*. This is not to be confused with the King's Lynn team that Dave rode for, who are the Stars.

About speedway

Speedway motorbikes have no brakes, just one gear, a clutch and 500cc engines which run on methanol fuel. They can accelerate to 60 mph faster than a Formula 1 car. Races are around shale oval circuits of between 250 and 420 metres in length in an anti-clockwise direction. To get around the tight corners at high speed the riders have to accelerate to bring the rear wheel out and initiate a "skid". On their left foot on top of their riding boot a rider wears a specially made steel shoe so that they can slide round the corner. There are usually four riders in a race. If a rider breaks the starting tapes, or causes the race to be stopped (for example by falling off or colliding with another rider), then they can be excluded and the race rerun.

Tracks are different lengths and shapes, so the home riders usually have an advantage over the visitors. Some riders prefer small tracks, others like larger ones. One of the interesting points about speedway is that it is both an individual and a team sport. In some sports, such as cricket or baseball, the individual records are important, but are achieved as part of a team. In speedway, there are individual events, such as the World Championship in Dave's time as a rider and today the Speedway Grand Prix, and team competitions.

For almost all speedway meetings, the scoring is very simple – three points for a win, two for second, one for third, none for last. But in a team match, the two riders from each team are encouraged to ride together, to try to beat the two from the other team. To stop teammates racing against each other, and because riders are paid based on the points they score, in league and cup meetings, if two riders from the same team finish first and second or second and third, the one who follows his teammate home is given a bonus point. This counts toward their average and in their pay, but not the match score. There is no bonus point for a rider finishing last. In the text, the bonus points are shown (+1) after the rider's score. The CMA (calculated match average) for a rider is based on four riders per meeting. A rider who averages two points a ride has a CMA of 8 (4 x 2). Not all the riders have the same number of rides in a match, and this provides a way of comparing their performances.

As well as competing in speedway, Dave also rode in long-track and grass-track meetings. The circuits are longer, and the bikes have gears, but the basics of the sport are the same. We have not covered Dave's longtrack and grasstrack in as much detail, but have tried to include the major events he rode in.

Contents

1. Early years — 1
2. Starting out at Eastbourne — 5
3. Eastbourne and Rhodesia — 13
4. Wembley and Rhodesia — 23
5. Heat leader at Leicester — 33
6. World Final debut — 47
7. Top rider at Leicester — 57
8. Pastures new – Reading — 61
9. World Team Cup triumph — 69
10. So near… — 81
11. King's Lynn — 87
12. The greatest season — 93
13. England captain — 109
14. Wimbledon — 123
15. "The ultimate professional" — 133
16. Return to Saddlebow Road — 141
17. Finale at King's Lynn — 147
18. Mildenhall — 153
19. Finale at Mildenhall — 159
20. Management — 165
21. Playing golf for England — 177

Appendix: Statistics and records — 185

Bibliography — 194

Dave with some of the many trophies he won in speedway.

1. Early years

Dave Jessup was one of the top speedway riders in Great Britain in the 1970s and 1980s. For most of his career, speedway as a sport was doing well, with a far higher profile than today. Coverage on terrestrial television, regular coverage in the popular national newspapers and success on the track by mainly young British riders all combined to bring the crowds to watch their heroes in action.

The origins of this success can be traced back to the birth of the British League in 1965. In the late 1950s, the sport had almost collapsed at the top level. Less than a dozen tracks ran National League racing, with a handful more running Southern Area League meetings on Sundays. In 1960, the launch of the Provincial League saw new tracks emerge, and some others return to the sport. The Provincial League may not have had the top performers of the National League, but it bought a rough-and-ready vitality to British speedway, and attracted new young riders. But in 1964 the two leagues fell out, and The Provincial League ran outside the sport's official structures for a year.

The *Shawcross Report* into the future of the sport, and the launch of the British League in 1965 that came out of it, gave the sport a new stability. But it had one weakness; opportunities for new younger riders to take up the sport and then find a team place were limited. However, in 1968, Division Two was launched, initially running on 10 tracks, with the primary aim of providing more opportunities for young riders. Many of these venues were new to the sport, and the new league fulfilled its objective by providing plenty of openings for new young riders.

It was an immediate success. Writing in the *1969 British Speedway Handbook*, Peter Oakes said "No-one could have realised, in late April [1968] just how successful the new Division Two would be. After all, there hardly seemed enough riders around to fill half a dozen teams – let alone 10. By the time Canterbury rounded off the season in October all doubts had been dispelled. And there is no-one in speedway who can deny that the new division is the biggest fillip the sport has had since the formation of the Provincial League. Not only did the 10 new clubs bring speedway's roll-call to near 30 – but it provided racing that has rarely been equalled for thrills and enthusiasm. It may have lacked the professional skill of Division One but there is no-one who can say the RACING was in any way inferior."

Writing in the same publication, Eric Linden made the point that "in one season the youngsters of then 10 founder-member Division Two outfits got more experience in the business of speedway racing than they could possibly have got in the next 10 years of second half experience. Their careers were pushed forward at a staggering pace." Dave Jessup was one of the riders who took advantage of the new set up.

****

Dave was born in Ipswich – ironically a team that he never rode for – but when he was a year old his family moved to North Kent, where he still lives. He was an only child and says that his family "were not particularly sporting". His father John was a motor mechanic and later the transport manager for the Sunblest Bread Company who had 100 vans. Dave's grandfather ran a coach, van and taxi company.

Dave recalls that: "My dad never told me how to ride, what to do or who to beat. He did put his arm around me every time I raced and said 'mind how you go'. I assumed that he meant 'come back in one piece', which I did most of the time. He always said this to me at a meeting or beforehand if he wasn't going to be there. Sadly, he died aged 69 in 2001. My mother kept a scrapbook about my racing, certainly in the early years. In those days I rode with my boots over my leathers, and with my socks folded over the top of the boots. She stitched into the socks the colours of the team I was riding for. For many years my boots were sponsored by Ashman, who made them. She died in 2015."

Dave went to Higham Primary School. He remembers that Jean, his mother, played hockey, and would run at the School Sports day 'Mums and Dads' races in bare feet. His first sporting memory of a big occasion is "taking part in gymnastics at the Royal Albert Hall in 1962 in a National Association of Boys Cubs event. The singer Frankie Vaughan was their President." Dave also played football for Higham Primary School.

In 1964, Dave went to secondary school at Hundred of Hoo Secondary Modern, which is now an Academy. Founded in 1948, the school got its name from the Saxon Hundred and the parish of Hoo. At school he enjoyed cross country running, and ran for Kent. He also played football for the school, and for the Chatham District under-15 team – "but then I stopped growing" he says.

Another sporting memory from his early years is of watching grasstrack racing in Kent in the early 1960s. He recalls that "There was no speedway in Kent at that time, but grasstrack was very popular and often drew crowds of 10,000 on Sundays. The riders included Alf Hagon, Don Godden, Reg Luckhurst and Malcolm Simmons"

Dave got his first motorbike when he was about 14. His uncle, Jean's brother, was into motorbikes, and worked on the oil rigs. He would stay with Dave's family when he was not working, and would often buy a new bike, and Dave got one he was no longer using. Dave remembers: "It was a very rusty 197cc James Captain bike. We adapted it and rode it in the woods. Coming home once, I was stopped by the police, who said that the back wheel had to be off the ground. So, I built a trailer with pram wheels. One day, I was riding with a friend in a field, sliding round the corners. The field was in Hermitage Road and belonged to a local farmer, Mr Fred Humphreys. One day, a guy parked up and was watching us. He came over and showed us an advert in *Motorcycle News* about an under-16s motorcycle club. He gave me the page and I took it home to show to my dad.

The man we contacted at the Kent Young Motorcyclists Association (KYMCA) was John Claridge, who ran the club. He later became my father-in-law." Dave joined the club and went there with his James Captain road bike. He says that "At first I was one of the worst riders, but then I started to beat the established riders. Then Dad bought me a better bike, a 200cc Tiger Cub with a grasstrack frame. I started riding junior grasstrack events in 1967, when I was aged 14. I won more races and I remember Alf Hagon presenting the prizes."

Interviewed in the 1971 *Webster's Speedway Annual*, Dave recalled that he was getting on for 14 years old when he sat on my first real motor-cycle. It was a 200cc James Captain and I was all alone in a Kent field with John, who helped and guided my career, my prospective father-in-law, John Claridge. Dave says that "... had anyone told me that one day I would earn a living racing motor-cycles I would have laughed them out of sight.

Left: On a grasstrack bike with the Kent YMCA. Right: Alf Hagon presenting a prize to Dave, who is on his new Tiger Cub bike.

Dave (on right) riding with Alan Sage.

For at the time I was scared stiff. My hands were shaking so much that I could barely release the clutch. But I soldiered on, into the KYMCA, which John founded, and gradually found that motor-bikes were fun and not instruments of fear. John's training aid was a handkerchief as a small stake to ride around But I still didn't have any notions about racing professionally." Dave adds that "I met my wife Vicky at the KYMCA. She used to race against me."

The next important event in Dave's development as a rider was some trips to West Ham's Custom House stadium in the spring of 1968, to take part in interval races at some of the meetings there.

This was arranged through John Claridge, who was going to West Ham home meetings to help Malcolm Simmons, another Kent-based rider who later became a friend and team-mate of Dave's.

The West Ham programme mentioned Dave and Barry Thomas taking part in these races, organised through the KYMCA. Dave Lanning was the manager at West Ham at the time, and was a very effective journalist and publicist for his club and the sport in general. The *Daily Sketch* reported that Dave and Barry were "as fast as some of the London big-time juniors". A week later, the *Speedway Star* reported that "lads aged from eight to 16" were involved in the display races. Dave and Barry were described as '15-year-olds'. This was true for Dave, but Barry Thomas was in fact 18 months older, and could have signed for West Ham at that time. *The Sunday Mirror* reported that their times for three laps on 200cc machines was 60 seconds. To put this in context, the track record on 500cc speedway machines for four laps was around 70 seconds.

Dave and Barry were also given practice sessions after the meetings. Dave found that he was too small to reach the very wide handlebars on the track spare and all the bikes at that time. Dave remembers that "Ken McKinlay helped me a lot with starting techniques. Gordon and David Kennett were involved in the rides at West Ham, along with Alan Sage. We used to practice at the Kennett's farm near Sevenoaks on Saturday afternoons."

Dave recalls in the 1971 interview that these visits to West Ham showed him that there was a lot more to motor-cycling "than a giggle with the boys. I remember the crowd – the first big one I'd ever really seen. And that vital atmosphere in the pits." Before then, grasstracking had been something Dave had done for fun. Speedway had made a big impression on him. One particular memory is when "Ray Wilson broke the track record by more than a second one night."

Another motorcycle sport that Dave started to take an interest in was trials. Very different from speedway, he acquired his first trials bike around this time, and found the sport an enjoyable challenge and way of keeping fit in the winter for many years. Dave believes that trails riding "also helped with balance and getting grip when there were wet and slippery conditions. It also improved my starting."

In September 1968, Dave returned to school with the intention of studying for his 'O' Levels (GCSE today). But after three weeks he left, and got a job in a light bulb factory "earning £3/17/6 a week". His original plan was to get a job for the winter, and then develop his grasstrack racing. But the start of a speedway team at Eastbourne changed his plans and his future.

2. Starting out at Eastbourne

Eastbourne is a slightly sleepy, but very pleasant, town on the south coast. It has some sporting tradition – non league football teams, an annual tennis tournament in the lead-up to the Wimbledon Championships, and stages county cricket. But not somewhere that would normally be identified with speedway.

In fact, the Arlington Stadium is based a few miles outside the town near Hailsham off the A22 road. Speedway was first staged there in 1928. Up to the Second World War, open meetings were staged, although in 1938, they ran a team in the Sunday Dirt-Track League, which consisted of five teams. After reopening in 1946, and running open meetings, in 1947 they entered the National League Division Three and won it. However, the team moved to Hastings, where they were based at Hastings United Football Club until a court case over noise issues forced their closure in 1949.

Further open meetings were run from 1948 to 1953, but from 1954 to 1957 and in 1959 they competed in the Southern Area League. Further seasons of open meetings followed, although in 1964 they entered a team in the short-lived Metropolitan League, a Sunday training league. They had applied to join the Provincial League in 1961, but had been refused membership by the Speedway Control Board, probably because they ran their home meetings on Sundays.

The Stadium's main income came from stock-car racing. However, they applied to join speedway's Division Two for the 1969 season, and were accepted. So senior league racing returned to Sussex for the first time since 1949. Division Two had expanded from 10 teams in its first season to 16.

Dave attended speedway training sessions at Eastbourne in January and February 1969. He recalls "I was going to become 16 on 7 March 1969. [That was the age that a rider could get a professional speedway licence then]. Bobby Dugard asked me to sign for Eastbourne, and I became an Eastbourne contracted rider. I never had an approach from West Ham. Bobby paid me £25 a week minimum for riding for Eastbourne and 10 shillings a point and a start. I remember that we got paid on Sundays." Dave was slightly embarrassed to reflect that at the age of 16 he was earning more than his father, who was taking home "around £15 a week for 50 hours work."

Dave had purchased a JAP bike for speedway in October 1968, from someone in Bridlington. The house Dave and his family lived in at the time had a long drive, with two concrete strips and grass in the middle. Dave says that "It was 50 to 60 yards long, and ideal for practicing starts. With my grasstrack bike I would make a start then hit the brakes. But I forgot that a speedway bike doesn't have brakes. I went through the garage, hit the wall, wrecked the bike and cut myself. The front wheel was by the footrest. I didn't have any protective gear on. And then I had to tell my dad what had happened..."

Dave made his debut for the Eastbourne Eagles on 4 April 1969, less than a month after his 16th birthday, in a challenge match at Plymouth. The Eastbourne team was a mixture of youth and experience. Reg Trott, who had joined Wimbledon in 1949 and subsequently ridden for Norwich, had come out of retirement to have the rider-coach role which was common in the Second Division. Barry Crowson had experience with Canterbury and West Ham, and during the season returned to Custom House full-time. The rest of the team had some experience, and Dave was the only real beginner.

Dave started in the number seven reserve position. However, after a credible second in his first race, his engine blew up, putting him out of the rest of the meeting. Dave Lanning commented in the *Star*: "Dave Jessup, 16-year-old wonder boy down at Eastbourne, had a pretty sickening debut into team racing. In Eagles' match at Plymouth he finished a brilliant second in his first ride, then blew his motor completely in the second. "Over £100 worth of damage" he said. "It's a good job I've got a spare motor otherwise I'd be finished with speedway after only one race.". Steady-as a-rock Dave has a great future in the game, and quickly settled on his spare engine to notch seven points in Eastbourne's first home fixture." In fact, Dave borrowed money from his grandmother to get a new bike from Alf Hagon Motorcycles, and did pay her back.

Two days after his Plymouth debut, Dave scored 7+2 from five rides against King's Lynn II in a narrow Eastbourne victory. In the *Star*, James Oldfield reported that "South Coasters Eastbourne, a Sunday afternoon drive for many Londoners, are delighted with their early showings. Dave Jessup, the 16-year-old discovery, is already fulfilling the forecasts made about him by Eagles' boss Dave Lanning."

Although his scores were a little inconsistent, unsurprisingly given his lack of experience, by the end of April Dave had moved into the team proper, riding at number two with Reg Trott at number one. His first meeting in that position was at Doncaster on 27 April. Dave scored 5+2 from four rides, partnering Barry Crowson.

Of course, all the away tracks were new for Dave. Doncaster was particularly memorable: "Eastbourne opened the season at Doncaster. It was a new track. They just used road stone to make the track, no dirt or soil. It was like a motocross track with shingle and rubble. It was a real eye-opener. Nelson was another track that was never good. One end had a brick wall which was the changing rooms. The windows had wire mesh on them." Nelson moved to Bradford in 1970, but there Dave says that "I remember racing against Alan Knapkin on the first corner, on the banking, and spectators were leaning on the fence, which collapsed. But the meeting continued. At Romford there was a two feet high brick wall around the track, and at Canterbury people lent on the fence, although it was quite solid. But some of the Division Two tracks were quite primitive. At Eastbourne, the track was very good. Bobby Dugard prepared it; he rode for Wimbledon so knew how to prepare a speedway track. Riders of lesser ability needed a good track. I used to follow the white line and judge things from the inside, not on the safety fence. It is very different today with the air fence."

He also says that "Eastbourne got very good crowds and had a big following at away meetings. Canterbury did as well, many of the grasstrack fans went there. Graham Miles and Barry Thomas were a big attraction there."

At the end of May, in a review of Division Two in the *Star*, Peter Oakes said that: "Inconsistency among the second strings is the Eastbourne fault, although young Dave Jessup – once he cures his starting technique – will improve rapidly." Dave comments: "That's a bit cheeky! I was one of the best starters of all time!"

Left: Riding a JAP bike for Eastbourne in 1969.
Right: With Colin Pratt receiving the Gerry Hussey trophy at Rye House.

Eastbourne 1969: Reg Trott, Hughie Saunders, Arthur Nutley (team manager), Tony Hall, John Heddrick, Dave Jessup, Barry Crowson (on bike). (JSC)

Eastbourne proved to be one of the strongest teams in the league. In a 21-point victory over local rivals Crayford, the *Star* reported that "Crowson and Trott were as reliable as ever, while wee Dave Jessup's seven points provided solid backing." At home to Doncaster, Dave scored 7+3, and proved equally effective on the road at Nelson and Long Eaton. Dave was also now starting to get open bookings. Eight points from four rides in Rayleigh's Eastern Counties Championship was followed by winning the Gerald Hussey Memorial Trophy at Rye House with 14 points. A week later, he was third with 12 points in the Champagne Derby at Canterbury. The *Star* noted that "May and Jessup were the real bright spots of the evening." But at Eastbourne, Dave had less success in the Championship of Sussex, with just six points.

International speedway was introduced to Division Two this season, with the visit of a Young Czechoslovakia team. Dave was included in a list of 26 riders from which the Young England team would be chosen. He was the only Eastbourne rider in the squad.

Young England won two and drew one of the seven match series, although all the meetings were fairly close. Dave remembers that the Czech team came in a coach, and all had new JAWA bikes with clip-on handlebars, different from the ones the British riders used. In the seven match test series, Young England used 26 riders, which while it may have given more riders international experience, hardly helped build partnerships or teamwork. Dave rode in the first match at Canterbury, scoring 4+2 in a 14-point England defeat, and one from one ride in the last match at Reading, when the Czech side won by six points. However, these appearances did make Dave the youngest ever (at that time) speedway international, and was the precursor to a long international career.

As well as his commitments with Eastbourne, Young England and a little later in the season Young Britain against Young Australia, and various open meetings, Dave also found time to ride a handful of meetings for West Ham. He also appeared in a West Ham team photo in the *Star* in July. However, he had no official links with the Custom House outfit. Their end of season review in the *Star* said the team should try to sign him, he says that he would not have been ready to move up to the First Division after just one season in the Second Division. The approach never came anyway. From a speedway point of view, Dave would have joined a struggling side at West Ham, who ultimately withdrew from the British League at the end of the 1971 season when the stadium was sold.

Dave's form dipped slightly towards the end of the season. Dave Lanning reported in the *Star* in mid-September: "Dave Jessup, 16-year-old wonder boy of Second Division speedway, has an unexpected reason for a recent lapse in his point-scoring potential. 'I'm staying up too late at nights', he explained. 'At Speedway!'. With his guest bookings and appearances for West Ham, Dave has been one of the busiest riders in the country – and the travelling has been wearing him down. 'Let's face it, most 16-year-olds are in bed by midnight most nights,' he said. 'I spent nine of the last 14 days on the road. Once I catch up with my sleep, I reckon I'll start getting points again.'"

The five Young Britain test matches against Young Australia saw Dave back at his best. Again, 21 riders were used in the series by the British selectors. Dave rode in the third and fourth tests, scoring 11+1 from six rides at Crayford and 14+2 from six rides at Eastbourne. As well as riding at Crayford, Dave was a regular visitor for work and as a spectator.

West Ham 1969. Dave (on right kneeling) rode three league matches for the Hammers.

Hughie Saunders and Dave – Eastbourne's first home meeting versus King's Lynn II On 6 April 1969. (JSC)

He remembers that "On Tuesdays I put the safety fence up and on Wednesdays took it down. I was paid for two days work, but made more money from selling batteries, starters, dynamos and alternators that the stock cars and bangers had left for scrap after their events on Saturdays."

The season ended with a typical Johnnie Hoskins – the Canterbury promoter and founder of the sport in Britain in 1928 – and Dave Lanning publicity stunt. Lanning reported in the *Star* on 10 October: "Barry Thomas, teenager to emerge this season at Canterbury ... Johnnie Hoskins still reckons that Barry is the best rider in Britain at his age and challenges all comers to prove that he is wrong. NO takers to date – but dear old Johnnie seems to have forgotten that Eastbourne's 16-year-old whiz kid Dave Jessup who started speedway with Thomas at West Ham, has already beaten the highly-promising Isle of Sheppey lad many times this season." Dave Lanning, writing as Dave Lang in the *Daily Mail*, also publicised the 'rivalry'.

A match race series was arranged, which Thomas won. However, Dave points out that they were friends, and at the start of the 1970 season, Thomas invited Dave to practice with him so that Dave could test a new bike. Dave says there was "nothing sinister", they were rivals from their grasstrack days and tried to beat each other. Dave does say that they had different outlooks on life: "I didn't drink alcohol until I was 30" he said with a wry smile.

Dave could look back on a successful first season in professional speedway. Reviewing the 1969 Eastbourne season in the *Star* in February 1970, Angus Kix said "Eastbourne had five heat leaders on the books... Find number one was Dave Jessup. A little 'un. A good 'un. Above all a young un. Barely 17. Ready, in my estimation, for a crack at Division 1 any time he likes. Only previous speedway experience was riding a sub-power bike around West Ham the year before in races with his fellow teenager Barry Thomas. An international already. Must be a major star soon, all things being equal."

Dave's average for Eastbourne was 6.62. He had ridden 31 meetings for the club, more than any other rider. But given his lack of experience at the sport, and that every away track was a new one, it was clearly a successful campaign. He had also won international honours in his first season in speedway. The support of his family had been essential, with his father doing the driving, initially in a camper van, and then in a Cortina. However, Dave maintained his own bikes, cleaning them and gradually developing his skills as a mechanic. This was something he did throughout his speedway career, and continued to tune bikes when he retired from riding. He had also learnt from his team mates, and recalls that Reg Trott was supportive of the younger riders in his 'rider-coach' role.

His life had also developed off the track. In an interview in the *Star* with Pam Oakes in August 1969, Vicky Claridge, John Claridge's daughter, is described as his 'steady girlfriend'. Looking back, Dave accepts that his 'teenage' years were not the norm: "I missed out on some things. I didn't go the pub in the village. I didn't have a road bike or a scooter. I was too busy. But it was a job I liked, I got paid and never worried. I was up before 8am to start work in the garage. I always travelled home from meetings if I could. Then I could prepare the bikes and leave at 2pm if I was riding that night. I rarely stayed away if I could avoid it."

Eastbourne had finished mid-table in the league, but their crowds had been good, and the new riders had established themselves. Dave had much to look forward to in 1970, but also had the challenge of building on his achievements in 1969.

International action

Dave riding for Young England in 1969. (JSC)

Young England versus Young Czechoslovakia 1969 at Canterbury.

Young England versus Young Czechoslovakia at Canterbury 1969.
From left: Geoff Ambrose, Jan Klokocka and Dave. (JSC)

3. Eastbourne and Rhodesia

Over the winter, Dave could reflect on a successful first season in professional speedway. He had finished fifth in the Eastbourne averages, although two of the riders who were ahead of him – Alby Golden and Hughie Saunders – had only ridden 14 and 13 official meetings respectively for the Eagles, while Barry Crowson had only ridden in 15 meetings before leaving halfway through the campaign to join West Ham. To continue to progress, he needed to be a regular heat leader and preferably taken the number one position which had been held by veteran Reg Trott.

In the *Star*, Dave Stevens analysed the make-up of the Second Division in 1969. 115 riders had made their debut, of whom 73 were "more or less completely new", including Dave, for whom big things were predicted. Dave Lanning reported that Dave had ordered a 'Charles Atlas' bodybuilding course to build up his strength and stamina. Also, in the winter, Dave kept fit by taking part in trials riding. He was re-classified as an 'Expert', which was very good considering his relatively limited experience. Trials riding remained an interest of Dave's for many years. However, he does recall breaking his ankle while doing trials riding: "I was carried out of the woods on a frozen corrugated metal sheet. We waited 40 minutes for the ambulance to arrive in freezing conditions. The roads snow covered. I was riding my 350cc Montesa. It had been supplied by Roy Frances and Paul Smart, who was a road-racer, and Barry Sheene's brother-in-law.

Apart from his commitments with Eastbourne, Dave was also looking forward to the Young England team's planned visit to Czechoslovakia in May. The riders were going to be loaned Jawa bikes for the trip, so Dave decided to switch from Jap to Jawa equipment, so that he was familiar with it. He ordered the new machine from Barry Briggs, and used it in his pre-season practice sessions. Dave Lanning reported that Dave commented: "I wouldn't want the fact that I ride the wrong sort of machine to stop me winning a place in the Young England side". The new machine cost £400, and he then considered buying a second one, so he would have spare parts. He invested all his earnings from 1969 into new equipment.

Another issue facing Dave was moving up to the First Division. Some commentators felt that he was ready to make the move straightaway, however, he felt that he needed another season's experience with Eastbourne before making a move.

One new addition to the Eastbourne team was Gordon Kennett, the senior member of what was to become a famous speedway family, and another graduate from the KYMCA. Mac Woolford also won a regular team place, but Hughie Saunders left Eastbourne to join Rayleigh during the season.

The popularity of speedway at Arlington was not in doubt. For the first meeting, against local rivals Canterbury, there was a huge traffic build-up of people trying to get to the stadium, and "hundreds of fans" were turned away. The meeting saw the rivalry between Dave – now riding as the Eagles' number one – and Barry Thomas resume. Dave won heat 10 to stop Thomas getting a maximum, and the Eagles won the meeting comfortably by 12 points.

From left: Barry Thomas, Laurie Sims, Graham Miles, Dave.
Canterbury versus Eastbourne 1970. (JSC)

Dave waiting to ride in 1970 while his dad John works on his bike.

Dave was soon in the wars as far as injuries were concerned. In a narrow win for the Eagles at Crayford, Laurie Sims fell in heat 11. Dave, his partner, could not avoid him, and despite a "severe shaking up" and damage to his bike, won the rerun. The meeting was tied going into heat 13. Dave was so far ahead that he slowed on the last lap to allow Derek Cook to score a maximum. Two weeks later, Dave was blinded by flying shale against Canterbury, and had to go to hospital after the meeting. Doctors advised him to rest for a week.

In May, the question of the rivalry between Dave and Barry Thomas arose again. Rye House, who ran Sunday open meetings involving Division Two riders, offered to stage a neutral track match race between them. The *Star* reported that: "As a first step in the matter both Dave and Barry were approached as to their willingness to take part in such a race. Both, however, declined with the explanation that while each is always keen to win as many races as possible no matter who they may be racing against, the rivalry said to exist between them is no greater than that they feel for any other opponent they meet on the track."

In fact, the two remained friends off the track, and would on occasions practice together. Dave recalls that "I took my brand new Jawa to Barry Thomas's field to practice. We had to walk half a mile to get there, carrying our tools and pushing the bikes. When we got there, we found it was flooded. It was heart breaking..."

Eastbourne were battling with Canterbury and Rochdale for the Division Two title. Dave and Gordon Kennett were leading the charge. At Rayleigh at the end of May, the Eagles won by 16 points, and they were "most impressive" according to the *Star*. By the end of June, they were Eastbourne's opening partnership, aged 17 and 16, and believed to be the youngest pairing ever seen in the sport. Keen for publicity as usual, the Eagles advertised that they would challenge any club pairing against Dave and Gordon, one heat home and away, with a £50 side-stake going to a charity nominated by the winners.

In early June, Dave's immediate future was decided when Wembley's bid for him was accepted by Eastbourne. It was agreed that he could ride for Wembley in 1970, but that the Eagles' fixtures would take priority. Three other teams were interested in signing Dave, who recalls having very little say in the matter, but was obviously pleased to have the chance to take part in First Division racing. That part of his career is covered in the next chapter.

As well as his success with Eastbourne, Dave was now being offered more open bookings. In June, he won the Olympiad at Crayford with 13 points. The *Star* reported that: "With twice having to come from a handicap of 15 yards and two starts from 10 yards back, Eastbourne's Dave Jessup proved himself a worthy winner of tonight's Olympiad with a 13 point total." In July, Dave won the first Division Two London Riders Championship at Romford, with 14 points from five rides, after Romford's Phil Woodcock fell and was excluded in the last heat to finish runner-up with 12 points. In August, Dave was runner-up to Malcolm Shakespeare in the Arlington Open handicap meeting. In October, he won the Recorder Trophy at Romford with 14 points.

One title that Dave missed out on was the British Junior Championship. Held at Swindon on 2 September, Dave was beaten by Reading's Mick Bell in heat five, but then beat Barry Thomas in heat 11; so both riders finished on 14 points. Thomas gated from the outside in the run-off to win the title.

Winning the Recorder Trophy at Romford in 1970, with runner-up Ross Gilbertson. (JSC)

Left: 1970 in Eastbourne colours. (JSC). Right: First trip to ride in Europe, Dave was runner-up to Ivan Mauger, but beat Garry Middleton into third place.

Eastbourne Eagles 1970: Dave Jessup, Reg Trott, Alby Golden, Gordon Kennett, Derek Cook, Mac Woolford, Laurie Simms. (JSC)

1970 British League Division Two Riders Championship: Barry Crowson (runner-up), Dave (winner) and Gary Peterson (third) at Hackney. (JSC)

The *Speedway Star's* headline on page 13 was "Jessup shock move" reporting that he had been banned from the Hackney meeting. Six pages further on, Martin Rogers's report was headlined "Jessup storms to Success" as he outlined how Dave had won the meeting. The Second Division promoters had met before the meeting, and overturned the SCB decision.

However, Dave had experienced major problems in actually reaching Hackney that night. He recalls: "There was a crash on the A2 and we were delayed. All the roads were blocked. We arrived as the parade started. I had got dressed in the car. Gary Petersen was the best rider in that line-up." Petersen finished top of the Division Two averages, but could only finish third at Hackney, having been beaten by Dave and Ross Gilbertson in heat 12. Dave won his first race in heat one, beating Barry Crowson who finished as runner-up, and went into his final race, heat 20, knowing that one point would secure the title for him. He settled for second place behind Paul O'Neil. Rogers's report said that "The diminutive Eastbourne rider, yielding years in terms of both age and experience, rode with the sagacity of a seasoned campaigner and was a deserving British League Riders Championship title winner."

Writing a history of the whole series of second tier riders championships in 2019 and 2020 in the *Star*, Phil Chard's records showed that, at 17 years and 203 days old, Dave was the youngest rider up to 2019 to win the title. The second youngest was Tai Woffinden in 2008, who was 202 days older than Dave.

Dave Lanning claimed that Dave asked to borrow a comb before he was presented with the Championship Trophy so that he would 'look his best'. The controversy around the meeting and Dave's status continued. Danny Carter wrote in the *Star* that Dave was a "victim of stupidity" over whether he could ride at Hackney. Meanwhile, Dave Lanning was charged with action "not in the best interests of the sport" by selecting Dave to ride for the Eagles at Teeside the night before the Hackney meeting.

The BLRC Division Two title was a fitting finale to Dave's time with Eastbourne, who finished as runners-up in the league table, just two points behind Canterbury. Dave's last league meeting for the Eagles saw him score a maximum at Arlington against Teeside on 18 October.

The review of Eastbourne's season in the *Star* said that "Dave Jessup, their golden boy among a team which was struck through with golden touches" was expected to join Wembley full-time in 1971, especially given the "whopping great tail the Lions have". The article also said that Gordon Kennett might turn out to be even better than Dave, and that there were other youngsters waiting to come forward.

As well as his performances for Eastbourne and in individual meetings, Dave also added to his experience on the international scene. He did not make the trip to Czechoslovakia in early May with the Young England team, who lost the test series 3–0. Maybe this was because he did not actually have a passport of his own, something that came to light later in the year. He had travelled abroad, but was on a joint passport with his parents.

In July, Dave rode three times for Young England against Young Sweden. His best meeting was at Teeside, where he scored 13+2 from six rides. The next night, at Workington, his return was 8+2 from five rides, although he suffered an engine failure. At Berwick, he fell and was excluded in his only ride. England won the first two meetings and drew the third.

Richard May, John Louis and Dave riding for Young England against Young Czechoslovakia on 8 August 1970 at Canterbury. (JSC)

The series continued in the south, Dave scoring 8+3 from five rides at Reading and 12+3 from six rides at Ipswich. The England team won both meetings for a 4.5 to 0.5 series win. Tommy Johansson led the way for the Swedes, scoring two full maximums. Tommy Jansson rode twice and Christer Lofqvist once.

At the end of August, Dave rode three times against a Young Czechoslovakia side who won the series 3–2. His best performance was at Reading, where from reserve he won four races and suffered an engine failure in a narrow defeat for the England team. He recalls Reading promoter Reg Fearman, who would play a significant role in Dave's later career, being very annoyed with him over the engine failure, which was from Dave forgetting to turn the fuel on. This happened in heat 14, which was a 4–2 to the Czechs. However, England went into the final heat needing a 5–1 to tie the meeting and the series. Dave won, but fellow reserve Barry Thomas could only finish third behind Miroslav Verner.

Martin Rogers's interview with Dave in his 'Man of the Week' column in the *Star* gives us a picture of Dave's development at this time. Rogers wrote: "But mark how this boy won his championship at Hackney. He won it because he was the most cool, collected character on view. He won it – despite the terrible psychological hazards of being told hours earlier that he would not be allowed to ride ... and following a nerve-stretching late dash into the Stadium..." He continued: "Jessup is not a spectacular, thrill-making rider. He is neat and tidy, because he realises full well that he hasn't the advantages which enable some riders to pull all sorts of capers and get away with it." The article concludes: "Dave Jessup, nevertheless, is a youngster who takes things both seriously and thoroughly. Speedway is becoming so much more of a professional enterprise these days, for the competitors if not some of the administrators, and this young man looks well equipped to make a very big impact at the highest level of the sport."

When he left Eastbourne, he recalled in an article for the 1971 *Webster's Speedway Mirror* that a group of supporters gave him a bracelet saying "Please Remember Us". He said that he would, and that the 1970 season had been "mostly milk and honey for me". The challenge he faced now was developing his experience at the top level of British Speedway, but there was an unexpected international trip and an important personal event to come before he would return to Wembley's colours.

Dave's popularity among the younger female fans was also shown at West Ham one night. He recalls scoring 13 points and "being carried from the pits to the changing room by a pack of girls".

***

The 'important personal event' for Dave was the announcement of his engagement to Vicky Claridge. Dave Lanning wrote that she was "Dave's schooldays sweetheart" and was the daughter of John Claridge, the former organiser of the KYMCA, and the man who had set Dave on a speedway career. She was actually a year older than Dave, and passed her driving test before he did. He recalls that he would drive when they were on the road together, with L-plates before he passed his test, while Vicky did the motorway driving. The couple are still together – Vicky does say that it was less stressful after Dave retired from speedway.

Before joining Wembley full-time, Dave was presented with the opportunity to ride in Rhodesia (now Zimbabwe) for three months.

There had been some speedway in Rhodesia in the 1950s, mainly linked to activity in South Africa. Most of the meetings were staged at Bulawayo. Trevor Redmond had been involved in promoting speedway in South Africa in the 1950s, and had come close to taking South African citizenship. He visited the Rhodesian venture that Dave joined.

Dick Barrie was the organiser of the group at the British end. The *Star* reported that eight riders were to make the trip, and were expected to leave for Rhodesia in December. It should be pointed out that in 1965, the white minority government led by Ian Smith had declared 'unilateral independence' from Great Britain, and the British government applied trade sanctions to Rhodesia. But in 1970, the Conservative British Government were trying to resolve the situation, which does not seem to have created any difficulties for the British, Norwegian and Australian riders. Later, a civil war developed as African-led liberation movements attempted to overthrow the Smith regime, but at this time the country was relatively peaceful.

The main driving force behind the relaunch of speedway in Rhodesia was former Edinburgh rider Alex Hughson, who had emigrated there at the end of the 1969 speedway season. There were plans to run meetings at the Glamis Stadium in Salisbury, the Showground at Bulawayo and the Central Sports Stadium in Gwelo.

Dave was not among the riders originally chosen for the trip, but was added to the party at the last minute. He did make sure he had a return ticket before making the trip. There was no time to arrange for a bike to be sent to Rhodesia, so Dave would use borrowed equipment. It was still a great opportunity for him to get some overseas experience.

The party finally left for Rhodesia from at 6pm on Christmas Eve. However, Dave had nearly missed out on the trip because he did not have a passport of his own. He applied on 18 December, but because he was only aged 17, a licence for this had to be approved by a magistrate sitting at the famous Bow Street Court, near Covent Garden. This was duly done on 23 December, just before Dave was due to fly out. He had the support of John McNulty, the Speedway Control Board manager in making the application, and his father believed that without Mr McNulty's presence, the application may not have been granted. Another condition of his being involved in the touring party was to report regularly to the welfare services in Rhodesia, and to report back to the police when he returned to England.

The season was due to open in Rhodesia on 30 December, and racing would take place at the three tracks until early March. Dave made a good start to his time in Rhodesia, finishing third in the BAT Embassy Silver Helmet, which drew over 12,000 fans to the Glamis Stadium. The meeting was, not surprisingly, dominated by the overseas riders.

Speedway Star journalist Dave Stevens visited Dave's parents to see what they had heard about his time in Rhodesia. His father said that he was "living the life of Riley", with 'super' accommodation, the use of an American car and a swimming pool. His parents were also pleased that Trevor Redmond was there to offer support. Dave was also writing regularly to Vicki, and his parents kept in touch with her so they had a 'full picture' of what he was doing.

The three tracks staged both team and individual meetings. Over 7,000 attended the Bulawayo Open Championship, where Dave, Laurie Etheridge and Oyvind Berg all tied on 12 points. A three-man run-off saw Etheridge successful, with Dave as runner-up.

The tourists were split between the three tracks to make up teams with the locally based riders. Dave was allocated to Gwelo, with Oyvind Berg and Jimmy Gallagher. Dave scored 12 in the team's first match, a 36–36 draw with Bulawayo. Three days later they went down 39–33 at Salisbury, with Dave scoring six and suffering the frustration of an engine failure when leading.

As well as the team and individual meetings, Dave was involved in a series between the Rhodesian League and a South African select team, led by former Wembley rider Dennis Newton, who had settled in South Africa. In the first match, Dave top scored for the South Africans with nine. He was a late guest replacement for Tony von Visser, who had been injured while practicing. Five days later, at Gwelo, Dave switched sides and came 'from his sick bed' to score a 'magnificent' 15 point maximum in a comfortable win for the Rhodesian League team. He did not ride in the final match of the series, but did ride for 'The Champions' against Bulawayo, scoring six points and winning the JD Mackay International Shield in the second half. One interesting partnership in a pairs meeting was Dave riding with Peter Prinsloo, who Trevor Redmond would recruit to the Wembley Lions for the forthcoming season.

Gwelo did reach the final of the National Trophy, and despite Dave scoring 11 and 10, narrowly lost on aggregate to Salisbury. Dave flew home on 10 March, giving him a four week break before the Wembley Lions' season started.

One highlight soon after his arrival was an 18th birthday party, secretly arranged by his parents. Dave told the *Star's* Dave Stevens that "Rhodesia is a fine place – its somewhere I would really like to live at some time in the future. What I'd really like to do is get good enough so that I could go out there to live each winter and have a British promoter pay my fare back to England for each British League season." Stevens also reported that Dave had come close to meeting Ian Smith. Dave visited the sister of one of his family's neighbours in Higham once or twice a week, and on one occasion just missed the Rhodesian Prime Minister.

Looking back, Dave believes that the trip to Rhodesia, and living away from home for almost three months, was an important experience for him. He recalls "After a couple of weeks I moved to share with Geoff Curtis and Bob Young. When I returned the next year, I stayed in the same place with Bob Valentine and the other Australians. They involved me in things. We had a rota for cooking and spent £5 a week on food, so I would go shopping. I came home and tried to cook; it was a wide awakening for a 17-year-old. I enjoyed that.

I remember it was always packed at Glamis speedway. The meetings were mainly the tourists, with some of the locals – Peter and Chris Prinsloo and Abe Koekemoe. From South Africa, I remember Dennis Newton, Vic Pretorious and Donny Fourie."

Dave did return to Rhodesia at the end of the 1971 British season. But before then, he faced the challenge of establishing himself as a full-time Division One rider with Wembley.

4. Wembley and Rhodesia

The Wembley Lions! One of the glamour names of British speedway. The sport had started at Wembley in 1929, but it was in the post-war period that the Lions became the top team in British speedway. Based around two 'veterans' – Tommy Price and Bill Kitchen – team manager Alec Jackson and the managing director of Wembley Stadium Ltd, Sir Arthur Elvin built a team based on young riders who had had come out of the Armed Forces. Wembley attracted massive crowds, and dominated the sport until the mid-1950s. As the crowds dropped, and the sport itself declined to a handful of tracks, the sudden death of Sir Arthur Elvin in February 1957 saw the rest of the directors withdraw the team from league racing due to the financial losses it had been making. The stadium continued to stage a major World Championship meeting each year, and occasional international meetings.

Trevor Redmond had been one of Wembley's stars from the early 1950s until 1956. He had become a speedway and stock car promoter, and had kept in contact with the management team at Wembley Stadium. He teamed up with local businessman Bernard Cottrell to bring the Lions back to league racing in 1970. Their very presence in the British League gave the sport a boost. Redmond and Cottrell had bought the First Division licence of Coatbridge, who had been struggling financially since their enforced move from the Old Meadowbank stadium in Edinburgh, which was being redeveloped to stage the 1970 Commonwealth Games. The Lions' first home meeting, against Hackney, was attended by over 20,000 fans, and the Saturday night meetings regularly attracted over 10,000.

The bulk of the team – Reidar Eide, Bert Harkins, Wayne Briggs and Brian Collins – came from Coatbridge. Eide was the top Norwegian rider and an established 'number 1'. Bert Harkins had come through from second-half appearances at Edinburgh to be one of Scotland's top riders and was an established heat leader. Wayne Briggs was also a heat leader, but had never reached the top levels of the sport. Brian Collins had established himself in the Edinburgh and Coatbridge teams, but was still a second-string in Division 1.

Redmond also managed to tempt five times World Champion Ove Fundin out of semi-retirement to join the Lions. While past his peak, Fundin was still a big draw. The team's weakness was at reserve. Tim Bungay had a regular place, and Des Lukehurst rode in some of the early meetings. The team also was quite old – Brian Collins was the only youngster at the age of 22, although he had three years experience at First Division level.

In 1953, an ageing Wembley team had started the season poorly. To provide some new impetus, the Lions signed Brian Crutcher – one of the top English prospects at the age of 18 – from Second Division Poole. Now the new version of the Lions was repeating history by signing 17-year-old Dave Jessup from another south coast team, Eastbourne.

It was clear to everyone in speedway that Dave was heading for the First Division. Four teams were interested in signing him, but Trevor Redmond had been promised by Bobby Dugard first option on Dave and took it. It was the largest cash transfer at the time for a Division Two rider to move to the top flight. Dave says that "I wanted to go to Division One. It was a bigger league and I had the opportunity to go to Wembley.

Left: Dave in the famous Wembley colours. Right: The programme from his Lions debut.

I didn't think about it, such as the problem of the track opening later than everyone else [because of the football fixtures at the Stadium]. Wembley was a big name."

Dave was signed as Wembley's 'number 8', which meant that he would only ride if another rider was injured. Danny Carter wrote in the *Star*: "Negotiations may have been completed by now but I hear that Eastbourne are looking for a new home for Dave Jessup. Oh, they aren't giving him away, they are facing facts. They know that Dave will be ready for Division 1 racing next year ... so they are offering him to a Division 1 club this year.

They had in mind giving a club first option on his transfer by allowing him to race as their number 8 right now.

'All we want is a guarantee that Dave will be given regular second half rides. It will be understood, of course, that he will only be available for a Division 1 match IF HE IS NOT RIDING FOR EASTBOURNE' said manager Dave Lanning. First track to snap up the bait was Wembley. They were sniffing around this tempting lure last time I heard."

In fact, Dave rode regularly for the Lions for the rest of the season, completing 19 official fixtures. Dave remembers listening to Freddie Williams's advice, the Lions team manager, former Wembley rider, and double World Champion in the early 1950s, and to Trevor Redmond. He also got a new bike and was guaranteed to be paid for four starts, even if riding at reserve.

Wembley Lions 1970: From left: Dave, Bert Harkins, Tim Bungay, Freddie Williams (manager), Wayne Briggs, Reidar Eide, Brian Collins, Ove Fundin (captain, on bike).

Dave was supported at Wembley by George Yule who was his mechanic from when he joined the Lions until he retired in 1987. Dave says that George was "very, very loyal to me". George's daughter Jane ran Dave's fan club while he was at Wembley.

One issue he had to deal with was riding with Ove Fundin. The Swedish veteran had agreed with Trevor Redmond that he would always have the inside gate. Dave says that "I was not happy with this, and once left the pits before Ove and took the inside gate. He was annoyed and tried to nudge me out of the way, but I stayed there. Then I got to the first bend ahead of him and he complained to Trevor Redmond. Freddie Williams told me to keep Ove happy, and I got an extra £5 for letting Ove ride from the inside. But later in my career I must admit that I did the same when I was a heat leader." By the end of July, Fundin had left the Lions; the logistics of running a business in Sweden and riding for Wembley meant he missed too many meetings, and he was released.

Dave, not surprisingly, found the First Division harder, and faced stiffer competition. He says that he enjoyed going out to dinner with the rest of the team at *The Captain's Table*, a local restaurant who sponsored the team. "My Mum and Dad were invited" he recalls. He does say that "Wembley was the best stadium –only Hampden Park was bigger." However, he has mixed memories of the Scottish track, having to travel there three times in short succession to compete in a World Championship qualifying round which was twice rained off.

Dave ironically made his Wembley debut against West Ham, where he had first ridden on a proper speedway track back in 1968, just two years ago. The *Star* reported that "... Most pleasing feature of all for Wembley was the debut of Eastbourne's teenage wonder Dave Jessup. He won the reserves' race and picked up two more points later in the meeting for a more-than-useful five points." Renewing an old rivalry from the 1940s and 1950s, Wembley won 47–31 in front of a crowd of over 18,000.

Had Dave joined West Ham, he may well have been on the trip to Lokeren in Belgium which saw speedway's biggest ever disaster. A group of riders, along with Phil Bishop and mechanic Roy Sullivan were on a trip to Belgium when their minibus was involved in a major road accident. Four riders were killed, along with speedway legend Phil Bishop and the minibus driver. The injuries Colin Pratt sustained finished his riding career. Dave sombrely reflects that "I was lucky to miss the Lokeren trip." We met to work on this book on the 50th anniversary of the accident. Sad memories indeed.

Wembley also strengthened the team by signing Brian Leonard, who was also looking for one of the reserve places. Another former West Ham rider, he was aged 24 and had extensive top flight experience. Despite the pressures of 'doubling up', the extra travelling and riding on away tracks that he had not seen before, Dave's scores for the Lions gradually improved. In mid-July, Trevor Redmond was said to be delighted at the progress shown by Brian Collins and Dave. He said that they were taking note of the advice passed on by 'highly experienced' ex-riders around Wembley – and the improvement in both is noticeable."

In early September, Dave scored 8+1 from five rides in a 41–37 victory over Coventry, and two weeks later topped that with 11 points from five rides against Cradley Heath, including a win against experienced international Roy Trigg. By the end of September, Dave had moved up to number two in the team, and scored six points against Newcastle.

Dave's final appearance for the Lions in 1970 was in the London 4s at Hackney, when he told Dave Lanning that he rode his best-ever race, beating West Ham's Christer Lofqvist and Wimbledon's Trevor Hedge. He finished sixth in the Wembley averages, with a figure of 4.76, ahead of both Brian Leonard and Tim Bungay.

Over the years, Dave rode regularly in Europe, both at speedway and long track meetings. He reflects that "From very young, I wanted to gain experience in both sports". In 1970, he remembers that "I made my first trip to Ruhpolding in Germany. I wrote to the promoter asking for a start and finished in second place. Another time, four of us drove in a Capri to Longio in Italy. It took us an extra 10 hours because of German holiday traffic. When we arrived, it was one o'clock in the morning. The club president gave me the keys to his chateau in the mountains as we had been travelling for 24 hours. He could see that we were shattered. We had not eaten or drank anything, so I think we probably drank some of his wine."

An interesting experience was going with Garry Middleton to Hungary. He recalls "We shared the driving. He arrived in a Mercedes, with the back seat out. It was overweight, but we put my bike in the back as well. The tyres were bald. We were going through Germany to Hungary. Halfway across Germany, I was driving, aged 17, without a full licence. I had never driven a Mercedes before. I went over a crossing a bit quickly, and was pulled over by the police. There were two of them at first. They asked to see my licence, but they let us go. Driving back, after the meeting, I was driving with Garry asleep in the front seat. He woke up and grabbed the wheel. We nearly hit the barrier. We had a puncture. He tried the boots of various Mercedes, nicked a wheel and used it to change our wheel and we drove home. He also told me how he kept a trophy in the car so that if he was asked how he got on at the meeting by fans at home, he had something to show them!"

Angus Kix reviewed Wembley's 1970 season in the *Speedway Star*. He commented that "Wembley made one effort to do something about the future with the signing of Dave Jessup from Eastbourne. He was a great success. A smallish bundle of talent willing to have a go with anyone, and delighting the crowd when he took 'em on and beat 'em. Now that he has got his dive into Division I over, he can concentrate on two improvements. The first, his points average, which I confidently expect him to push up by at least half. The second, which will follow, his regular place in the team ... and not the reserve berth." He continued "The experience Jessup got was invaluable. It brought him on much faster than if he had stayed as the number 8, the original intent."

In an article in the *1971 Webster's Speedway Mirror*, Dave reflected that "... I'm riding for a club, Wembley, that most kids only read about in storybooks. I just hope I don't let the Lions down in the years ahead. I certainly never dreamed five years ago ... that one day I would be on nodding terms with the pit commissionaire at mighty Empire Stadium..."

After a couple of months off, Dave resumed his speedway career in Rhodesia, as was covered in the last chapter. He returned to Britain early in March 1971, ready for the challenge of riding solely in Division 1.

One issue that he faced immediately was that the Lions home season did not start until 5 June, although one 'home' match was ridden at neutral Newport, against Belle Vue. The Lions lost to the league champions, but there was "some fiery riding from reserve" by Dave, according to the *Star*, to secure 9+1 points from his five rides.

Meanwhile, there were plenty of changes at Wembley. On 24 April, Eric Linden revealed in the *Star* that Bernard Cottrell would not be involved in the forthcoming season, and that Trevor Redmond would be running the Lions on his own. Despite running Wembley, Redmond lived in the south west. Dave recalls the Wembley riders stopping off at his house on their way back from Exeter for some food and drink. Dave remembers being "so impressed" with Redmond's home, and this showed him what he could achieve through speedway. Years later, towards the end of his career, Dave invited the Mildenhall riders to his home on their way back from a meeting at Canterbury, to offer them something to eat and some hospitality.

The team also showed changes from the previous campaign. Reidar Eide had moved on, and Wayne Briggs was released. Tim Bungay also retired after a couple of meetings. Tony Clarke joined the Lions from West Ham. Redmond reflected that even if Hasse Holmqvist, who had been allocated to the team, did not join the Lions – he never did – with Bert Harkins, Tony Clarke, Brian Collins and Dave Jessup "Wembley have the possibility of four heat leaders". Soon, Sverre Harrfeldt joined the Lions, having fallen out with West Ham, and another former World Championship runner-up, Gote Nordin, was also recruited. Tommy Jansson also had an early season spell at Wembley, but was released. In retrospect, he was a better prospect than some of the riders who Wembley used after Nordin stopped riding due to business commitments.

The upheaval at the top of the promotion was maybe the reason why Wembley did not have any challenge matches to warm up for the new campaign. However, apart from his Wembley commitments, Dave also entered the World Championship for the first time. His best meeting was at Wimbledon, with nine points from his five rides. But scores of five at Halifax and three at Glasgow, on a track of mud following a day of rain, were not enough to see him through to the British semi-finals. On 22 May, Dave was top scorer for Wembley with 11+1 from five rides in a 39–39 draw at Cradley.

One unexpected benefit came Dave's way in June – seven sets of very smart red Wembley leathers. By mistake, the set for the team had all been made in his size. Dave said that he had a set for each race. At the age of 18, he was still the youngest member of the team. Team manager Freddie Williams realised that he won his second World Championship in the year that Dave was born. Freddie said that this made him feel "almost pre-historic".

The 1971 Wembley Lions was very much a team. Bert Harkins had his best ever season, and Gote Nordin was clearly a class above the rest for the spell he had with the Lions. But just over two points separated Sverre Harrfeldt in the averages on 7.80 from Brian Leonard who was seventh on 5.72. Dave finished fourth with a figure of 7.43, which in most teams would have made him a heat leader.

Wembley Lions 1971: From left: Dave, Tony Clarke, Brian Leonard, Gote Nordin, Sverre Harrfeldt, Brian Collins, Peter Prinsloo; on bike Bert Harkins (captain), Freddie Williams (manager).

His development is reflected in the reports of the Lions' meetings. At Wimbledon, he was second highest scorer; a week later at Sheffield "The Lions relied almost solely on Bert Harkins and Dave Jessup" according to the *Star*. At the end of June, in a 52–26 win over Halifax, Dave scored 10 from four rides, and "has never been sharper". At home to Cradley, when the Lions again topped 50 points, he was top scorer with 10.

Dave Lanning was now saying that he deserved an England cap. At Sheffield again in July, Bert Harkins and Dave "both rode extremely well". At Reading, in a narrow defeat, he was "particularly impressive". In July, the *Star* reported how Wembley had improved, and "Dave and fast-improving Sverre Harrfeldt are the current quick-gating kings at Wembley."

Dave was also getting more open meeting bookings. He scored five points in the Hammerama at West Ham, but found more success in the Southern Riders Championship, scoring 11 at Hackney and 10 at West Ham in the qualifying rounds. The final was at Wimbledon on 12 August, and Dave finished with six points in a strong field.

One title that Dave missed out on was the British Junior Championship. Although he was now not eligible for 'Young England' and 'Young Britain' which only included Division Two riders, he could still ride in this meeting. He was runner-up by a point to Kings Lynn's Ian Turner. The decisive race was heat two. Turner went from last to first, and won all his other races from the back.

Another new tournament for Dave was the London Riders Championship. He scored eight from his first four rides, but then was brought down in his last ride and broke bones in his foot. This meant he missed the last few weeks of the season.

In the *Star's* review of Wembley's 1971 campaign, Danny Carter said that "Dave Jessup tackled his Division I first full season with a deal of enthusiasm and verve and was aiming higher and higher when he was pitchforked out of the season, early like, with a foot full of busted toes. Dave was more scientific than spectacular, but, like all game nippers, he looked spectacular even when he wasn't!"

A return to Rhodesia

Even before the season had ended, and with his foot still in plaster, Dave signed up to return for another spell in Rhodesia. Trevor Redmond's visit to the country earlier in the year had paid dividends with Peter Prinsloo joining the Lions. He rode in 11 meetings, but was clearly out of his depth in Division One at that time. Another familiar face heading south for the winter was Wembley colleague Brian Collins.

In 1970, Dave had been a last-minute addition to the squad of riders visiting Rhodesia. This time, he had signed up for the trip in mid-September, which meant that he could arrange for his own bike to be sent to Rhodesia. He went with Laurie Etheridge to Southampton to drop off their bikes. Dave recalls that they had the bikes on a trailer, and after going over a hump-back bridge, the trailer disconnected from the car, and went into someone's garden. They had to stop, re-secure the trailer and return to Etheridge's place to repair it before finally getting to Southampton.

Dave, along with Oyvind Berg and Bob Young was allocated again to the Gwelo team. Another British rider who joined Gwelo was Norman Strachan. Peter Prinsloo and Brian Collins both were lodgers in Strachan's house, and he got so fed up hearing about their plans to ride in Rhodesia in the winter that he decided to join them.

In 1970–71, Dave and the other international riders left for Rhodesia on Christmas Eve. This time, Gwelo's season started on 19 November. Another addition to the party was Australian Bob Valentine, who went to Rhodesia to ride on a freelance basis, and would start in the second-halves. He was also planning to work in Rhodesia in a motorcycle shop.

Valentine ended up staying in the same place as Dave and his Australian colleagues from the previous season. Dave Lanning reported that Dave, Bob Young and Valentine had been sharing a Honda 90 motorbike. They went into the bush for some 'joyriding', all got on the bike together, and it turned over backwards. Valentine was worst affected; his legs were trapped and he lost skin from his back. They all used the sauna at their digs to try to ease their aches and pains.

Dave also recalls another incident with Bob Valentine. They went to meetings in a jeep, and Valentine had a cross bow and said he was going to do some hunting. Dave says that "I'm not into killing animals", and was upset when Valentine was aiming at some guinea fowl and wild chickens with his cross bow. Dave threw a Coke bottle to scare them and hit and killed one of the animals. They were both upset for different reasons, and Valentine didn't speak to Dave for a few days.

On the track, Gwelo's season opened at Bulawayo, with a narrow defeat in a challenge match. Dave won three heats and suffered an engine failure in his other ride. Over 6,000 fans came, despite heavy rain in the four days before the meeting. Five days later, Gwelo lost their first league fixture 37–35 at Salisbury. Bob Valentine was now riding for Gwelo. Dave scored seven from his three rides.

Just before Christmas, Dick Barrie reported in the *Star* that the three Australians and Dave were staying in a cottage owned by Bill 'Paddy' Powell, the head groundsman at the Salisbury Showgrounds. Dave, Bob Young and Geoff Curtis had stayed in the cottage on their previous visit to Rhodesia, and had asked to stay there again. The same edition reported that Trevor Redmond was having problems securing enough dates at Wembley to run a full season, and was looking for an alternative venue for some meetings. Some riders had raised this issue during the season, and it was one that Dave was concerned about.

Trevor Redmond visited Rhodesia again, looking for possible riders for Wembley. He was also in the crowd that saw Ian Smith and British Foreign Secretary Sir Alec Douglas Home come out onto a balcony after successfully concluding peace negotiations between their two countries. Trevor's main concern was that this would make it easier for Peter Prinsloo to ride again for the Lions.

Gwelo won their next league match. Dick Barrie reported that "Dave Jessup was in sparking form in the races his machinery lasted the pace." Two wins and two engine failures were the result of his night's work. At home to Bulawayo, Gwelo won by 18 points in the 12-heat match, with Dave scoring a 12-point maximum and winning the second half final.

In early January, all Wembley supporters were shocked to read that Dave had asked for a transfer. The lack of home meetings was the reason, and – looking back – Dave says that it would have undermined his development as a rider to stay with the Lions. Wembley riders probably lost out on eight to 10 home meetings a year, and for the World Championship would have to ride all their qualifying meetings away from home. Dave's father had written the letter requesting the transfer on Dave's behalf, and sent Dave a copy in Rhodesia to give to Trevor Redmond.

Dave Lanning reported that Dave's preferences were to go to Cradley Heath or Ipswich, but that Eastbourne would be possible if they were promoted to Division One. A few weeks later, in early March, Trevor Redmond suspended the Lions for a year and loaned out the riders, because he could not secure enough dates to run a league season at Wembley. A year on, and the Lions withdrew permanently from league racing. One of the sport's greatest names was consigned to the history books.

Dave's immediate future on the track was halted when on 10 December, he broke his collarbone in his first race for Gwelo at Bulawayo. His injury responded well to treatment and he was back riding in January. During the Christmas break, Dave and his Australian friends visited the bush in the Zambesi Valley, watching animals there who were not in a game reserve or wildlife park. The trip was arranged through Ian McMillan, who was a tobacco farmer about 90 miles north of Salisbury, as well as riding speedway. It was a wild and remote place to visit.

Just after Christmas, there were political protests over the Pearce Commission proposals for Rhodesia's future, which would have meant parity in Parliament for the white and African populations by 2040. The population at this time was 250,000 whites and five million Africans. Alex Hughson postponed a couple of meetings at Gwelo until things had calmed down.

Dave returned to action on 14 January, top scoring with nine points for Gwelo in a narrow defeat at Bulawayo. Five days later, Dave won his first race and then had three last places for Gwelo. However, their 37–35 win at Salisbury meant that they had – more or less – clinched the National League title. This was confirmed a couple of weeks later. Gwelo and Bulawayo tied on seven league points each, but Gwelo had the better racing points difference.

In early February, it was also confirmed that Dave would remain a Lion for the 1972 season, but this time a Leicester Lion. Graham Plant left Blackbird Road as part of this move, but never actually rode for Wembley.

After riding in a three-team tournament, Dave made an unusual international appearance. He rode for a 'Sassenachs' side against a World Select. He scored five in a 53–36 defeat, with Brian Collins top scoring for the World team. Collins also won the Rhodesian Open Championship, Dave again scoring five points. His final meeting in Rhodesia was for Gwelo in a three-team tournament. He scored seven points in Gwelo's victory. The crowd was lower than usual because Prime Minister Ian Smith was speaking on television that night.

Writing in the *Star* on 19 February, Dave said that it was great to be back home. He was getting married to Vikki on 25 March, and was shocked to find that his best man, John Louis, was no longer available because Ipswich needed him for a special practice and press day. Dave's friend Judd Drew stepped in. He was a former grasstrack rider.

On his transfer, he explained the reasons for his request for a move: "My transfer request away from Wembley may have given the impression I was not happy at the Empire Stadium. That's not so. I've enjoyed every minute there, and as at Eastbourne earlier, I've had every assistance, encouragement and help I could have wished for. When it comes to economics, however, 34 meetings in a year is not a lot of good to a professional rider. With a bit of luck, I could double that number with Leicester ... which should please my bank manager no end."

On Rhodesia, he said it was unlikely that he would ride there again, as he would have family responsibilities. He said that some meetings were cancelled because of rain, and he was disappointed that a track at Umtali didn't open. Also, Gwelo shut down early – not through political troubles – the crowds had dropped before then. He also thought that the political issue was exaggerated by the British press. He had enjoyed a visit to the Victoria Falls and Kariba Dam, which he said were "sights not to be missed".

Undoubtedly Dave had benefitted from riding in a very different environment to British speedway, and from being away from home for long periods for the first time. But back in Britain, new challenges awaited him at Leicester.

Dave and Vicky got married on 25 March in Sittingbourne, her home town (see photo above). One of his new Leicester colleagues, Malcolm Brown, was also an accomplished singer, and added to the entertainment with two songs, including *There's Always Something There to Remind Me*, which Sandie Shaw had made famous. Dave recalls that Brown "stuffed a cushion up his jumper" while he sang, but Dave says it was not a 'shot-gun' wedding. In fact, David Jessup – their son – was born in 1976. The couple are still together and celebrated their 48th wedding anniversary while working on this book. Among the guests were Freddie and Pat Williams, and Graham Miles. One change for Dave was that he would no longer need to keep his road bike going – he had mainly used it to ride to Sittingbourne when he was courting Vicky.

5. Heat leader at Leicester

In moving to Leicester, Dave was joining a club that had only been in Division One since 1968, when promoters Ron Wilson and Reg Fearman closed Long Eaton and moved the team a few miles to Blackbird Road.

Speedway had a tradition in a very sporting city. Leicester City Football Club, the Leicester Tigers Rugby Union team and Leicestershire County Cricket Club all vied for support. Speedway had started in Leicester in 1928, but disappeared after two seasons of league racing in 1929 and 1930. The sport returned in 1948, and lasted until 1962.

The Lions finished 12th in 1968, and since then had gradually improved, finishing runners-up by four league points to a powerful Belle Vue side in 1971. They were let down by their home form, with four defeats and a draw. Winning three of these matches would have made them champions.

Dave's move was a rider-exchange with Graham Plant, who had won the first Division Two Riders Championship in 1968. However, Plant never rode for Wembley, and ended up at Newport for the 1972 campaign. The Leicester team was built around Ray Wilson, one of the top English riders who consistently averaged over 10 and John Boulger, one of the top Australian riders whose 1971 average was just under nine. Alan Cowland, Norman Storer, Malcolm Brown and Geoff Ambrose – who had been exchanged for Tom Leadbitter – had the second-string and reserve team places. Malcolm Shakespeare was also under consideration. Ambrose had ongoing knee problems that saw him only ride in 10 league meetings for the Lions, and saw him temporarily retire from the sport.

Dave recalls that he was given little say in the move to Leicester: "I was still young, and wanted to leave Wembley because of their late start to the season. I was told that Leicester wanted me, and that Reg Fearman was going to phone me. No special reason for Leicester – that was what happened. I didn't know Ron Wilson and Reg Fearman, I was just trying to win races. I didn't know this at the time, but there was a consortium – Allied Presentations – and Reg was part of that, along with Maury Littlechild and Len Silver. When I moved from Leicester to Reading, Len Silver was involved, although I always associated him with Hackney.

In hindsight, a weekday track was better, there was more chance to do open meetings, especially at the Saturday night tracks. If a Saturday night track had a big open meeting, I couldn't ride if my team was riding on a Saturday. I wasn't doing so many European meetings then, that came later. When I moved from Reading to King's Lynn, a Saturday track, that was a problem. I had to pay airfares. I preferred to drive to European meetings.

Leicester was a fantastic track to ride. It was well prepared, and was perfect, always perfect. After meetings, I often stayed with George Gower, who looked after the track. It was convenient for me, especially if I didn't need to go home to work on my bike.

In terms of the riders, Ray Wilson was a top rider, I remember seeing him at West Ham in 1967 and 1968. I was always impressed with him. John Boulger was a great character, but laid back. He would arrive just after a meeting had started. He was number three in the team at that time, and so didn't ride until heat four. I think he could have been even better, to me that wasn't the best build up to a meeting. I always arrived early.

Malcolm Brown was the funny man of the side. He could sing as well. After he retired, he opened a night club in Durban. Norman Storer was a nice man, very quiet."

As well as preparing for the new season, Dave was also working on his new home, which he would share with Vicky, a caravan on the Hoo Marina Estate near Rochester.

Ray Wilson wrote a column in the *Speedway Star* at this time. He said that "Our new boy, Dave Jessup, now an old married man of course [of two weeks], really looks the part. Perhaps his good form is explained by the fact that he is taking his new responsibilities very seriously." In fact, Dave's early scores as he settled down with a new team and a new home track were not that high. But his first home meeting was on 28 March, over two months earlier than it had been the previous season with Wembley.

Three weeks later, Wilson said that Dave was "clicking into gear". He got his first double figure score against Ipswich at Blackbird Road. However, in the Midland Riders Championship qualifying rounds, Dave mustered 21 from three meetings, but did win a place in the Final. At the end of June, at Coventry, he scored four from five rides, but that included a win.

In May, Dave's scores gradually improved. At Wimbledon, he was top scorer for the Lions for the first time. A couple of weeks before, he had ridden in an open meeting at Rupholding in Germany. Accompanied by Vicky, and his mum and dad, he left for Dover straight after riding at Oxford on Thursday 27 April. They arrived back at Dover on 2 May at 5am, and Dave was riding at Leicester that evening. Dave did the fastest times in practice, and then finished runner-up on 14 points to Ivan Mauger, who won the meeting with a maximum. When they met, Dave had led for two laps before Ivan overtook him. However, his display impressed the promoters so much that two more contracts were agreed, with air travel to be provided.

Dave's World Championship challenge started at Reading. He tied with Wimbledon veteran Ronnie Moore, who had ridden in a World Final before Dave was born, and Mick Bell. In the run-off for top spot, Moore overtook Dave for the second time in the meeting. His second meeting was at Coventry, and a fall and an engine failure left him with just four points from his five rides. But in his final round, at Leicester, he was top scorer with 13, and reached the semi-finals with 29 points, the lowest score to qualify. Dave was one of six riders who had ridden in Division Two to reach the semi-finals.

Now settled in to his new team and home track, double figure scores were becoming the norm. At Hackney, he scored 14 of Leicester's 32 points, and the report said that Leicester "relied heavily on young Dave Jessup who only missed a maximum through a defeat in his last race". At Reading, in a 20-point defeat, he was "the pick of the visitors". As well as winning races, Bill Cooper reported in the Star that Dave and Malcolm Brown were having a competition to see who could get the most stickers on their car, and Dave was winning.

Dave's semi-final was at Sheffield, and nine points from five rides saw him qualify for his first British Final. He won two heats. Curiously, all three Leicester riders rode at Sheffield, while Sheffield's Arnie Haley was at Leicester. This might have been 'fair' to the other riders, as no one had home track advantage, but it can't have helped encourage the local supporters to attend. However, all three Leicester riders did qualify for the British Final.

Bill Cooper, the *Star's* Leicester correspondent commented that it "looks like young Dave Jessup is riding well enough for international recognition. Apart from his World Championship form, his scoring for the Lions for the six matches previous to the encounter with Hawks was ahead of his skipper's … which can't be bad seeing his skipper's international standing." A couple of weeks later, he reported that Dave had undertaken a 2,000 mile return trip to Italy for a long track meeting. He won two trophies, one of which was for the fastest time in practice. These trips, while demanding, were both important in building up experience of different racing conditions and types of competition, but also were lucrative financially.

To help cope with his growing riding commitments, Dave recruited a young mechanic, Mick Lipscombe, who he had met while riding at a junior grasstrack meeting. Incidents travelling to and from meetings could sometimes be as problematic as those on the track. Dave remembers driving home down the M1 when his bike fell off the back of the car near Harpenden. It had not been secured properly. Another time, he was with another rider coming back from Exeter. They were running low on fuel, so his colleague got a hammer out of the boot and broke the lock on a closed petrol station to fill up!

At the end of July, Eric Linden previewed the British Final in the *Star*. He said that: "I'm finding it difficult to believe that wee Dave Jessup has yet reached the glory heights. He is improving all the time. He is obviously going to be one of the lads who gets better and better and better and better. Gradually easing his way right to the top. So I'm forced to believe that Dave won't beat the form book this year either." Three riders in the British Final had come up from Division Two – Dave, Peter Collins and John Louis.

Ten days before the British Final, Dave made his senior international debut for England against New Zealand at Wimbledon. The home team won 51–26; Dave contributed six points from three rides at reserve. His old friend and Division Two rival Barry Thomas was the other reserve. Dave did win the second half event from Ray Wilson and Ronnie Moore, and the report said that he could be a real threat in the British Final.

Bill Cooper pointed out that seven of Dave's double figure scores for the Lions had been away from Blackbird Road; while Ray Wilson reported that Dave had got a new bike, his first for three years.

Only five of the 16 riders who lined up at Coventry's Brandon Stadium on 2 August would qualify for the World Final at Wembley. Although called the British Final, this was the route for the top Australians and New Zealanders to reach the sport's biggest meeting of the year. Five of the riders were from 'down under' and they took two of the five qualifying places. Dave ended up with seven points, missing out on a final place by three points. However, he scored the same as his Leicester colleagues Ray Wilson and John Boulger, who had far more experience at this level. Wilson commented after the meeting that for Dave, the British Final was "all good experience" and that "One way and another he has been one of the successes at Leicester this year and the fans think a lot of him."

As well as riding regularly for Leicester, Dave was starting to receive more invitations to ride in big open meetings. His former London affiliation saw him finish fourth in the London Riders Championship at Hackney.

Dave, Ray Wilson and Nigel Boocock on parade before the 1972 British Final at Coventry. (JSC)

John Louis and Dave watching the action in 1972. (JSC)

The night before, he had turned out for a Wembley Lions team in a four-team tournament, and reminded the Lions fans of what they were missing with 11 points from his four rides. And then in Leicester's Golden Gauntlets meeting, he was runner-up to Ole Olsen. A week later, he scored his first paid maximum for Leicester in a 47–31 home win against local rivals Coventry. His best performance was in one of his last meetings of the season. In Wimbledon's The Laurels, Dave beat Ole Olsen in the heats and tied on 14 points with the former World Champion. However, Olsen won the run-off for the top spot.

Dave also continued to ride in European meetings. In September, he went to Germany for a sand track meeting. He expected the track to be 500 yards, but found it was actually 700. He said that he needed to improve his 'metres to yards' calculations. Despite not having appropriate equipment to compete, he still reached the finals. He also got a stone in his eye, which left him with Henry Cooper type scar tissue. Cooper was a British boxer in the 1960s and 1970s who was vulnerable to cuts around his eyes.

Dave's international career continued at Halifax, where England faced Scotland in September. It was a young England team, with Dave's teammates including Peter Collins, Doug Wyer and Eric Broadbelt. Six of the riders in the meeting had ridden in Division Two. Dave contributed 13 points from his six rides to England's 66–42 victory.

Leicester finished fifth in Division One, with 39 points from 34 matches. But they were a long way from Belle Vue, who dominated the league and ended up with 63 points. But one success on the track was winning the Midlands Cup. In the Final they faced Wolverhampton, who won the first leg 41–37. Dave had engine problems in the second leg at Blackbird Road, and had to sort things out after his bike had fallen off the back of his car the week before. However, the Lions won 45–33, with Dave scoring 5+2 from his four rides.

Dave's final meeting in a memorable season was another appearance for Wembley, in a four-team tournament at Hackney. However, for Leicester he had added over a point to his average from 1971, despite taking time to get used to the track at Blackbird Road. In the *Star*, Ray Wilson said that: "One rider who has not had the publicity he deserves is ... Dave Jessup. Our Dave Jessup came so close to causing what would have been one of the shock results of the season in The Laurels when Ole Olsen – whom he had already beaten – pipped him in a run-off for the title. When you consider that David is still only 19, the progress he has made is really remarkable. He's so mature. You wouldn't think that he wasn't even out of his teens, because he must be the classic case of 'having an old head on young shoulders'.

When he joined the Lions from Wembley at the start of the season, we didn't know quite what to expect. He had done well – very well– in the Second Division and had a quiet, but quite effective first full season in the top flight. On the face of it though, it looked as if Leicester might be losing something because his average was about a point and a half less than Graham Plant, the man he was replacing.

As events turned out, quite irrespective of the fact that Planty has had the sort of season he would probably prefer to forget, Dave Jessup has exceeded expectations. His final figures are certainly comparable with those Graham had last year. And he has shown real touches of class against the best opposition available. Jessup doesn't go crashing and banging around like some of the highly praised hot properties who have hit the headlines. He has been riding a motorcycle for quite a number of years, and doesn't it show?

Dave has done his share of meetings on the continent this year. That sort of experience is invaluable, too. Needless to say, Leicester fans couldn't be happier with him and I'm sure that the England selectors will quickly come to regard him as an automatic international choice for years to come."

Bill Cooper's end-of-term report on Leicester said that 1972 had been disappointing with a fall from second to fifth. He added: "To put it bluntly, there were many doubts as to whether Dave Jessup would be able to fill the vacant heat-leader spot created by the transfer request of Graham Plant. My own doubts were among them. But the young 'un shook us all, and even had a spell where his scoring was as good as his skipper's. He's certainly and Englishman with a very bright future."

In the *Star,* Danny Carter reviewed Leicester's season. He wrote that "Dave Jessup arrived from Wembley with a fine reputation. Leicester knew he was good. His figures showed that. His talent, when they'd seen him in action, underlined it hard. But was he good enough to replace the outgoing Graham Plant?

Jessup soon showed that he was able to bridge that gap ... Dave took a couple of meetings to settle in – then started flying and kept that way right through to the end. This was no wild-hair Harry of a teenage terror. This was a controlled tearaway who brought the art of collecting points to a fine, planned state of affairs. And was still damned good to watch. There was little doubt that he would end the year as a heat-leader. But the fact that he scored as many points as John Boulger – second only to the mighty Ray Wilson – truly delighted the Lions fans.

They took him to their hearts and they kept him there. It was as well that Dave came off so well or Lions could have slid far more than three places down the table from their previous runners-up slot. For they developed a bit of a tail and aspiring champs can't do that."

Dave continued his international trips until the end of the season. Booked for a long track meeting at Homburg in Germany, he found there were three places with this name, and another three spelt with a 'u'. There was also Homburg-Bracht-Bellsscheidt and Mount Homburg in Switzerland. When he got there, the track was tarmac. A more successful trip to Germany, saw Dave win third prize in a meeting at Krumbach. His prize was two gallons of Martini, and Dave was a teetotaller.

Dave also rode while on holiday with Vicky and her brother, Rayleigh's Peter Claridge in Majorca. Ian Hoskins was promoting a speedway track there. Dave did some exhibition rides on the 350cc Bultaco bikes the riders were using. The bikes had been built by Reg Luckhurst. He says that "What I earned from riding paid for the holiday."

On returning home, he had stomach troubles which resulted in him having his appendix out. He was at home at 7pm, and being operated on two hours later. When he came out of hospital and was fit, there was a return to his usual winter hobby of trials riding.

In December, Dave was included in the Division One 'Honours' in the *Star*. He was 'Mister Shaker'. Eric Linden explained his selection: "Straight off let me say I expected Dave Jessup to make Division 1 sit up and take notice. He'd shown he had what it takes when he topped 200 points for Wembley the year before. Level headed, steady– the real old head on young shoulders – it was all Lombard Street to a china orange that his career would continue going up, up, up and away. What I did not expect was that he would score as many points for

Leicester as their No. 1 Aussie, John Boulger. But that's what he did, with one more meeting under his belt. That's not decrying Boulger, whom I rate as great and due to get greater. It's purely a compliment to this pint-sized hunk of British talent. And the best is yet to come."

Dave could look back at his first season at Leicester with a lot of satisfaction. Still only aged 19, he had established himself as a top flight heat-leader; won senior international honours, reached his first British Final, and performed well in open meetings both in Britain and on the continent. And with more England matches planned for 1973, there would be the opportunity to consolidate his England place, and look to improve his scores for Leicester.

1973

In January, Dave Lanning reported that Dave was going 'flat out' to achieve the 'expert' grading in trials. He was still categorised as 'intermediate'. He was again using a 250cc Bultaco bike, and had missed three events because of his appendix operation. By the end of March, he had achieved the 'expert' rating. He won a second-class award, finishing 16th in a field of 180. He had also won four 'novice' awards, although he had to give one back because riders were only allowed to win three. The night after Leicester's first meeting, he rode trials from 10am to 6pm, and said he was "so numb" that he "couldn't feel his rear".

Trials riding is very different from speedway. Motorcycle trials, also known as observed trials, is a non-speed event on specialised motorbikes. The bikes are extremely lightweight, lack seating – they are designed to be ridden standing up – and have a short suspension travel compared to a motocross or enduro bike. The sport requires very good throttle, balance, and machine control.

A trials event is split into sections where a competitor rides through an obstacle course while attempting to avoid touching the ground with their feet. The obstacles may be natural or constructed. The route is designed to test the rider's skill. In many local observed trials events, the sections are divided into separate courses to accommodate riders with different skill levels. In every section, the competitor is scored by an observer who counts how many times the competitor touches the ground with the foot, or any part of their body. Each time a competitor touches the ground with a foot, the penalty is one point.

The possible scores in each section are 0, 1, 2, 3, or 5. If a competitor goes through the section without touching the ground with a foot, their score is 0. They are said to have 'cleaned the section'. If they touch the ground once, they have a score of 1, twice and their score is 2. If they touch the ground three or more times, their score is 3 —if they complete the section without stalling, dismounting, going out of bounds or backwards. If the competitor fails to complete the section, the score is 5. The winner is the rider with the least points at the end of the event. Some events are timed with penalty points given to late riders.

Dave says: "The bikes had to be roadworthy – we did 30 to 50 miles on the road. It is a winter sport and is often in freezing conditions.

For the national championships in Shropshire, the start was earlier and we did 60 to 80 miles on the road. It was a great effort after the course, your body temperature drops – I remember shaking with cold."

Left: On a Bultaco 350 trials bike at Watling Tyres, who sponsored Dave in trials riding.
Right: Briggo's Boys: Barry Briggs, Martin Ashby, Dave, Graeme Stapleton and Scott Autrey.

Dave's plans for the 1973 season were hugely disrupted by a fire at Don Godden's workshop in Maidstone in February. Dave had been preparing his bikes there for the forthcoming speedway and longtrack seasons. This was severe financial blow, and Dave and Vicky were also buying a house at the time. Halfway through the season they moved from Hoo to Shaw Close in Cliffe Woods, near Rochester.

A couple of weeks after the fire, the Leicester supporters held a dance and film night to raise funds for Dave to buy new equipment. The bikes had not been insured. Interviewed in the *Star*, Dave said that he had been using Godden's workshop to avoid disturbing the neighbours where he lived. He had been planning to sell the bikes and buy a new one.

He was also waiting for Barry Briggs to return from New Zealand to see if Briggo would be sponsoring him. This deal was agreed, and Dave become one of 'Briggo's Boys'. The other riders involved were Martin Ashby, Phil Crump, Scott Autrey and Graham Stapleton. Briggo was the Jawa importer at the time. All the riders bought two bikes from Briggo, and were given various accessories, including matching seats, leathers and helmets

Dave had also become a director of his father's car engineering business. He was also anxiously waiting for the speedway fixtures to come out so that he could plan more trips to European meetings. While he could get to the meetings, which were on Sundays, when there were very few Leicester fixtures, if he had to ride on a Saturday night, then he had to fly out on Sunday morning, which was an extra expense.

One further honour he had received was the 'Most Improved London Rider' at the London Speedway Honours Ball. How he qualified for this, living in Kent and riding for Leicester, is not clear. Maybe it was his past Wembley connections. Another 'honour' was being invited to play for the Speedway International XI football team, although this depended on his trials commitments.

Leicester had released Alan Cowland from the 1972 team, who had moved to Second Division Hull. Brian Foote rode at reserve, and another new recruit towards the end of the season was Frank Auffret. He replaced Foote who returned to Rayleigh in Division Two. Otherwise, the team was similar to 1972, with a strong heat-leader line up, with Malcolm Shakespeare and Malcolm Brown both providing the main second-string strength. Both riders improved their averages from 1972, as did Dave.

Dave showed good form from the start of the season, as did Ray Wilson and John Boulger. At Cradley in a challenge match he scored a full maximum, which included beating Cradley guest John Louis twice. In the second leg of the East Midlands Bowl, Dave achieved another full maximum, with all three heat leaders in 'brilliant form' according to the report in the *Star*. He was chosen for an Under-23 Great Britain squad to ride in Poland. Ray Wilson commented that "Dave Jessup ... in such good form at the moment that his must be one of the first names pencilled into the test teams ... in fact I reckon he must have a great chance of being named captain of the under-23 side against Poland as well. He's young, but very sensible and mature in his outlook. It would be quite an honour if he does get that captaincy job."

Dave Lanning reported that Dave was disappointed with a return of eight points from five rides at Hackney, which most visitors would have been satisfied with. Dave showed his frustration, saying that "... in my last two matches I've returned a round dozen, and they were challenges so relatively unimportant. This is a league match which counts on my average and I've had one of my poorest nights of the season. It simply won't do." However, he did return to form very quickly, with full maximums at home to Hackney, and then against King's Lynn riding as a guest for Oxford. Two days later he rode for Leicester at King's Lynn, and scored 10+1. Bill Cooper said that if Dave continued this level of scoring, he would not receive many guest rider bookings because his average would be too high.

Dave's good form continued, and he took over the number one race jacket from Ray Wilson. But in the first heat against Ipswich at Blackbird Road on 17 April, disaster struck. Ipswich's Alan Sage, a former KYMCA rider who had ridden with Dave at West Ham back in 1968, fell on the slick first turn. Dave hit his bike, somersaulted over the top and hit the safety fence. The ambulancemen put his leg into splints. He had dislocated his knee and torn his ligaments. However, there was no bone damage. The track doctor thought he would be out for six weeks. In fact, it turned out to be three months before he could return to action. In May, the *Star* reported that he was in plaster from groin to ankle. He was hoping to be fit for the World Championship qualifying rounds.

Alan Sage was very upset by the accident, and apologised to Dave, who Alan said was 'an inspiration' to him. He phoned the hospital regularly for the first few days Dave was there. Dave said that it wasn't Alan's fault, but just 'one of those things'. The Leicester fans collected £142 for Dave, and in May he travelled to Blackbird Road to thank them. Ray Wilson said that "there cannot have been many more popular riders at Leicester in the last few years." For the match against King's Lynn, Dave travelled with his Kent neighbour Malcolm Simmons. He had had a new plaster fitted after the original one moved. He worked with Harry Aldridge, who had been the trainer for the Harringay Racers, to try to get fit.

Top: Dave, Barry Thomas and Hughie Saunders at the 1973 London Riders Championship at Hackney. (JSC)

Left: Dave wearing the individual race jacket given to him by his fan club at Leicester. (JSC)

42

1973 Great Britain World Team Cup winners at Wembley with Ed Stewart. Top: Terry Betts, Len Silver (manager), Dave; middle: Peter Collins, Ed Stewart, Malcolm Simmonds; bottom: Ray Wilson (JSC)

He also used a physiotherapy bike. He said it was "hard work", but at least "you don't fall off 'em and very rarely get involved in accidents."

His left knee caused Dave problems for the rest of his career, and still does. He says that: "I only have 17 degrees of movement in my left knee. [A knee usually has 135 degrees of movement]. It can be very painful and gets stiff. My leg was trapped in Alan Sage's bike and pulled my knee out of the socket. I damaged the cruciate and medial ligaments.
I was told by the Polish doctor who treated me in Leicester that I may not walk again. He rebuilt my knee, but said that 'my riding days were over'. When the tracks were bad it was a bigger problem for me.

Vicky stayed in Leicester while I was in hospital. One of the supporters used to help me in the pits, and she stayed with his family. That was very kind of them. When it was time for me to go home, we took the front seat out of our Capri and Vicky drove us home. I was in plaster up to my waist.

I was 19 years old and had been married for a few weeks. It was a worrying time with no money coming in, but we got over it. The injury doesn't affect my golf, only walking, so I now use a single seat golf cart."

Dave finally returned to racing in a Four-Team-tournament at Leicester on 10 July, scoring a 'creditable' seven points from his four rides. His scores gradually improved over the next four weeks. However, although he was named at number eight for the England versus Sweden International tournament final at Wembley, he missed out on the other England meetings for which he surely would have been included.

By mid-August, Dave scored a full maximum against Oxford and according to Bill Cooper was "back at his best". In the *Star* on 1 September, Jeff Chaucer interviewed Dave about his domestic and international racing: "Dave Jessup was a decidedly unhappy man after his recent none too successful longtrack trip to the Montaganna circuit to Italy. The knee injury sustained in the early weeks of what promised to be a most successful season for 'Wee Dave' of Leicester was playing up and he was far from happy. 'The knee just didn't stand up to the half-mile plus Montaganna track, the engine was slow and the field much tougher than I'd expected', he said. But three good British League scores to see out the week, plus the useful addition of a coffee percolator to the recently set-up Cliff Woods (Kent) home, had David in a very different frame of mind at the weekend.

Back with Montaganna he had trouble staying with his track rivals, but at least managed to score in every race for seven points, and before he left an offer for 1974 was made. 'Next time I'll go better prepared', he says. 'Longtrack racing needs a different approach and different equipment to British track racing. I'll just have to organise myself better.' Immediate fears though were of having to quit racing for Leicester before the end of the season and to re-enter hospital for further surgery on his knee. But that was immediately after returning from Montaganna. After a Leicester maximum against Oxford, a paid 13 when guesting for Wolverhampton in a Speedway Star Cup match against Swindon and a paid 11 in a second appearance of the week against Oxford – this time for Belle Vue – may change his way of thinking.

A couple of good scores, including cleaning up the Belle Vue second half, which won him the coffee percolator and a trophy, plus establishing the fastest time of the night at Hyde Road had David back to his usual perky self.

'A good winter's rest is probably what I need more than anything,' he said. And that almost certainly rules out a close season tour to America, Australia, New Zealand, Rhodesia or elsewhere.

'I've had one or two offers and invitations, but they all demand too much time away from home,' said David. 'I want to spend Christmas with my family in my own home this year.'"

After his maximum against Oxford, Leicester staged a double header, against Coatbridge and Coventry, and Dave scored paid maximums in both matches. More prestigious open meetings were coming his way. In the Welsh Open at Newport he was runner-up, and finished fifth in the Golden Gauntlets at Leicester.

More international honours also came Dave's way. In the World Team Cup at Wembley on 15 September, Dave was reserve for a Great Britain team consisting of just English riders. In the past, Australians and new Zealanders had ridden under the Great Britain banner. They beat Sweden, the USSR and Poland to win the title. The *Star* reported that "Diddy Dave spent the evening ministering to the mechanical and psychological needs of his colleagues, and was as much a part of the team as anybody. Complimented on having the one unmarked body colour in the pits, he grinned 'I feel as if I've ridden all four races though'". The night before the Wembley meeting, Dave scored 14 from six rides, including an exclusion, for an England Select team against a Scotland Select at Coatbridge. The home team won by six points.

In the London Riders Championship at Hackney, Dave tied with Barry Thomas on 14 points. Thomas won the run-off for the title on his home track, but the *Star* said that "Jessup was superb throughout." He returned to Hackney three weeks later to win their Bonanza Pairs meeting in partnership with Ray Wilson.

Leicester again reached the final of the Midlands Cup, but lost to Wolverhampton over two legs. An unusual international appearance was for an England team in a four-team tournament in Germany. Dave scored 10 points, and had driven there with his dad and the bikes. And there was one final appearance for the Wembley Lions. On 18 October, an 'Ex Wembley' team lost 43–35 to Wimbledon. Dave scored eight from his four rides.

In September, Dave had the experience of a shattered windscreen on the way to a meeting. In October, he was involved in a more serious accident close to home on the way to Ipswich. An oncoming car spun in front of him, and Dave hit a wall. His car was wrecked, but neither he or Vicky were injured. He quickly phoned his father who took him to Malcolm Simmons's house. He was riding in the same meeting so Dave travelled with him and rode in the meeting.

After the end of the speedway season, Dave resumed his trials riding. He 'jabbed' his knee at an event, and had some work to do to get it right for 1974.

This season had promised much for Dave. However, in many ways it was a frustrating one. He missed out on the World Championship altogether, and on the International Tournament and other meetings, when he surely would have won a place in the England side. Would he have ridden in the World Team Cup Final if he had not been injured? As it was, his average for Leicester improved to 9.24, with five full maximums and two paid. The Lions improved by one place in the league, finishing fourth, nine points behind champions Reading.

Danny Carter's review of Leicester's season in the *Star* was headlined "DJ's loss decisive". He said that "They have no doubts about it at Leicester. There was only one reason why they moved up a place to finish fourth this year. That was Dave Jessup. Or, to put it more bluntly, the lack of Dave Jessup. But for him, they would have won the title. They are convinced of that. Or, to put it correctly, but for the lack of Dave, they'd have won that title. It could be. I'm not convinced. After all, before he copped that early injury which out him out of action for a vital nine league match period, they hadn't been doing all that well. I mean to say they had actually lost a match." He goes on to point out that while Dave was injured, the Lions continued to win at home, but were not so strong away from Blackbird Road. He pointed out that Dave made an "extremely good comeback" although he was not sure if the Lions would have beaten Reading to the title if Dave had not been injured. He felt that the second strings and reserves were not strong enough for a league-winning team.

However, the importance of Dave's contribution to the Leicester team was very clear. He could now look to build on his first two seasons at Leicester, and look for further progress in the World Championship and for England in 1974.

6. World Final debut

Dave was now an established heat leader at Leicester, and Dave Lanning said that he "was expected to make the breakthrough to world class in 1974." In the speedway close season, he kept his fitness by again doing trials riding on his Bultaco 325. His growing status in speedway was shown by an invitation to the Motor Cycle Show in London along with Terry Betts and Ray Wilson in January to link up with Phil Read Developments in 1974. The company supplied equipment including helmets, bags and jackets.

In March, Dave and Malcolm Simmons took part in the Mutton Lancers trials event at Barham in Kent. Simmons won the best performance award, while Dave was among the First-Class Expert awards. Dave Lanning commented on how this showed the all-round motorcycling ability of Britain's speedway stars.

There had been speculation linking John Boulger with a move to Cradley Heath, and in March this was borne out. Ray Wilson commented that there would be "a fair amount of responsibility" on him and Dave Jessup. Boulger was replaced by Frank Auffret, but he never really reached the heights required of a third heat leader.

On 7 March Dave had reached the age of 21, at the start of his sixth season in professional speedway. A party was held for him a few days before his birthday. The event was organised by his Leicester-based fan club, and he was "absolutely inundated" with presents according to the report in the *Star*. The ones from the fan club itself included a race jacket with his name on, the Leicester Lions crest and a Union Jack for him to wear in open meetings. There was also a bottle of Champagne for his birthday and a birthday cake with models of speedway riders. He was also given back protector to wear when riding. The fan club secretary, Hazel Mathers, was given a bouquet of flowers by Vicky.

One issue to be settled before the new season was Dave's contract. He recalls that "Reg Fearman was a very good boss. He was straightforward to deal with. We would argue about my contract and other things while sitting in his Rolls Royce. That car was something to look up to. He was an impressive manager and was widely respected in the sport. There were the 'Three Fs' – jack Fearnley at Belle Vue, Charles Foote at Poole and Reg. They travelled abroad to test matches with us to support us. Once Charles Foote came down to Poole to speak on my behalf in court to get me off a ban for speeding.

That year at Coventry, at about 7.10pm we made an agreement. I wanted to ride in the meeting, but also wanted to make 1974 a good year. From then on, I always wanted a lump sum at the start of the season to sign on. It gave me a guaranteed figure and points money on top of that. We always had to sign a BSPA contract in those days before we could ride." It was a financial arrangement that Dave continued throughout his career. His accident in 1973, when he had been married for three week and suddenly had no income, meant that he wanted security.

Dave started the season in top form. In his first six meetings for Leicester he only failed to score double figures once, and that was when he got nine points against Exeter. This was despite the *Star* reporting on 6 April that he had not yet agreed terms with the Leicester management and was "very upset with things". Presumably the dispute was resolved.

Leicester struggled early on; Ray Wilson was injured and the team often used rider-replacement, which while it meant extra rides for Dave did not adequately cover the skipper's absence. The Lions lost at home to Halifax despite a five-ride full maximum from Dave. Four days later, another defeat followed at King's Lynn, where Dave contributed 15+1 from 6 rides and "rode manfully".

The first major meeting of the season was the *Daily Express* Spring Classic at Wimbledon. Dave scored 12 from 5 rides to finish as runner-up to Malcom Simmons on 13. Philip Rising reported in the *Star* that "At one stage Dave Jessup, a lovely rider to watch round Plough Lane, looked set for the title. He needed a win from his last race to finish on 13 points, but John Louis pipped him to the post. Jessup did gain some consolation when he took second place overall, Olsen's machine playing up in the run-off."

The World Championship qualifying rounds for the First Division riders started at the beginning of May. Dave scored 37 from his meetings at Leicester, Poole and Oxford to comfortably qualify for the British semi-finals, the next step on the road to the Ullevi Stadium in Gothenburg.

One area where — according to Dave Lanning's report — Dave was not the leader at Leicester was in telling jokes in the dressing room. "I'm terrible at joke telling. I'm still trying to remember the punch-lines of two gags I started last season," he had told Lanning. The established jokers at Leicester were Malcolm Brown and Norman Storer.

Dave continued to regularly score double figures for Leicester, who at times struggled away from home. At Belle Vue, he scored 14 from five rides, over half of Leicester's 27. One triumph was to knock local rivals Coventry out of the Speedway Star Knock Out Cup. Leicester won by eight points at home, and went down by six at Brandon to go through by two points on aggregate.

Apart from speedway, Dave also regularly rode in longtrack meetings. Often these were in Europe, a more local one was the Lydden International 600 yarder. Dave was runner-up to Malcolm Simmons, despite having to borrow a bike from Dave Galenby.

In the World Championship, Dave was drawn to ride at Sheffield in the semi-final. The first attempt to stage the meeting was rained off, which suited Dave because he had flu. When it was restaged, Dave won the meeting with a 15-point maximum. He won heat 18 against Jim McMillan and Ray Wilson to complete "a brilliant maximum to finish on top of a star-studded field" according to the report in the *Star*. Previewing the British Final, the *Star's* James Oldfield said that he expected Dave to be in the running for the title. Winning the British Final was an achievement in itself, but Dave's priority would be to qualify for the British-Nordic-American Final in August.

The weekend before the British Final, Dave won the Littlechild Trophy at King's Lynn, beating local favourite Terry Betts in a run-off after both riders had finished on 14 points. The night before the big meeting at Coventry, Dave scored his second consecutive full maximum for Leicester at Blackbird Road. He continued this good form in the British Final, finishing third with 11 points from his five rides, comfortably qualifying for the next round.

As well as his commitments for Leicester, Dave was becoming a regular selection for the England team. He was joint top scorer with 15+1 from six rides in a 71–37 win over Sweden. At Poole, England won 66–42 with Dave scoring 13+1 from six rides, despite cracking his frame in one race. Overall, Dave averaged 15.72 (six rides) from his four meetings against the Swedes, scoring 58+5 points. He was top of the England averages for riders who rode regularly in the tests – Richard Greer had an 18-point average from winning his one ride!

At the beginning of July, it was announced that Dave and Peter Collins had been selected to represent England in the Best Pairs World Final at Belle Vue. The *Star* commented that "Jessup has a fine record on visits to Manchester." Ray Wilson added: "Dave Jessup has certainly been tremendously consistent this year, with double figures in all the internationals he rode against Sweden, third place in the British final and convincing performances in plenty of other big meetings. And when Leicester were up at Hyde Road earlier in the year, he was the one man to really impress." Barry Briggs also supported Dave's selection, commenting: "Young Dave is a clever rider who I have always rated very highly and he has a good record at Belle Vue."

Dave was also selected for all seven test matches against Poland, which meant him having eight meetings in nine days, including the Pairs Final. Dave and Peter Collins finished fourth in the meeting, on 20 points, with the Belle Vue rider contributing 12 and Dave 8+2. Dave did beat Ivan Mauger in heat three, with Collins taking third place against Barry Briggs. But a 5–1 defeat to the eventual champions, the Sweden pair of Anders Michanek and Soren Sjosten in heat seven made their chances of a rostrum finish less likely. A further 5–1 loss to the runners-up, Australian pair of Phil Crump and John Boulger in heat 16 made their task more difficult. However, had Dave beaten Zenon Plech for second place in the final heat would have given the British pair a run-off against New Zealand for third place. Ivan Mauger had lent a bike to Plech for the crucial final heat. Dave remembers that "I only had one win. Peter Collins was the big star at Belle Vue. It was his home track. But it was not bad for a first World Pairs final."

The tests against Poland were generally even more one-sided than the series against Sweden. At Ipswich in the fifth test, Dave scored a full maximum from his six rides, as part of a 78–30 victory on a track that he liked riding. In the first test, which England won 88–19, Dave scored a paid maximum, 14+4 from his six rides partnering Peter Collins. Overall, Dave scored 80+18 from his 41 rides. While this was clearly a strong England side, maybe the results also reflected the lack of international experience the Polish team had.

A third international series was staged, with England taking on the USSR. Dave was selected for the first test at Swindon, scoring 16 from six rides. The selectors seem to have used this series to give more riders international experience, using 25 riders over the six tests that started – the last one at Newport, which was Dave's second meeting in the series – was abandoned after six heats. England won the series comfortably 5–0.

Dave's opportunities to ride for Leicester in this busy period were relatively few. One disappointment was a 40–38 home loss to Ipswich in the second leg of the Knock Out Cup second round. The Lions would have fancied their chances of making up the six-point deficit they faced from the first leg at Foxhall, but Dave, for once, had a poor night. Riding against doctor's orders, he scored just six points from his four rides, and was "far from his best" according to the report in the *Star*.

The first two weekends in August saw more international action. On 4 August, Dave and his Leicester team mate Ray Wilson, who was reserve for the meeting, were in Frederica in

Denmark for the British-Nordic American Final. The top eight riders went through to the European Final at Wembley. Dave was drawn at number 9, and the preview in the Star said that he "will be hoping to get all his equipment back in working order". An 11,000 crowd saw Dave qualify in sixth place with 10 points. Eric Boocock had been involved in a nasty crash in heat two, and Philip Rising reported in the *Star*: "For a horrifying split second it looked as though Dave Jessup was going to follow Eric in heat 3. He had led Peter Collins quite comfortably for almost the whole race when the Belle Vue ace came under him on the last bend and set Jessup towards the fence. Fortunately, Dave clipped the boards and he actually crossed the line while temporarily out of control. Collins was lucky to escape punishment, but had Jessup actually fallen the Swedish referee would have been compelled to act." Martin Rogers commented that: "Dave Jessup ... had only four points after three rides the sickener being heat five when he shed a chain. Like the great little rider he is, Dave Jessup hit back with two fine victories to earn himself a long-awaited return to Wembley, where he hasn't ridden since being a member of the now defunct Lions in 1971"

The four British riders who qualified from Frederica – John Louis, Terry Betts, Peter Collins and Dave – made up the four riders, along with captain Ray Wilson at reserve, made up the England team for the World Team Cup semi-final at Ipswich. England won the meeting comfortably and qualified with 41 points. Australia, Scotland and New Zealand – who were missing Mauger and Briggs – missed out. Dave scored 10 points from his four rides, with two wins and two second places.

At the end of July, Leicester beat Wimbledon 51–27 at Blackbird Road. Dave scored one of his six league full maximums that season. In his column in the *Star*, Barry Briggs wrote about Wimbledon's meeting at Leicester: "...Not a good night for Dons but I enjoyed it ... But when Dave Jessup beat me in heat 11, I was more determined than ever to get my own back in the last race. But the ears of the clutch broke off which left me in a hopeless position. I came up against Dave again in the second half and gated ahead of him. I attempted to run him off the line and made a very good first corner. But Dave turned back under me in terrific style and this was just about the best 'speedway' move pulled on me this year."

Leicester only won two away league meetings all season. Both were in August, and both were notable for Dave. At Coventry on 17 August, the Lions won 50–28. It was the home team's biggest ever home defeat in the British League at the time, and Dave "raced to a splendid maximum" according to the report in the *Star*. And a week later, the Lions won at Cradley 40–38. Dave "... smashed the four-year-old Dudley Wood track record with a time of 66.2 in the opening race of this British League match. Jessup went on to complete a faultless maximum."

On the last Saturday in August, British speedway fans took advantage of a rare opportunity to watch speedway at Wembley, with the European Final being staged there. Martin Rogers said in the *Star* that Dave had waited three years for the chance to ride at Wembley again, having been a member of the Wembley Lions team in 1971. Eleven riders would qualify for the Final. Rogers said that Dave was "another ice-cool character and a snappy starter, he's had a couple of little knocks recently, but nothing to interrupt his progress."

In the event, Dave qualified for his first World Final in eighth place, with eight points from his five rides. Paul Parish reported that "Dave Jessup packed up while lying third in his first ride and was last to Terry Betts's third in heat 20. In three other rides he looked every inch a World Finalist". Dave also gave Ole Olsen a shock in heat 14, leading for the first lap before Olsen passed him. Dave said at the time: "It was my first actual meeting here since 1971 and very enjoyable, especially after the first race! Getting to Sweden makes up for missing so much last year."

The World Final was dominated by Anders Michanek, who won comfortably on home soil with a 15-point maximum. The top English rider was John Louis who finished fourth with nine points. Dave finished 13th in his World Final debut, with five points from his five rides. According to the *Star*, he "…never got to grips with the circuit at all, and a style more suited to delicate throttle control did not serve best on what is basically a full-throttle circuit."

Dave recalls that "It had rained for a week. The Swedes used a helicopter to dry the track, and a land speed car to dry it out, with hot air from the turbine. It was still wet and miserable. I was friendly with John Louis – I was from Ipswich originally. He suggested I have a massage and sauna, but it didn't improve my riding. I never did it again. I rode well at Gothenburg later on in my career."

Nine days later, Dave was part of the England team that comfortably won the World Team Cup at Katowice in Poland. They finished on 42 points, 11 clear of Sweden who were runners-up on 31. Poland finished third on 13, three clear of the USSR. Dave Lanning commented that "Dave Jessup showed the English style with as breathtaking a ride as I've seen in heat 10." Peter Collins and John Louis both scored full maximums, Dave got 10 points and Malcolm Simmons eight in front of 80,000 disappointed Polish fans. Reg Fearman, chairman of the BSPA, said that "This is the greatest ever achievement by a team from the British Isles. There will be champagne celebrations tonight."

Dave is very proud of his record with England: "All the World Team Cup wins were fabulous. I was extremely proud to wear the England jacket. I rode in four World Team Cup wins and was reserve in two more, so won six gold medals."

Despite all the meetings he was riding in at this time, Dave did not neglect his fan club. On 7 September, Bill Cooper reported in the *Star* that Dave had attended a fan club dance, and turned down a riding booking to do so. He had planned to stay in Leicester after a Blackbird Road meeting to attend the event, but problems with his bike undermined that arrangement. He returned home to Kent to repair his bike, then drove to Leicester to enjoy the dance. Cooper said that the evening was a success, and club secretary Hazel Mathers looked very happy.

Also, away from the track, Dave and Vicky's interest in greyhounds continued to develop. In January, Dave Lanning had reported that Dave – in fact it was Vicky – was walking the dogs that belonged to his father-in-law John Claridge. Now he broke the news that Dave had invested in a greyhound puppy – Davick's Racer – which was expected to make its racing debut at Catford soon. Lanning also added that Dave had also acquired a goldfish, won by Vicky when Dave was invited to open a garden fete at Sibley in Leicestershire which was raising money for the local scouts and guides.

Left: John Louis, Ron Bagley, Dave, Reg Fearman and Ray Wilson at the 1974 British-Nordic-American Final at Fredericia (JSC)

Below: Dave and Peter Collins lead Dag Lovaas at the 1974 European Final at Wembley. (JSC)

Dave, Peter Collins and John Louis at the 1974 World Final in Gothenburg. (JSC)

England 1974 World Team Cup Winners at the RAC Club in London:
Terry Betts, Peter Collins, Ray Wilson, Malcolm Simmons and Dave. (JSC)

Leicester's form continued to vacillate. Two heavy defeats home and away to Sheffield were followed the next week by a 53–25 home win against Swindon, with Dave contributing a full maximum. Although Leicester could only finish 10th in the 17-team league, with 27 points from their 32 matches, they did win the Midland Cup. Wolverhampton were their opponents in the final. Leicester won by six points at Blackbird Road, and then by eight at Monmore Green. Dave contributed 10+1 from his four rides.

Another sign of Dave's progress was that he qualified to represent Leicester at the British League Riders Championship ahead of Ray Wilson. Dave finished top of the Leicester averages on 9.66, 0.32 ahead of Wilson. At Belle Vue, Dave finished in sixth place, with 10 points from his five rides.

The British League Riders Championship is the only major British meeting that Dave never achieved a rostrum place. Looking back, he reflects that "I did have some good meetings at Belle Vue. I used to do all the driving, leave the south east and drive to the north west, the sun was coming through the front window. If you were driving in the other direction, the sun was behind you. The track always seemed to be wet and cold in late October. I often was tired at the end of a long season. In hindsight, I should have prepared a bike specially for that meeting, and mothballed it. I always wanted to be number one in any team I rode for. I'm sorry for the fans who came to support me that I didn't do better. I did try hard, but never got the result I wanted. Another meeting near the end of the season was the Golden Helmet in Prague. Even when I was a Jawa works rider, I didn't enter it. Again, that's something I regret."

To complete Leicester's dominance of Midlands speedway trophies, Dave won the Midland Riders Championship at Coventry with 14 points. Only Martin Ashby beat him in a memorable win of a longstanding speedway trophy. Dave was the pre-meeting favourite.

Another notable success was at Wimbledon, where Dave won the prestigious Laurels meeting. Again, Dave won with 14 points, to take the prize of £100 and a Favre Leuba watch. Dave says that "I loved that watch, but it was stolen in a burglary at our house in 2019. It was one of the best prizes I ever won."

Despite "being up to his eyeballs in speedway bookings", Bill Cooper reported that Dave was also finding time for his trails riding. He had brand new equipment for the forthcoming winter season, and was sponsored by Barrie Rodgers Motor Cycles of Derby, who had supplied him with an Ossa bike. And his longtrack meetings could also be lucrative. Dave Lanning reported that at a meeting in Krumbach in West Germany, Dave had gone through the card, and won the meeting trophy, a garland and a huge box of cassette tapes. Now he was hoping to win a cassette player so he could listen to them.

Dave reflected on a successful season in an interview with Dave Stevens in the *Star* at the beginning of November. After considering his successes in the World Championship, and whether winning the meetings or qualifying was the priority, Dave said that getting to the Final in Gothenburg made up for the disappointments he had in 1973. He also said that he would have liked to have done better in two meetings at Belle Vue: The World Pairs meeting and the British League Riders Championship. He also said that his final British League average had fallen by about a point because of "a calculated experiment with machine preparation which just didn't pay off. It proved a dear lesson and one I'll never repeat."

An informal photo of Dave in the pits in 1974.

For 1975, he said that the World Final at Wembley, he would be "striving to win the title". He was also building up a stable of four bikes, having at one stage in 1974 not had a working bike. He was planning a short holiday and to work for a couple of months so that he could use the money he had earned this season towards his equipment for 1975.

Dave and Vicky had their holiday in the Canaries, but the trip back was marred by their plane having to make an emergency landing at Stanstead instead of Luton when the front wheel would not secure into position. They were relieved to have landed safely.

Also, Dave had some health problems at the end of the season. He had x-rays on a problem with his rib cage, which he thought had been caused when he looped at the start at King's Lynn in the England versus Poland match. He didn't take much notice of the injury because he didn't want to stop riding, but now had the chance to get the problem dealt with properly. In fact, the x-rays showed problems with his spine, and that there had been damage to his vertebrae in the fall at King's Lynn. The injury had not knitted together properly and caused him discomfort. Despite this, Dave was still planning to do some trials riding in the speedway close season, and wanted to compete in the national trials in January.

Although it had been a successful year for Dave, it had not been for Leicester. Winning the Midland Cup was enjoyable, but overall, the team was weaker than in 1973. Frank Auffret, in his first full season in the First Division, was not really ready for a heat leader spot, although his average of 6.46 was respectable. Danny Carter's review of the season in the *Star* said that Dave "started like a bomb and finished up like a bigger bomb." However, the team could not cover adequately for when Ray Wilson was injured early in the season, and his scores were slightly down on the previous season. The team also missed Malcolm Shakespeare, although he was replaced by Mick Bell, and Malcolm Brown had a poor campaign. Leicester fell from fourth to 10th in the league. They would face a new challenge in 1975 to climb back up the table.

7. Top rider at Leicester

Dave spent the winter keeping busy on a motorbike with trials riding, and off one on the golf course. Much of this activity was in the company of near neighbour Malcolm Simmons. They entered the Vic Britten National Trial, but found it tougher than the local events they had competed in, and were up against real experts. On the golf course, they were playing at the Deansgate course twice a week. The four-mile walk was a challenge for them, particularly when it became longer as balls went into the rough. However, they were improving, and what was a nine- or 10-mile walk for 18 holes was getting closer to seven.

Another new interest for Dave and Vicky was being the owner of a greyhound puppy. It had been given to him by his father-in-law, John Claridge. Davick's Racer was planned to run at Catford or White City.

As in 1974, there was speculation that Dave would be leaving Leicester. In February, it was reported that Bobby Beaton and Barry Crowson had been allocated to Leicester, but in the event neither became a Lion. Ray Wilson hoped that Dave would stay at Leicester, saying that he had been an 'outstanding' member of the side for three years, and was "getting better all the time".

Dave's efforts were appreciated locally. In March his fan club again held a disco to celebrate his birthday. The next day he was invited to the local Variety Club awards. He was also in the running for the Leicester Sports Personality of the Year award. At the end of March, it was announced that he had won the award, which was a trophy worth £800. He bought an evening suit specially for the presentation. He beat top gymnast Avril Lennox, Olympic diver Helen Koppell, Steve Whitworth of Leicester City FC, Leicester Tigers rugby union club's Peter Wheeler, sprinter Chris Monk, cricketer Ray Illingworth and road rallyist Roger Clark.

The Leicester team which started the season showed several changes from the 1974 line up. Dave, Ray Wilson, Frank Auffret and Norman Storer were all still present. Dave had agreed to stay with the club for another year. Mick Bell had returned to parent club Reading, who were back in action after a season absent from the sport while their new stadium was being built. Malcolm Brown and Malcolm Ballard had also left. Keith White, who had ridden in nine meetings in 1974 claimed a regular slot. Other new arrivals were Tony Lomas and Ila Teromaa, a promising Finnish rider. The clear weakness was in the third heat leader position. After Dave and Ray Wilson, Teromaa was the next highest scorer in 1975 with an average of 5.91. This was commendable for a new rider in the British League, but not enough for a heat leader. Tony Lomas was expected to fulfil the heat leader role, having averaged over seven in his last two seasons at Exeter, but was inconsistent and his average fell to 5.70.

Dave started the season with a string of double figure scores for the Lions. Perhaps the best was a 15-point maximum at Cradley, when Leicester lost 42–35. Ray Wilson said in his column in the *Star* that Dave had "been scoring maximums all over the place and he's going to take some beating at this rate." He was – maybe not surprisingly – at times almost unbeatable at Blackbird Road. In April he only dropped one point in five home meetings.

However, a long-track injury in a World 1,000 metres event at Vilshofen in West Germany cut across his progress. He injured his shoulder and bruised his kidneys. Dave remembers the incident well: "It was my first ride. Preben Eriksen, who rode for Belle Vue, took me out on the corner. The track was wet. This was by the pits, and I ended up in the fence at Vicky's feet. The track doctor thought it might be spinal damage. I couldn't stop shaking – I had trapped a nerve. It took a long time to treat. For the rerun I rode with a broken shoulder.

I really thought it was a serious injury. I was waiting for the X Rays in hospital and Otto Lantenhammer came in. His spark plug lead had come off and he tried to put it back. He caught his fingers in the chain and lost three fingers. There were two nurses with him and a towel wrapped round his hand. There was blood all along the corridor. There were no chain guards in those days. A rider's instinct was that if something went wrong, you try to fix it. I didn't want to stay in Germany, so we drove home. It was a very long drive, 12 hours. When we got home, I had my shoulder fixed." Otto Lantenhammer did return to long-track racing despite his injury, and then became a well-known engine tuner.

Dave decided not to ride again until the World Championship qualifying rounds. He had been due to partner Peter Collins in the World Pairs semi-final in Yugoslavia on 25 May, but was replaced by John Louis.

The original draw for Dave to ride at Reading as his first World Championship qualifying round meeting, but he was switched to Belle Vue 12 days later. In his first meeting back from injury, the qualifying round at Leicester, he rode with his shoulder heavily strapped, and scored just seven points from five rides. But 14 points at Oxford nine days later, and then 10 at Belle Vue saw him comfortably into the semi-finals with 31 points. However, he did miss out on the prestigious Internationale meeting as well as some Leicester meetings.

A short trip to Poland followed in early June. Dave remembers that "We all arrived at Heathrow after midnight on the Saturday night. People had been riding all over the country. We dossed down as best we could and flew out first thing on the Sunday morning with our bikes on a charter flight."

England fielded 'A' and 'B' teams. Dave rode twice for the 'A' team, first in a 71–37 defeat at Bydgoszcz, he scored eight points to be the second highest scorer. The next day at Gorzow, he scored 15 in a 58–50 England win. The 'B' team won both their matches.

The next week, England, represented by John Louis and Peter Collins, finished fourth in the World Pairs Final. The *Star* reported that Dave was "bitterly disappointed and disillusioned on return from England's Poland trip. Dropped from the World Pairs semi-final and final, Dave Jessup, in spite of an injured shoulder blade, still showed that he could turn in good performances. What must have made the pill more bitter to swallow was ... that on this last trip, Dave's return was much better than John Louis's, the man who replaced him in the pairs event. And no doubt, with all this in mind, John Louis's original outburst concerning the Pairs selection, didn't help leave Dave Jessup in any better frame of mind. "In any case" said Dave, "I was never given an official explanation about being dropped." Some more positive news was that Dave had been offered sponsorship by Century Oils Ltd and British Steam Specialities Ltd.

Although overlooked for the Pairs meetings, Dave was named in all five England squads for the forthcoming test series against Sweden in July. In the World Championship semi-finals, he was drawn to ride at Sheffield, and comfortably qualified for the British Final with 13 points.

In July, Dave was riding almost every night at times, commitments with Leicester being combined with appearing for England. In the England versus Sweden series, he rode in all five matches, along with John Louis and Ray Wilson. Louis was top scorer for England with 84 points, Dave was second with 65. England won the series comfortably 5–0; the Swedes' best result was a 62–46 defeat at Hackney.

In the middle of the test series, Dave rode for England in the World Team Cup UK qualifying round. England comfortably qualified with 37 points, 13 ahead of Australia. The final was scheduled for the end of September. More England appearances followed, in the *Daily Mirror* Inter-Nations series. Dave rode in three England victories, against Sweden, Australia and against the Rest of the World team. The tournament was decided on a league basis, and England won it comfortably.

With the World Final scheduled for Wembley, the British Final at Coventry was a tough challenge, with only four riders going through to the big night at the Empire Stadium. In those days, one bad meeting – or even a bad ride – could finish a rider's chances, and sadly that is what happened to Dave on this occasion. Last place in his first heat, against Martin Ashby, Gordon Kennett and Doug Wyer, made his job difficult. Another last place in heat six effectively finished his chance of a qualifying spot. As it was, John Louis, Peter Collins, Malcolm Simmons and Ray Wilson (after a run-off with Ashby) went through. Howard Jacobi's report in the *Star* said that "Dave Jessup alone failed to live up to expectations". Ivan Mauger commented that it was a shock that Dave didn't get through to World Final: "He usually gates so well and is so unflappable that I thought he would certainly qualify for the World Final."

One compensation for Dave was that he raced for the Golden Helmet for the first time, and won it. In those days it was run monthly, with a new challenger being selected each month. Dave beat Ole Olsen 2–0 at Wolverhampton in the first leg, and then repeated that scoreline at Leicester. Olsen's bike packed up in the second race, but it was still a very creditable result for Dave. In August he faced John Louis, and lost 2–1 at Leicester and by the same score at Ipswich.

For Leicester, Dave and Ray Wilson held the team together. In early August, Danny Carter pointed out in the *Star* that the two of them averaged 20.92 per match, the rest of the team scored 26.81. The Lions had some good away wins, with a 48–30 victory at Hackney particularly notable. Dave scored a 12-point maximum, and was "outstanding". A few weeks earlier, he had won the London Riders Championship at the same stadium with a 15-point maximum. How he qualified for the event – maybe his old Wembley Lions connection, or that he lived near London – is not entirely clear, but it meant that he won one of the sport's historic trophies.

In early September, Dave saw more international action. He and Ray Wilson were selected for the last three matches on England's five test series in Sweden, so they did not miss Leicester's Tuesday night meeting. England won the series 5–0 again. However, for the World Team Cup Final at Norden in West Germany, Martin Ashby was selected ahead of Dave, who was chosen as reserve. This was largely based on his good form in the test series in Sweden.

England won the meeting comfortably, with 41 points, 12 clear of the USSR who were in second place. Dave did not get a ride.

However, at the end of the meeting, Dave recalls that "There was a ballot on whose engine was going to be stripped by the machine examiner to check it. My name was pulled out, even though I had not ridden a race. They stripped the engine with the bike on my trailer, and measured it. I was incensed. Of course, the engine size was ok."

For Leicester, Dave was involved in a controversial home defeat to Exeter. Tony Lomas walked out of the meeting because of the wet state of the track, and Dave and Ray Wilson both declined tactical substitute rides. Bill Cooper's report said that "the Lions, Jessup apart, looked all at sea on a wet track." Although the Lions were not in a position to challenge for the league title, they had success in the Speedway Star Knock Out Cup. After beating Hackney in the second round, the Lions beat Halifax home and away in the semi-final, with Dave scoring 15-point maximums in both meetings. However, in the final Belle Vue were too strong, winning by two points at Blackbird Road, and 14 at Hyde Road.

Dave again qualified for the British League Riders Championship, and finished eighth with eight points from his five rides. The preview of the meeting said that Dave had "...such a fine season, but disappointed both us and himself when it came to the World Championship." Dave recalls that "I tried out the first four valve JAP at the British League Riders Championship. However, I hadn't really had long enough to get the set-up right for such a big meeting."

Towards the end of the season Dave was using a Jap engine for some meetings, and also trying out a Weslake in some open meetings. In his last meeting for Leicester, he scored an "immaculate" five-ride maximum at Cradley. However, in November he asked for a transfer from Blackbird Road, citing the amount of travelling from his Kent home as the reason. There was speculation that he could replace Barry Briggs at Wimbledon, but this did not happen. By Christmas, the transfer had still not been resolved. He returned to Leicester, but only for his fan club's Christmas dance.

There were other things to look forward to. Vicky was pregnant and the baby was due around Christmas. Dave was again doing some trials riding, and had a new BKR Bultaco. And their greyhound, Davick's Racer, won his first race at Rochester.

The review of Leicester's season in the *Star* said that Dave was "every bit as good, and better, as we expect. Despite a cracked shoulder in May, he ran through the season in tremendous high style." Writer Angus Kix also said that Dave was "one of the finest British riders to appear in years".

Dave had joined Leicester as third heat leader, behind two very experienced riders. He finished his four years at the club as their top rider, with an average of 10.41, which put him at seventh place in the British League averages. It was his second season as Leicester's top man, and it would be hard for the Lions to find a replacement for him. During his time at Leicester he had also reached his first World Final, and ridden regularly for England, in test matches, the World Team Cup and the World Pairs.

The challenge for him now was to become one of the world's top riders. But it was also time for him to move on to a new club, preferably one nearer his Kent home.

8. Pastures new – Reading

Despite four successful years at Blackbird Road, it was clear that Dave would be moving to a new club nearer home for the 1976 season. However, thoughts about where Dave would ride in the new season were overshadowed by the birth of David John Jessup on 8 January. So, Dave was a dad at the age of 22! Two days after the birth, he won a trials meeting for the first time, the Barham Combine at Canterbury.

Dave reflects on why he left Leicester: "It wasn't just the driving to home meetings, a lot of their fixtures, challenge matches, Midland Cup and so on were midlands based. I hadn't fallen out with Reg Fearman. I didn't have much to do with Ron Wilson, if I had a problem, I would see Reg. He also had shares in Reading, and they were looking for someone to replace Anders Michanek. They gave me a good deal; in fact, I had a wonderful deal at Reading. I rose to the challenge. The track was good, and it was a new stadium. Overall, it was a good set up. The track was smaller, it suited me as a more technical rider. It was 83 miles to get there, going through London and picking up the A4 and then the M4.

Wimbledon, Hackney and Reading were all possible moves for Dave, but at the beginning of February it was announced that he had signed for Reading. He had also been looking to appoint a business manager to develop his continental racing, and make the travelling arrangements. Reading's home meetings were on Monday nights, which fitted in well with longtrack racing in Europe.

Dave also appointed Dave Phillips, Anders Michanek's former mechanic, to work on his bikes. Dave says that "I was travelling all over Europe, and having Dave Phillips involved made me more confident, because of the experience he had working for Anders. George Yule still helped at almost all my meetings. I would pick him up on the way, at Fuller's Brewery on the A4 for Reading. When I was at King's Lynn, he would drive up there with his wife. He even went with me to the World Final in Los Angeles, and paid his own way. I bought him fish and chips. He was a great asset for me."

Reading had been one of the new teams that made up the inaugural Second Division in 1968. There had never been professional speedway in the Berkshire town before, although there was a Southern Area League team nearby in the 1950s in the same stadium which had staged some meetings in the 1930s. In 1971, having acquired Newcastle's First Division licence, the Racers moved up to the top flight. Their Tilehurst stadium had then been sold from under them, and the team did not ride in 1974 while their new stadium at Smallmead was built.

Dave got on well with his new team-mates: "John Davis was the same age as me and we got on well, both trying to be good. I enjoyed Mick Bell and Bernie Leigh's company. I was best man at Bernie's wedding. Bob Humphreys lived in a caravan at the track. I usually arrived early and used have a talk with him. Bengt Jansson was there for a couple of years. He was coming to the end of his career, and I got on well with him.

As well as his speedway commitments, Dave also found time to develop his golf skills. He got 'steady returns' according to Dave Lanning, but did not have an official handicap yet. He was also aiming to hit a golf ball more than 350 yards, a lap at Reading's Smallmead home.

The transfer fee for Dave's move from Leicester was £4,500. The preview of Reading in the *Star* said that "Dave Jessup for Anders (Michanek) is no loss in my book since it should result in Racers getting their own Number 1 around for up to another dozen matches or more. And Dave is still a rising force, even if he is not a Michanek force." Replacing Michanek, who was a Reading legend, would be a challenge.

However, Dave could not have made a better start for his new team. He gave a "faultless display" in the Racers' opening meeting against Hackney, with a full 12 point maximum. Three days later, he did the same at Plough Lane in a 46–32 win for the Racers, showing the Wimbledon fans what they had missed out on. He scored his third full maximum at home to King's Lynn; the match report said that "He was so fast away from the tapes that even by the first bend Jessup looked a certain winner." He repeated this feat at Saddlebow Road in another away win for the Racers.

His good form continued in April. The first big individual meeting of the season was the Spring Classic at Wimbledon. Dave won his first four rides, and took the third place he needed to win the meeting in heat 18. Philip Rising's report in the *Star* said that "Dave Jessup got both his tactics and his arithmetic right" in the meeting, and continued "On the night Jessup was the deserved winner of the trophy and a cheque for £500. From the word go he had looked very sharp, very fast and nicely at home on a track he rides particularly well…" Rising also said that Dave was one of very many riders who would have a say in the World Championship in 1976.

More success came with a paid maximum at home to Birmingham, and a full one in a 51–27 Racers win in the return meeting. The report said that "Dave Jessup was in a class of his own – a clear second faster than anyone else on view." His young son was also attending many of his dad's meetings in a specially designed carry cot. Apparently, he slept right through the Spring Classic.

At the end of April another individual trophy came Dave's way – the Superama at Hackney. This time he won with 14 points, and the prize was presented by television star Dennis Waterman. The Superama was unique among the big open meetings, because Hackney had an away meeting on the night it was staged, so no rider had home advantage. It was also announced that he was back in the England World Team Cup side, having been reserve in the final at Norden in the 1975 Final.

Dave was also successful in May in the Nulli Secundus Best Pairs at Reading, riding with Bob Humphreys, and still has the trophy, which was a clock that still works. Dave scored 16 points, with Humphreys scoring eight. They tied with John Davis and Mick Bell, but Dave beat Davis in a run-off to win the trophy. Dave still has the trophy on show in his living room at home.

As with Ray Wilson at Leicester, Dave found himself in the same team as another leading English rider at Reading, John Davis. Reading promoter Reg Fearman commented: "Rivalry between Dave and John is fierce within the Reading camp. They are perhaps the best two young English prospects in the game, and we're very, very lucky to have them both in Racers' colours. There's no reason why BOTH shouldn't appear in future England teams. Jessup is established in the top flight; Davis still has got a bit to do."

The World Team Cup and the World Championship both started for Dave in May. In the latter, he was drawn at Poole in the British quarter-final, and won the meeting with 14 points.

Left: Winning the 1976 *Daily Express* Spring Classic. (JSC)

Bottom: A family photo at Reading.

However, 11 days later in the World Team Cup, Australia qualified from the British qualifying round at Ipswich with 40 points, five clear of England. Dave contributed eight from his four rides, and fell in one race. As the holders, this was a great disappointment to both the riders and British speedway overall. The Final was scheduled for White City in August, and the Australians won in front of a crowd of 9,000. There would have been a far higher attendance had England been there.

Also in May, Dave competed for the Golden Helmet for the third time. At Reading, Dave won the first race, then Tommy Jansson won the second, when the rocker arm on Dave's bike broke, and the third. Three days later at Wimbledon, Jansson again won 2–1. Sadly, it was Jansson's last meeting at Plough Lane. The following week he was killed in a track accident in the Swedish Final. In July, Dave rode in a special second half at Wimbledon to help raise £780 in his memory.

Dave returned to Leicester for the British semi-final in the World Championship. He scored 12 from five rides, and comfortably qualified for the British Final in fourth place; the report said that he was "not as dominant as anticipated".

The British Final was at its traditional venue, Coventry's Brandon Stadium. Only the top five riders would qualify for the Inter-Continental Final at Wembley. Malcolm Simmons dominated the meeting with a 15-point maximum; Dave scored 10 points from his five rides, not quite enough. He finished sixth, and had the reserve spot for the big night at Wembley. With only one win in his five rides, he conceded too many points to the riders who qualified.

A couple of days later, Dave was taken to hospital after a collision at Hackney in his second ride. He was lucky to avoid serious injury, and withdrew from Reading's meeting against the USSR the following Monday after winning his first two rides.

Dave sat in the pits as reserve at the Inter-Continental Final at Wembley, watching as the five qualifiers from the British Final all reached the World Final, with Anders Michanek and Ole Olsen eliminated. His challenge for the rest of the season was to get Reading as high up the table as he could, and win as many individual trophies as possible. One was the *Daily Mirror* Grand Prix, which involved qualifying rounds, and the awarding of premium points before a Final at White City in August. Dave scored 13 points on the track at Wimbledon, Reading and Hackney, and then 10 at Halifax. He accumulated 31 premium points, and finished fifth in the final at White City, with 10 points. His 61 premium points also left him in fifth place in the competition overall. A formula like this had been tried in the early World Championships before the War. The *Star's* report said that the scoring system showed how it was possible for an 'unfancied' rider such as Dave – presumably because of his premium points total prior to the meeting – could come through to fifth place. But for bike trouble in heat 13 he could have had a place on the rostrum.

After a very busy summer on the international scene in 1975, there were very few test matches for Dave to represent England. One came at Vojens in Denmark towards the end of July, when Dave scored four points for England against a Rest of the World side who won the meeting 43–41.

Dave usually steered clear of controversy off the track. However, in the *Star* on 17 July, he was critical of the refereeing system. Their report said that he had "…joined the growing band within the sport and on the terraces, lobbying for sweeping changes as to the men appointed to control meetings … Among Jessup's complaints he cites a strong home bias at particular tracks, inconsistency with decisions, or being unsuited to the job. 'I didn't pay much attention as to who was 'on the button' before this year, but since being appointed captain of the Racers I've come into more direct contact. I'm not at all happy with the overall position. The inconsistency doesn't vary from referee to referee. The same man will make different decisions on identical incidents at various tracks and often as not involving the same riders in the same week." He went on to say that this could not been good for the sport, and that there were too many referees chasing too few meetings. He recognised that they have a difficult job to do, and make personal decisions. He said that more meetings would make them sharper. He also called for the weeding out of those not up to standard.

Three weeks later, in a crucial league meeting at Hackney, Reading walked out of the match in protest at the referee's decision when Dave was excluded in heat 11, with the scores tied at 30–30. He was excluded for unfair riding after Dave Morton fell on the third bend and went under the safety fence. Reading's Boleslaw Proch was excluded under the two minutes rule in the rerun, and the Reading team then withdrew from the rest of the meeting, saying that they had no bikes fit to race.

Dave commented after the meeting: "My exclusion was just another example of amateur refereeing. I'm truly sorry for all the disappointment Reading's walk-out caused our own supporters and those of Hackney, but the court of inquiry which will come will serve to highlight the generally low standard of refereeing professional speedway riders must combat these days." He argued that Morton had gone too wide into the bend too fast, and says that "I did try to pass him, his bike was stopping. The race was stopped and no one checked his bike. The referee didn't want to listen."

Reading were top of the table at the time, and a win at Hackney would have boosted their championship hopes. Despite Dave's best efforts, they finished sixth, 14 league points behind an all-conquering Ipswich team that did the League and Cup double. Some of the reports of those meetings show how important Dave was to the Reading team. Away to a struggling Leicester, he scored a 12-point maximum in a 47–30 win. Another maximum followed at home to King's Lynn, combined with the fastest time at Smallmead by a Reading rider that season. At Poole, in a narrow Reading win, he was "in brilliant form", and the next day at Sheffield, in another away triumph, was the "star of the Reading side". Another seven full or paid maximums came in the rest of the season, including 18 out of 38 for Reading at Wimbledon. The *Star* reported that on a wet and miserable September evening, "Dave Jessup was singularly unconcerned by it all and slithered to an 18-point maximum." Dave also scored a 15-point maximum riding as a guest for Exeter at Hackney, when he was "immaculate".

All this led to some busy periods. In August, in the week before scoring a maximum against Poole at Smallmead, Dave rode in three Swedish meetings and then a grasstrack meeting in Germany before dashing back to Reading. He told Dave Lanning that "I enjoy this kind of routine. If I'm away from racing for three or four days I seem to go rusty." Dave had also found success in the longtrack competitions on the continent, and reached the World Championship Semi-Final in Aalborg in Germany in August. Dave never made it to Aalborg. He recalls that "There was horrendous traffic in Germany, north of Hanover. I had to make a deadline – 6pm on the Saturday to sign in for the meeting. I had ridden at Hackney on the Friday, but it was clear that we would not get thee in time. We came home and never got to the meeting. I had incurred great expense, paying the fares and so on, for no reward.

Dave preferred to drive himself to meetings, putting his bike on the back of his car. He says that he "Used a trailer occasionally, but there was a 40mph limit. With four-wheel trailers, you could do 70mph, but not drive in the outside lane. I preferred to use the car; it was more comfortable. I could borrow a bike if necessary. Riders didn't use transit vans in those days, they were more difficult to drive. I had a van once, put a V6 engine in it, and three seats in the front, but generally it was not for me."

Dave also found success in open meetings. In July, he won the Yorkshire TV Trophy at Hull with a 15-point maximum, and "upset all the odds in a star-studded meeting." In August he was runner-up to Peter Collins after a run-off in Swindon's Silver Plume, and five days later won the Geoff Curtis Memorial Trophy at Reading. Another success in Yorkshire followed in September, when he beat Ole Olsen in a run-off to win the Yorkshire Open Championship at Sheffield. He also won the Wimborne Whoppa, one of the biggest grasstrack meetings in England, which attracted a field of the top speedway and grasstrack riders.

Dave qualified for the British League Riders Championship, and finished fifth with 11 points. Dave and John Davis had also qualified for the British League best Pairs Final at Ipswich, but missed the meeting because Davis was injured.

Interviewed by Dave Stevens in the *Star* before the big meeting at Belle Vue, Dave reflected on the good and bad points of his first season with Reading. He said that the British Final had been "a bitter disappointment", but that he had "upped his average" and therefore was not too upset. He added that "I was one of the first to use the 'Catapult' tyre. It's a bit narrower than the Dunlop and has a slightly deeper tread. They scored me plenty of points although there's not a lot of difference between the two. I wasn't sure though in the weeks leading up to the British Final and went back on the Dunlop. No, I can't say that was my failing on the night, but perhaps I switched too late, for I've done well enough since."

Dave also said that he had had engine troubles, as had a lot of other riders. He said that there were a lot of new innovations becoming available, and that the only way to test them was on the track. He added that he aimed for "100 per cent mechanical perfection and that "... my problems this year have caused a great deal of heartache, let alone all the extra work. I like to do my own equipment. It makes for more work but that way I know what's going on; I can tinker with the engine ... and I only have myself to blame if things go wrong." He said that trying to foresee metal fatigue had been a problem, but that he had received some help from Weslake.

Dave accepted that he was criticised for only taking one machine to most meetings, but said that any 'blow up' usually happened towards the end of a meeting. Driving with a trailer would greatly add to his travelling time. In team events for Reading, he could borrow a bike although they were usually set up for someone taller than him, but he could still win. Hazards for speedway riders were not only on the track. With the amount of driving Dave did, he was involved in several accidents over the years. He recalls that his only one in 1976 was on the way to Poole. A car hit the side of his car at Winchester, and knocked Dave's Weslake bike off the frame at the back of the car.

He said that he had enjoyed his season with Reading, although replacing Anders Michanek was a challenge. He had also enjoyed being the team captain as well. He was disappointed that the Racers had not won the league title.

Top: The England Lions team at Leicester in April 1976 with comedian Freddie Starr.
From left: John Louis, Terry Betts, Freddie Starr, Reg Wilson, mascot, Malcolm Simmons, Martin Ashby, Dave, Len Silver (manager), Ray Wilson (on bike). (JSC)

Left: Winning the grasstrack Wimborne Whoppa in 1976.

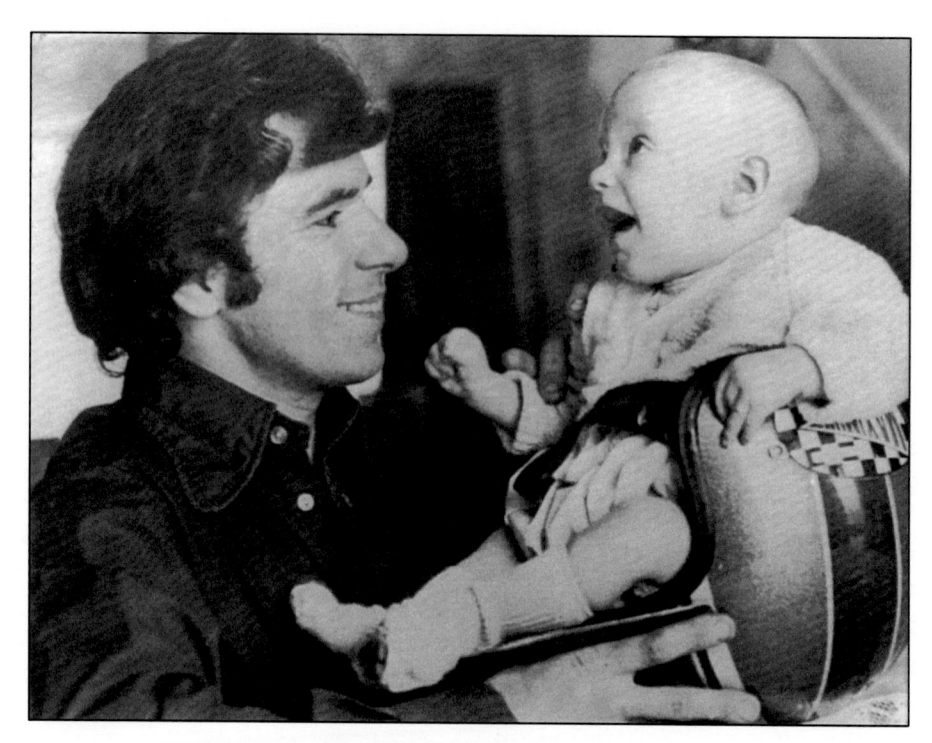

Dave and a young David.

On the home front, he and Vicky had moved to a new family size house during the season, but were now settled at Parbrook House in High Halstow, on the Hoo Peninsula in North Kent.

He had no winter racing plans, but hoped to continue his trials riding. He was also planning a family trip to the States in early February and hoped to attend the Daytona road racing meeting. He was also hoping to run some speedway training events.

Overall, Dave could look back on a successful season. Reading had finished sixth in the British League on 41 match points. Two home defeats and two draws at Smallmead were offset by five wins and a draw on the road. Four of their away defeats were by two points. A 100 per cent home record and winning those four matches lost so narrowly would have put them equal to Ipswich.

Dave's average had fallen fractionally, from 10.41 at Leicester in 1975 to 10.35 in 1976. But given he was riding a new home track, it was very impressive, as was his total of 13 maximums – nine full and four paid – in 38 league and knock out cup meetings. Reading's weakness, as with his last season at Leicester, was in the third heat leader slot. John Davis averaged 9.33, but the next best rider was Reading stalwart Bernie Leigh on 6.74, although Bob Humphreys also averaged over six points, as did Bengt Jansson in the 10 meetings he rode for the Racers.

It was something to build on for the future. However, for 1977 Dave would also look to improve on the individual front, in particular to reach a second world final to follow up his first appearance in 1974. It was easy to forget that he was still only aged 23, but had eight years experience as a professional speedway rider under his belt.

9. World Team Cup triumph

This was an important season for Dave, who was happily settled at Reading. On the team front, Bengt Jansson had returned to Reading. Although he was not the top-class heat leader he had been in his younger days, especially for Hackney, he was still a useful third heat leader, with an average of just under seven points. West German Hans Wasserman, who had a good reputation as a longtrack rider, was another useful addition. Boleslaw Proch joined Leicester midway through the season and Reading stalwart Mick Bell moved to Coventry. Proch's move was the end of a dispute between Reg Fearman and the British Speedway Promoter's Association (BSPA) who said that Reading were too strong, and had to release a rider. Fearman disputed this, and for a period used a rota system to stay within the national points limit. His appeal against the original decision was rejected in August, resulting in Proch joining the struggling Leicester side. Doug Underwood joined the Racers from Leicester. Underwood and Ian Gledhill both rode at reserve. The challenge for the team would be to improve on their sixth place in the league the previous season.

Once again, the World Championship figured high in Dave's priorities. For England, there was a test series against the Rest of the World, and the World Team Cup. He also had regular invitations to high profile open meetings, the VW-*Daily Mirror* Grand Prix and longtrack and grasstrack meetings mainly in Europe, but also on some occasions in the UK.

After an abandoned meeting at Swindon, Reading's season opened with a challenge match against the Polish side Stal Gorzow. Dave scored a 12-point full maximum in a comfortable win for the Racers, and repeated the feat 24 hours later riding for Leicester as a guest against the Polish visitors. Three days later, the *Daily Express* Spring Classic was held at Wimbledon. It was very early in the season for such a meeting; Dave finished third with 13 points, behind Billy Sanders and Peter Collins. Interviewed in the *Star*, he said the track was bumpy, and he would not watch the highlights on television.

As in 1976, Dave made an excellent start to the season. Almost unbeatable at Smallmead, he scored a "superb" 15-point maximum at Hackney and notched the same score in the restaged challenge match at Swindon. His good form continued throughout April, with double figures in each meeting for Reading. A minor controversy for Dave arose at Bristol on 29 April. Speedway returned to the city for the first time since 1960. The team was using the Eastville football and greyhound stadium, and the speedway track, which was made of sand, was on top of the greyhound circuit. A crowd of 18,200 attended the first meeting, the *Daily Mirror* Open. However, Dave and Martin Ashby both withdrew after taking one ride. Three riders were injured in heat 13, including John Davies. The report in the *Star* said that John Louis was "very suspicious" of the track. This issue, along with legal challenges to speedway being held at the stadium, were problems for the team during their two years in Bristol.

On 25 June, in his Letters column in the *Star*, Dave was asked about the Bristol track. He replied: "... it is obvious that the dual-purpose surface at Eastville did not work out as envisaged – even the Bulldogs management admit that. I must add that my much-publicised withdrawal from the opening meeting at Bristol was caused mainly by a badly wrenched knee first time out – there was very little likelihood of my continuing on any track."

At the Speedway Honours Ball at the Seymour Hall in London, winning a 1976 Award. Mick Hines is in the background. (JSC)

Reflecting on the incident today, Dave outlines that "The track was pre-laid, with sand. I couldn't get my foot on the ground, it was too rough and ready. Barry Richardson was the referee. I never used to look at who was the referee until I became a team captain. The doctor said that my knee was aggravated, that I would struggle and was unfit to ride that track. It was a very successful venue for crowds, but needed a different stadium."

A week after the Bristol meeting, Dave scored 17 points from six rides at Ipswich to help the Racers to a six-point win. The report said that "Reading were brilliantly led by Dave Jessup." Dave was still hosting a letters page in the *Speedway Star*. While some of the letters were about the sport's history, others asked Dave for his views on current issues. In response to one about speedway bike engines, he said that he liked Weslake best, although one of their engines cost £520, and a complete bike was £1,000.

On 17 April, Dave rode in an usual longtrack meeting. Instead of heading for Europe, he drove up the M1 and M6 to Chasewater Stadium in Staffordshire. He was riding for a Great Britain team against the Rest of the World. There were 10 riders on each side, and both teams included top speedway riders as well as longtrack specialists.

Competing in the Collier Cup Trial in 1977.

Longtrack at Chasewater: Dave and Mike Beaumont on parade. (JSC)

The Great Britain side included Peter Collins, Malcolm Simmons, Chris and Dave Morton and Don Godden. The Rest of the World line-up included Ivan Mauger, Anders Michanek, Barry Briggs and Egon Muller. The Rest of the World won 171–136 in front of a 10,000 crowd. Dave scored 19 points from his five rides.

Dave's first appearance of the season in a World Championship came in the Sand-track 1000 metres event. He won his qualifying round at Pfarrkirchen in West Germany. A week later, he started his speedway World Championship campaign at Hackney, and ran into more controversy. Hackney rider Keith White was excluded in heat 18. In the rerun, the report in the *Star* said that Dave "team rode Bernie Leigh home" to deny White the chance of a run-off for a qualifying place. Hackney promoter Len Silver said that Dave and John Davis could have a run-off for third place, but he would not pay them any start money. Dave declined his offer. A couple of weeks later in his letters column in the *Star*, he commented: "What sort of club man would I be if I didn't have the interests of my team-mates at heart? Naturally I'm not going to break my neck racing a chum when I've already qualified; but there was no question of 'fixing' anything. You might think the draw system is wrong that allows three riders from the same club in the same round."

Len Silver complained about the race to a tribunal, but the decision went in Dave's favour. Writing in Len's autobiography, *As luck would have it*, Dave said that Len "...took me to a tribunal once because he claimed that I didn't make a bona fide attempt to race a team-mate in a heat during an individual meeting featuring one of his Hackney riders. At the end of the day he would have done the same as I did. Unfortunately for Len, he lost at the Tribunal and I won because I had made a genuine attempt to beat the Hackney rider, but didn't try to pass my team-mate." The two didn't fall out over the issue. Dave rode for Len when he was England team manager, and today he often attends the meetings Len promotes at Sittingbourne, and presents the prizes in individual events.

Meanwhile, the test series against the Rest of the World had started. In the first meeting at White City, England won 63–45. Dave scored 10 from five rides. The *Star's* report said: "Dave Jessup also rode wonderfully well. After suffering machine failure in his first ride when placed second behind Billy Sanders, and missing his second, he then raced to three heat wins in his remaining four rides." England lost the next two meetings, with Dave scoring 14 from five rides at Ipswich and then 10+3 at Coventry. The report said that "Only the Jessup-Lee pairing measures up to the job at hand."

The following Monday at Reading, England lost the match – and therefore the series – by 16 points. Dave had one of his worst meetings for years, failing to score from four rides. The *Star* said that Reading promoter Reg Fearman expressed his disgust at the team's performance, and continued: "His criticism must have been largely directed at his own skipper, Dave Jessup, who failed to score at all. Jessup, with 34 points from the previous tests, had a real nightmare in front of his home crowd, finishing last in three heats, doing a cartwheel at the start of another, and being replaced by reserve Gordon Kennett in two others." The *1978 Speedway Yearbook* said that "...there was no real explanation for the nightmare return from the usually so-consistent Dave Jessup." Dave comments that "I had ridden in a 1500 metre longtrack event on the Sunday and had beaten Egon Muller. My engine was so fast that I thought I would try it at Reading. What an error! It was not suitable for the 350 metre track at Reading." However, overall England had a bad night, with Malcolm Simmons being top scorer on 11 points. The *Star* said that the Rest of the World's domination was clear by heat eight, but the score after that race saw the visitors only in front by four points. The gap only widened after heat 13, when Dave had his last ride.

England won the last test at Hull by two points to at least restore some pride. Dave returned to something like his usual form, with eight from four rides, including a fall in his final outing. And he set a new track record in heat two. A sixth test was originally scheduled for the Friday that week, at Bristol. However, problems with the track and international commitments for some riders saw it rescheduled for 22 July. In the event, with ongoing concerns about the track, which involved Reading later in the season, meant the test match was never staged. Dave and Malcolm Simmons had both said they would not ride for England at Eastville, although Dave later issued a public denial of the reports of these comments. Dave was one of four English riders to take part in each test, and finished with 42+3 points from his 25 rides.

On Saturday 18 June, Dave won the Dews Trophy at Halifax with a 15-point full maximum. The *Star* reported: "Dave Jessup rode to an immaculate maximum despite the fear that his clutch might come apart in his last race because the stud was showing signs of shearing. He was first away each time and made clear his intentions of taking the £100 first prize by clocking 65 seconds in Heat two, the fastest time of the night."

Less than 24 hours later, Dave was at Reading on a Sunday afternoon for the World Team Cup UK qualifying round. Only the winners qualified for the final. Dave continued his good form of the previous evening to win the first heat and go on to compete a 12-point maximum. The *Star* said that he "full atoned for his unhappy display for England against the Rest of the World." England qualified for the final with 42 points, nine ahead of Australia. It should be said that New Zealand were missing Ivan Mauger and Barry Briggs, and were well beaten.

In the World Championship, Dave was drawn at Poole in the Semi-Final. He won the meeting with "a superb maximum" and took home the £200 cheque. The British Final at Coventry came two weeks later. Twice before Dave had failed to qualify from this meeting, and there must have been concern among the Racers supporters when he finished third in his first ride. But he won his other four comfortably to finish as runner-up to Michael Lee and qualify comfortably for the Inter-Continental Final. Bob Radford commented in his column in the *Star:* "Success, too, for Dave Jessup, who made it third time lucky at Coventry. Twice Dave has failed to negotiate this hurdle, when all club form suggested that he'd get through easily enough. It looked dodgy for the Racers skipper after he was relegated to third place in his first outing, but he recovered to finish in second place."

However, Dave did not fare so well in the World 1,000 Metre Sand-track championship. He failed to qualify from the semi-final in Scheessel in West Germany. The meeting was won by Egon Muller; Anders Michanek won the Final.

For Reading, Dave continued to regularly score double figures, and was rarely beaten in a league or cup meeting at Smallmead. In the Knock Out Cup, Halifax were beaten by 30 points on aggregate, with Dave scoring 25+1 from his nine rides, as well as a 12-point maximum in the home league match against the Yorkshire side.

1977 Reading team: Hans Wassermann, Bengt Jansson, Bernie Leigh, Bob Humphreys, Boleslaw Proch, Frank Higley, Dave (on bike) (JSC).

Dave, John Davis and Bob Humphreys – a second half presentation at Reading.

England versus the Rest of the World at Ipswich 12 May 1977.
From left Michael Lee, Egon Muller, Dave and Ole Olsen. (JSC)

England World Team Cup riders at Reading for the qualifying round: John Berry (manager), Michael Lee, John Davis, Peter Collins, Malcolm Simmonds and Dave. (JSC)

The thorny issue of the Bristol track raised its head again on 12 August, when Reading were there for a league meeting. After three heats, the score was 9–9, but then Proch fell and John Davis came in third in heat four. The *Star* reported that the "majority of the Reading side then decided that conditions were too bad and staged a 30-minute delay, threatening to walk out." The referee spoke to both teams, then put Dave and Bob Humphreys on two minutes for heat five. Both failed to beat the time allowance, and were replaced by Proch and Ian Gledhill. Dave only took one more ride, and the report said that only Bernie Leigh, Proch and Gledhill put any effort into racing. The final score was 57–21 to the home team.

The following week, a report by Trevor Davies, who covered the west country for the *Star*, was headed "Jessup is blamed". He said that the referee had declared the circuit to be "rideable and raceable". The problem was bumps on the first bend and home straight. The referee, Barry Richardson, had issued a statement saying that "The mandate of any professional speedway rider should be to ride to the best of his ability for the sake of the paying public but at the same time having regard for the prevailing conditions. Certain Reading riders failed to meet that mandate and have been reported to the Control Board." Dave had said that "My dislocated left knee just cannot cope with the bumps. I only came down here to give it a try." Reading promoter Reg Fearman told his riders to continue, and ride "according to the conditions." Bristol promoter Wally Mawdsley blamed Dave: "Jessup was undoubtedly the ring leader, he should be ashamed of himself not only as a professional rider but as a Reading team man and England international." He said they had spent thousands of pounds on the track, and that Wimbledon had won at Eastville, showing away teams could ride there. He added that Dave would not be given any open bookings at Bristol. One suspects that Dave would not have accepted them anyway! Interestingly, the Reading manager Frank Higley said that the track needed a solid base to prevent it cutting up.

Part of the problem with Bristol was the duel-use of the surface, for speedway and greyhound racing. This had never been tried before, and did mean that the track could vary quite considerably from week-to-week. So, it may have been raceable when Wimbledon rode there, as Wally Mawdsley claimed, but different a few weeks later.

Anyway, a few days later, Dave was in the Inter-Continental Final at White City, with the top seven riders qualifying for the World Final in Gothenburg. In the *Star's* preview, Eric Linden wrote: "Equally as determined to get to Sweden is Dave Jessup, racing brilliantly for Reading but just missing out on the big ones. He says it is high time he started finishing first again, rather than being the great trier and real threat who cops for the runners-up stuff. He can move around this strip as well as most and better than many. But can he move around it better than all?"

Dave started well, winning heat two, but two third places and a second saw him on seven points with one ride left. Finn Thomsen was on eight points from his five rides. John Davis was on the same total after completing his rides, having been controversially excluded in heat 16. So, Dave needed just two points to qualify, and one for a run-off with Thomsen. However, Dave fell in his last ride to finish on seven points. He was unfit to take part in a run-off against Davis, so his Reading team-mate would be in Gothenburg as reserve. The report of the meeting said that Dave's starts were not up to his usual standard.

Top: Crashing out of the 1977 Inter-Continental Final at White City

Left: On the way back to the pits accompanied by a concerned John. (Both photos JSC)

However, Dave's international season was not finished. It was announced that he was selected for the World Team Cup Final in Poland on 18 September, along with Peter Collins, Michael Lee, Malcolm Simmons and John Davis at reserve. The first eight heats were very close between England and Poland, with Czechoslovakia and Sweden never in contention for the title. England took the lead in heat nine and in the end won comfortably with 37 points to the Poles' 25. Dave scored nine, with two heat wins.

In September and October, the Volkswagen-*Daily Mirror* Grand Prix event was run again. Interestingly, the report in the *Speedway Yearbook* said that "Ole Olsen [the winner of the competition] is a vociferous advocate of the growing lobby in favour of the World Championship being organised on a Grande Prix basis." This was to come later, after Dave had retired. This is not the place to fully debate the pros and cons of the Grand Prix system the sport has today compared to the 'old' World Championship of Dave's time. It could be argued that the Grand Prix system would have suited Dave better, as he was a consistent points scorer. We will never know.

After qualifying rounds in September, Dave made it through to the Final at White City on 5 October, and finished fifth on the day with 30 competition points. He had won the rounds at Reading and Poole to earn 10 competition points in each, and was second at Ipswich. Overall, in the competition he finished fourth, with 66 points. A problem with the competition was that it started immediately after the world final, and was crammed into 19 rounds in 19 days. Riders withdrew from some of those meetings, and maybe it would have worked better over a longer period.

It was a busy end to the season for Dave. In individual meetings, he was runner-up in the Poole Blue Riband with 13 points, and scored 10 in King's Lynn's Pride of the East. However, in the British League Riders Final at Belle Vue he finished with five points and 11th place. In the British League Pairs Championship, Dave rode with John Davis. They finished third in the Semi-Final with 13 points, but fourth in the Final with 10.

It had been the Queen's Silver Jubilee, which meant an unexpected bonus for Dave: "There were a lot of open meetings connected to the Jubilee. They often had a prize for every race, and I won clocks, toasters and decanters which I still use today."

On the team front, Reading finished third in the league on 53 points, the same as Exeter and two behind champions White City. While Reg Fearman's tactics over rider selection had worked, Eric Linden said in the *Star's* review of the season that "Proch's departure did upset the team balance for a short while. Reading immediately went through four matches without winning one. They dropped a point each at home to Poole and Exeter. They lost away to both of them. In fact, it was the three points they lost in the Poole matches, within 48 hours – their first two non-Boley matches – that might well be said to have cost them the title. It really was that close."

The Racers had worked their way through three two-leg rounds of the *Speedway Star* Knock Out Cup. Then they faced Bristol in the semi-finals. The first leg was at Smallmead, and the Racers established a 16-point lead for the return match. Dave led the way with a 12-point maximum. In the second leg, he repeated this score, albeit from five rides. The Racers lost by six points, but were safely into the Final. There they faced King's Lynn.

Above: 'That bit goes in there'. Dave and John Davis repairing John's bike in the 1977 World Team Cup Final. (JSC)

Left: Winners again! The 1977 England World Team Cup winning side. (JSC)

The first leg was at Smallmead, and Reading could only establish a two-point lead. Two days later, despite Dave's 15-point maximum, the Stars won 41–37 to take the trophy.

Reading fared better in the Spring Gold Cup. This was an early season tournament, and they qualified for the Final against Poole by winning the Eastern Sector. The Final took place in October. Poole won the first leg by six points, but the Racers won 48–30 at home to take the trophy on the last day of October. Dave scored 12 at Poole from five rides and 11 from four in the home leg. It was a good way to end the season.

The *Speedway Yearbook* said that Dave "Continued his tremendous league form" and "Skippered Reading to an impressive performance in both major competitions." As well as reaching the Cup Final, Reading had finished third in the league. For 1978, the World Championship, with the Final at Wembley, would undoubtedly be Dave's major target.

10. So near…

The focus for the top British speedway riders this season was the World Championship Final at Wembley. It proved to be a memorable one for Dave, for good and bad reasons.

Only four qualifying places would be available from the British Final at Coventry to reach the big night. Dave had started the season with a broken – "shattered very badly" he recalls – ankle from a fall in a trials meeting in February. But he was back in action in early April.

The World Championship started in May. Dave was drawn at Wimbledon, Reading and Poole. He finished third at Wimbledon with 13 points and was then switched to Hackney for his second qualifying outing. He won the meeting there with a 15-point maximum and then finished fourth at Reading with 12 points. He comfortably qualified for the semi-finals with 40 points. He was only headed by Peter Collins on 43 and Gordon Kennett on 41. He was drawn at Poole in the semi-final on 12 July. The top eight would go through to the British Final at Coventry, and Dave again qualified comfortably with 11 points from his five rides. Tony Davey won the meeting with 12; Dave beat Reading team-mate John Davis in a run-off for third place.

Dave had missed out at this stage before. In the preview of the meeting, Philip Rising wrote in the *Star*: "Dave Jessup needs to master his nerves at Coventry to get to the World Final. He still has restricted movement in his ankle, and can't run. He is still enjoying golf, and watched Jack Nicklaus win British Open." He also said that Dave was unsettled by Reg Fearman leaving Reading, as he had a long association with the veteran promoter.

The British Final was rained off on the original date, and then again. It was finally held on 16 August, less than three weeks before the big night at Wembley on 2 September. Michael Lee won the meeting with 14 points. Dave was runner-up with 12 and Malcolm Simmons and Gordon Kennett were the other qualifiers, along with Steve Bastable as reserve. Dave's Reading team-mate, John Davis, was one of the riders who did not make it, along with the 1976 World Champion Peter Collins. The latter had two engine failures in the meeting, and there were reports later that a sugar-like substance had been found in his fuel.

The riders' practice session for the big night was on the Thursday before the Saturday night meeting. Dave decided not to take part in the practice because the engine he had decided to use was not ready.,

Dave outlines that: "I missed the practice session for two reasons. Les Allison, the Managing Director of Kellands Industrial Machinery, who sponsored Phil Crump, offered me chance to play golf at Wentworth. It was a rare opportunity and I didn't want to miss it." The Saturday before the World Final, Dave had been riding in the Artdeans Trophy at Swindon. He continues: "I took my bike to Swindon to test an engine that I had specially prepared for Wembley. I had some special cams made by a friend, Gary Robinson, at this time. They were fast and worked well.

Sadly, something else went wrong, and Barry Dutnall, another friend who lived locally, had a frantic time looking for some spare parts in secret and found them in only a couple of days. He worked extremely hard to make things fit and ready for me to reassemble for the Saturday. We finished the engine on Friday morning.

On parade before the 1978 World Final. (JSC)

My mechanic, David Phillips, took out the pushrods to polish them, instead of holding them by hand, he put them in the jaws of a lathe, a bit too tight. In the first race, the steel cap split. It was an accident, a small costly error. He was trying to do his best. The pushrods had broken before. What happened was disappointing, and still grates now, but it's time to move on. I passed riders that evening and the bike was flying."

The preview in the *Star* said that Dave had "to show that apart from being a fine tactician, and a fiery rider, he also has the flair for the big occasions to match the heart." Three former title winners were in the line-up: Ole Olsen, Ivan Mauger and Anders Michanek. Dave's Reading colleague Hans Wassermann had won the Continental Final, which would have meant him riding at Wembley, but missed out after a serious track accident.

Dave's first ride was in heat three, and none of the other riders – Jerzy Rembas, Jan Verner and Jan Andersson – looked to be a great threat to him. The *Star* reported that he was "miles in front" when a push-rod broke on the final bend and he "glided to a halt." In heat eight, Dave had a "very accomplished" win and then in heat 10, "Jessup scorched round to defeat Olsen and Autrey in ... [a] track record time of 67.0 seconds" according to Robert Bamford and Glyn Shailes in their history of the World Championship. That time was the best of the evening. The *Star* said that "Heat 10 made us realise that Dave's bad luck in his opening ride could take on catastrophic proportions. He won heat 13 [against Malcolm Simmons, Jiri Stancl and Ivan Mauger] but was beaten by Kennett in heat 19." Olsen became World Champion for the fourth time. If Dave had beaten Gordon Kennett in heat 19, he would have been runner-up. As it was, he finished level with Scott Autrey and Rembas on 11 points, and lost the run-off for third place to Autrey.

The *Star* said that he was "desperately unfortunate" and "should have given England what she wants" in front of the 86,500 crowd. On the night a £2 part cost him a £2,000 cheque and the World Championship. However, with the commercial opportunities open then to the world champion, and the higher fees for open meetings and meetings on the continent, Dave reckons that the actual loss was probably around £100,000.

In the *Star* a couple of weeks after the final, Dave said that the cap on the pushrod had cracked, and must have been a bit brittle. He said that Weslakes were trying to strengthen them.

In most of his career, unlike many top riders, Dave maintained his own bikes. Critics often said that this was to save money; Dave says that he liked to take responsibility for his bikes, and also could make changes and keep them secret. But at this time, Dave Phillips was working for him anyway. Could the outcome have been different if Dave had attended the practice session? Maybe, but if his number one bike was not ready, what was the point in riding another bike? He knew the Wembley track well, and broke the track record on the night.

The question also arises as to whether Dave would have kept his nerve if he had needed second place in heat 19 to win the meeting? Dave was now a very experienced rider. This was his second individual World Final, but he had also ridden in the World Team Cup Finals as well as many other big meetings. Who knows? Speedway remembers Jackie Biggs in 1951 'just' needing third place in his last race to win the title, but finishing last and then losing the run-off to decide the title. So near, yet so far. Dave admits to being depressed for a spell after this meeting, and Vicky went away for a week to let him get it out of his system. He did ride for Reading against Leicester on the Monday after the World Final and got a paid maximum against his old team.

Dave helped lift his depression by some shopping: "After the World Final, I went to a car auction at Edmonton. I bought a Daimler double six V12 five litre car. It was practically brand new, but petrol had gone up in price and this car did eight miles per gallon. I treated myself to it. It was black with white leather seats. I used to take it to Wimbledon and Hackney. It was wonderful, the 'real McCoy'. I kept it for 10 years and then sold it for double what I had paid for it to a lovely gentleman in New Zealand. It was a very, very special car."

In the winter, Dave had run two training schools at Smallmead. He had continued his trials riding, and had amassed an impressive list of sponsors: Weslakes, Lewis Leathers, Century Oils, Ashman Boots, Venhill Cables, Maximum racing and Regina Chains. Also, his fan club had moved to Reading.

At the start of the season, Dave had taken the opportunity while he was recovering from his broken ankle to visit the Weslake factory in Sussex. They were increasing their support for him. The injury also meant that he missed a golf trip to Kenya with the Variety Club.

Dave missed six meetings at the start of the season. In his first meeting back, at Ipswich, he scored 13 from five rides, "a remarkable comeback from injury" according to the Star, and went one better at King's Lynn the next day. Reading had lost Bengt Jansson from the previous season, and did not look strong enough to challenge for the title. Bob Humphreys lost form compared to the 1977 campaign, and eventually moved to Milton Keynes. Hans Wassermann was injured at Ipswich in July and missed the rest of the season. A new signing was former Polish world finalist Henryk Glucklich. However, the 33-year-old, despite an impressive record, never got to grips with British league speedway and had an average of under three points in his 20 meetings.

As well as his commitments for Reading, Dave was chosen for the Masters of Speedway series. This was similar, albeit smaller, to the Grand Prix series in 1976 and 1977. There were only four meetings, two in Vojens, one in Bremen and one in Gothenburg. The series was organised by Ole Olsen and Peter Adams. They had hoped to run a meeting in Britain, but the BSPA did not agree. It was reputedly the richest ever speedway tournament. Dave didn't make a lot of impact in the first three meetings, in April and May, but in August tied with Olsen at Vojens on 14 points. He lost the run-off for top spot, but still finished with six competition points. He finished sixth in the standings, and earned 4,500 Danish Kroner, about £425.

In May, international racing came to the fore for Dave. In the World longtrack 1000 metres competition, he went through from his qualifying round in third place with 24 points and "rode very well" according to the *Star*. On 21 May, he was part of the England team that comfortably won the World Team Cup qualifying round at Reading. England finished on 43 points, more than Australia (21) and the USA (20) combined. Dave won three races and had one bad start.

The next World Team Cup meeting was the Intercontinental Final in June at Belle Vue. England won, and went through to the final with 33 points. They were joined by Denmark on 25. Dave only took one ride, and did not score. Bike problems forced him to withdraw from the meeting. He kept his place for the final in September in Landshut. Denmark won the Cup for the first time, with 37 points, beating England by 10. Dave was last in his first ride, replaced by reserve Michael Lee in his second, and then scored five points in his two final rides. The Danes were six points clear of England after four heats, and were never caught. It was a surprise result for English speedway.

For Reading, Dave continued to score consistently for a struggling team. He scored a 15-point maximum and "battled on bravely" in a 43–34 home defeat to White City and was "in sparkling form" at Belle Vue five days later. He scored 14 out of Reading's 32 points, and twice beat Peter Collins. Reading suffered eight defeats in a row in May and early June, although Dave scored double figures in every meeting except one. The run ended with a two-point win at Cradley in the Knock Out Cup, but that was not enough to overcome a four-point defeat in the first leg.

The Volkswagen-*Daily Mirror* Grand-Prix was run again. To make the fixture list easier to manage, the World Championship qualifying rounds also served as qualifying rounds for the Grand-Prix. The Final was at White City on 9 July. Dave had won the round at Hackney, was third at Wimbledon and fourth at Reading so went into the final with 25 competition points. He finished fifth in the final to earn another 30 points, so had 55 overall.

Dave's interest in the World 1000-metre longtrack competition ended in August, when he was knocked out at the semi-final stage in Pfarrkirchen. He finished 11th with eight points. Also, in August, test match speedway returned, with England facing Australasia in a five-match series. Dave was not chosen for the first test at Bristol – maybe after the problems he had experienced with the track there the previous season – but was chosen at reserve in the third test at Ipswich. The second test at Birmingham clashed with Reading's home match with Coventry, so presumably Dave was not considered for that reason. Local favourite Tony Davey was chosen ahead of Dave at Foxhall; Dave had two rides as reserve and did not score. He missed the fourth test at Hull when England fielded a weak team because the rearranged British Final was on the same night. He was recalled for the final test at Hackney, and scored 10 from six rides in a narrow England win. England lost the series 3–2, and had used 20 different riders in the five meetings.

Reading finished a disappointing 14th in the league table, with 29 points. Five defeats and two draws at Smallmead showed their vulnerability, and that Dave and John Davis could not win meetings on their own. Dave's average had dropped fractionally, but was still over 10 for the third season running with the Racers. Dave again represented Reading in the British League Riders Championship, but fell in his first ride and did not appear again. In October, Dave challenged Peter Collins for the Golden Helmet, but lost 2–0 at Belle Vue and 2–1 at Reading. One trophy for Dave was in the Bass Yorkshire Open at Sheffield, which he won with a 15-point maximum. He also won the Champions Chase at Hackney.

In November, Dave was part of a group of riders who went to Kuwait to stage two exhibition meetings. The venture was organised by Reg Fearman. Dave scored 7 and 11 in the two meetings, and also was able to visit a camel farm. Fearman had secured sponsorship from the Rothmans cigarette company for the venture. The meetings were held at the Kuwait Sporting Club Stadium, the national football stadium. It had an athletics track around the football pitch. This was adapted for speedway, with a sand racing surface. Dave remembers that: "The tracks were like walkways around football pitches, tarmac, put sand down to slide. Had to be careful. Didn't mind who won, main thing to get round safely. Joe Owen slid off and damaged his hand. The fence had steel spikes on top. We went ahead and did the best we could."

All the riders were British, which made securing visas for the trip easier. They left Heathrow on 19 November and were away for a week. The riders' bikes were airfreighted to Kuwait. Dave would return to the Middle East in 1979.

In December, it became clear that Dave's time at Reading was coming to an end. Reg Fearman had left, and one of the new promoters, Brian Constable, on behalf of the club, said in an interview in the *Star* that Dave had asked for a transfer on financial grounds, saying that "he wants considerably more than we could offer – and we have made important policy decisions in that direction ... Public opinion is that there is a rift between the two [Dave and John Davis], but that isn't the background to Jessup's request – it is purely and simply money. The two did seem to pull out all the stops against each other, but John Davis has had his time as an 'understudy' and now wants the number one spot ... Dave Jessup is 95 per cent certain to move on." In his interview with Tony McDonald in *Backtrack,* Dave said that he and Davis were rivals on the track, but friends off it. They were certainly different characters, with Davis being flamboyant in his appearance and Dave being more conventional, but as with Barry Thomas earlier in Dave's career, when the press tried to make more of a racing rivalry, there was not a personal split between the two riders.

The following week, the *Star* reported that King's Lynn were interested in signing Dave, but said that the £30,000 suggested transfer fee was unrealistic. King's Lynn general manager Martin Rogers said that they had been in contact with the Racers management. They were expecting Terry Betts to retire, and needed a top-class replacement.

Dave could look back on his three years at Smallmead with pride. He had clearly established himself as the number one, and had replaced the legendary Anders Michanek, hardly an easy act to follow. However, the departure of Reg Fearman from Reading had always made it likely that Dave would move on. New challenges would await in 1979.

11. King's Lynn

It was clear that Dave would be joining King's Lynn, but – maybe inevitably – it took a few weeks of negotiations before the transfer was completed. In mid-January, the *Star* reported that the move was still in the balance. The tracks had failed to agree terms, with Reading's valuation of Dave being beyond what King's Lynn were prepared to pay. Reading wanted to replace Dave with two riders of heat leader status. Dave said that he was only interested in a move to the Norfolk club, and was prepared to sit and wait.

In an interview in the *Star*, King's Lynn's general manager Martin Rogers said that they were interested in buying Dave, but that the £30,000 price quoted was unrealistic. He wondered if they were buying the Reading stadium as well. The price was apparently based on the transfer fee paid for a particular National League rider who had moved up to the British League in 1978.

Meanwhile, Dave was pursuing his trials riding. He had been sponsored by Watling Tyre Service Station to get a new 350cc Bultaco trials bike, and had won the Medway Motorcycle Club trial on Boxing Day.

King's Lynn's move for Dave had been prompted by the long-serving Terry Betts telling the Stars' management at the end of the 1978 season that he was planning to retire. Rogers recalls in his book *In My View* that they knew that Dave was unsettled at Reading and wanted to come to King's Lynn. Rogers said that "Peter Thurlow, who had sponsored Terry for a number of years, fancied the idea of backing Jessup. Dave was clean-cut, personable and obviously a rider of immense capabilities." Dave recalls that he had known Peter Thurlow for some time before he signed for King's Lynn.

Rogers also thought that having Dave, who was known to be very reliable, would be a good influence on King's Lynn's young rising star Michael Lee. Rogers says that "It would take a new British transfer record, quite apart from sorting out a deal with DJ who was renowned to be very keen on getting the right financial contractual arrangements for himself." Rogers said that King's Lynn clandestinely spoke to Dave before opening negotiations with Reading. Eventually, a transfer fee of £18,000 was agreed.

A few weeks later, Terry Betts changed his mind about retiring. However, by then King's Lynn had signed the riders they wanted for 1979, and Betts was transferred to Reading. The transfer fee paid by Reading for Terry Betts offset a lot of the funds they had spent on recruiting Dave. Betts was the third heat leader for Reading before finally retiring at the end of the season.

When Dave signed for King's Lynn, the club organised a reception for him at the Duke's Head Hotel in the town. They gave Vicky a bouquet of flowers, and it was reported that there was tremendous enthusiasm locally for the signing.

The King's Lynn fans could look forward to the new season with optimism. They had two of the best British riders in the sport as their top heat-leaders, with Richard Hellsen as an effective third heat leader. Club stalwart Ian Turner was an experienced second string, as was Bent Rasmussen. Peter Smith was the main reserve; the second reserve role was covered by Derek Harrison and Bob Garrad.

King's Lynn had joined the British League in 1966, Following the closure of Norwich in 1964, the club had run some open meetings in 1965 before joining the League. They had never won the title, and in 1978 finished in 13th place in the table.

Dave made his debut for King's Lynn against Hackney in the early season Gauntlet Gold Cup. Before the meeting, he said that "It's a big challenge and I realise that there will be a bit of added pressure. Still, I am looking forward to this year more than any previous season I can remember. It's been a long, long, winter … ".

Dave's early season form was uneven. In the opening meeting against Hackney he scored eight points from three rides, but then only five from four rides in the return match, although it was reported that he had flu. In early April, he secured his first double figure scores, both against Reading. In the home meeting, the *Star* said that King's Lynn won "because in Michael Lee and Dave Jessup they had that touch of class." The next week he finished third in the *Daily Express* Spring Classic with 11 points. He was excluded under the two minutes rule in one race and the *Star* said that "… for poor Dave it was another case of points lost through mechanical problems robbing him of a title."

Dave scored his first maximum of the season against Eastbourne at Saddlebow Road. The next day he scored 12 from six rides for England World Team Cup side against the English Lions at Leicester.

In May, the international season started. In the World Championship, Dave rode in qualifying rounds at Eastbourne, King's Lynn and Ipswich; his 31 points saw him comfortably into the semi-finals. He was also chosen as reserve in the World Team Cup UK qualifying round at Reading, and in the England team to ride in Vojens against Denmark. Dave and Mike Lee were the reserves at Vojens; both rode twice and didn't score a point. England lost 40–37; a four test series in England against the Danes was cancelled because of a financial dispute.

The World Longtrack Championship also started in May, and Dave won his qualifying round with 20 points in Farmsen in West Germany. However, he was knocked out in the semi-final at Korskro in Denmark in August. He scored seven points, three away from qualifying for the final. An engine failure in his last ride undermined his chances. Dave Lanning also said in the *Star* that Dave's goggles had been knocked off by flying mud, and he wanted legislation to have elongated rear mudguards on the bikes to stop this happening. However, the British speedway riders were at a disadvantage in this form of motorcycle sport, up against riders for whom it was their main sport.

In the World Team Cup, the UK qualifying round (now called 'Round A') saw England face tough opposition in New Zealand, the USA and Australia. The *Star* reported that the track at Reading was "greasy" and some riders said it was dangerous; Dave remembers that the track had "inches of water on it. The meeting should not have gone ahead. In those days there were no dirt deflectors which made a wet track more difficult to ride. It did stop raining, but then it started again."

England skipper Malcolm Simmons pulled out of the meeting after his first race, and Dave as reserve "was left … to try to salvage something for his country". Dave was winning heat six when his bike all but stopped. He "limped home for a point", but the *Star* said that that defeat was crucial in England's failure to qualify for the Inter-Continental Final. New Zealand, this time with Ivan Mauger, won the meeting with 30 points, the USA also qualified on 26 and England finished third on 22, ahead of Australia on 18. However, in heat six Mitch Shirra won the race for the Kiwis, with Australia's Phil Herne second. Had Dave won, England would have been closer to the USA, but would not have overtaken them. As it was, Dave finished as England's top scorer with seven from his four rides. Only he and Michael Lee won a heat for England. It was a poor result which contributed to John Berry losing his job as England manager at the end of the season. It was also disappointing for English speedway fans because the Final was at White City in September. New Zealand won the Cup by four points over Denmark.

Three days after the disappointing result for England at Reading, Dave qualified from his World Championship Semi-Final, scoring 13 points to be runner-up at Poole. His form was improving, and in early June, the *Star* reported that "... amongst those with smiling faces is Dave Jessup, confident that he is about to banish for good the mechanical trials and tribulations which have dogged his first two months with the club... Jessup, who despite several mysterious breakdowns still can point to a 9.50 average, believes that he has made the breakthrough at last after all those early season experiments with the 1979 works Weslake."

Dave Lanning reported in the *Star* that Dave had taken up another sport. He had entered the national Marlboro Masters Darts competition, and had even bought his own set of darts. How much time he had for his new pursuit is not clear.

This was a busy time for Dave. For King's Lynn, he scored 14 from five rides against Wolverhampton in the first leg of the Knock Out Cup first round. The Norfolk side had lost by just four points at Monmore Green and must have fancied their chances of going through to the next round. However, they went down by two points, with Dave scoring 7+1 after a tapes exclusion and an engine failure.

However, the following week, King's Lynn faced Ipswich twice in two days in the hard-fought East Anglian derby matches. Dave scored a 15-point maximum to help the Stars to a rare win at Foxhall Heath, and two days later scored a 12-point maximum in a six-point win at Saddlebow Road. The report said that he was "fast becoming one of King's Lynn's favourite sons" having led the way with his maximum.

King's Lynn had qualified for the finals of the national Inter-League Four-Team Tournament. Once again, Dave contributed a 12-point maximum, but King's Lynn finished two points behind Hull in the semi-final. Ian Turner and Michael Lee both missed the meeting and were suspended and fined by the club.

In the World Championship, Dave finished third at Coventry in the British Final with 12 points to comfortably qualify for the Commonwealth Final at White City less than three weeks later. In this meeting he again finished third on 12 points to qualify for the Inter-Continental Final on 5 August at the same venue. Again, Dave comfortably qualified with 10 points and fourth place. The World Final was to be in Chrozow in Poland on 2 September. The odds on Dave becoming World Champion had dropped from 10–1 to 6–1, but there was a lot of racing to come before the Final.

More honours came Dave's way with the test series against an Australasia team. With having two countries to choose from, the Australasian side used 15 riders, Ivan Mauger only rode once, and Phil Crimp and Larry Ross were their most consistent performers. Had they fielded their strongest team in each meeting, the series might have been closer. As it was, England won 5–0, and Dave rode in the first four tests in July and August. Younger riders were given a chance in the last two tests, with the final one at Halifax being in October. Dave scored 12 at Wimbledon, 15+1 at Swindon, 11+1 at Ipswich and 16+1 at Cradley. At Swindon early on in the meeting, Peter Foster in his *History of the Speedway Ashes* said that "it seemed that England had another tough match on their hands, but, led by Jessup and Lee, the Lions began to forge ahead." In the end England won comfortably. England also rode two tests in Poland in July, but Dave was not chosen for the trip.

Another international individual event for Dave was the Masters of Speedway series. Dave rode in the three rounds, in Kumla (Sweden), Bremen (West Germany) and Vojens. He finished eighth overall with 21 competition points, and won 2,500 Danish Kroner prize money. The Grand Prix event was run in Britain again, Dave qualified for the final, but missed the meeting, along with several other top riders.

Each track at this time had at least one high profile individual meeting. In July, Dave won the Traders Trophy at Reading with a 15-point maximum. It was "an impressive performance" according to the *Star,* especially given that he was still limping from a knee injury at Sheffield. Dave won four individual meetings on British League tracks this season, a performance only equalled by Scott Autrey.

However, the individual meeting that really mattered was the World Championship Final. Dave had worked with Trevor Hedge to prepare his Weslake bikes for the meeting. He was drawn at number 16. This meant he faced eventual winner Ivan Mauger in his first race. He would have expected to beat Finn Thomsen and John Titman, but suffered an engine failure. He finished in eighth place on eight points, including a win in heat 15. Even if he had finished second in his first race, 10 points would only have put him one place higher in the final rankings.

Dave had more success towards the end of the season. He won the Brandonapolis at Coventry with a 15-point maximum, the Duplex Litho Trophy at Swindon and King's Lynn's annual Pride of the East. In the latter, he beat Michael Lee and John Louis in a run-off. The *Star* said that "Jessup inched to a thrilling victory, which his overall sharpness, including the capture of the track record, probably just deserved."

King's Lynn finished fourth in the league table, their best position since 1973. They also reached the Inter–League Cup Final, losing to Cradley Heath over two legs. The *Star* said that "Dave Jessup has settled into the groove in splendidly consistent and vastly popular style". Dave finished second in the King's Lynn averages on 9.72, about half a point behind Michael Lee, and slightly lower than his last season at Reading.

Dave's final meeting of the domestic season was on 4 November. He scored nine points from his three rides for a Kent team in a 38–38 draw with Hackney in his old friend Barry Thomas's testimonial at Hackney. They had both come a long way from when they were riding in the interval at West Ham meetings in 1968.

In 1978 Dave had ridden in the Middle East for the first time. This year he was again invited by Reg Fearman to return to the region. The first two meetings were to be in Cairo.

With Bernie Leigh in Cairo in front of a packed stadium. Dave was best man at Bernie's wedding.

After two meetings there, the riders would go to Kuwait for another two meetings, and then on to Abu Dhabi.

The meetings were again in a football stadium. The first one nearly didn't happen because Fearman and his sponsors, Rothman's, had to negotiate the payment of a bond to have the bikes released by the Egyptian customs department. A large crowd gave the riders a very good reception. The stadium was packed to capacity for the second day's racing, with riot police in attendance in case things got out of hand. Dave says that "Cairo was a proper speedway track, and the place was packed." He scored nine points in the first meeting and six in the second, winning two heats. There was time for some tourism and a visit to the Pyramids before the whole show moved to Kuwait.

There, two meetings were held, again with good crowds. Reg Fearman recalls that the party were well entertained in their time in Kuwait, with tourism visits and receptions. The final leg of the trip was in Abu Dhabi. There the meetings were not well attended, partly because of a clash with football fixtures. One new experience for Dave was a flight in a helicopter: "I went up in the helicopter with Peter Collins and Chris Morton. We didn't know that the pilot was going to test it. We were looking around Dubai for possible sites for speedway and the engines cut out. It was frightening, but the pilot did restart it. It was a big helicopter, used as a transporter for the oil rigs. We didn't find any other venues."

The group then flew back to Heathrow, having been away for 19 days. It was an interesting end to the season, but sadly one that was not repeated.

At the end of 1979, it was announced that Martin Rogers was to leave King's Lynn. However, he would work with Dave again in the future.

12. The greatest season

British speedway fans of a certain vintage will look back on 1980 with fond memories. It was the first time that England won the World Championship, the World Pairs competition and the World Team Cup in the same season. And Dave was at the centre of this 'Grand Slam' of international honours.

The first international action of the summer took place in May, when England faced the USA in a five test match series. The England team was under the new management of Ian Thomas and Eric Boocock. The latter was designated as team 'coach', a title he did not like, but he did bring some riding experience to the management team, which Ian Thomas lacked.

Dave missed the first match of the series, a thrilling 54–54 draw at Wimbledon on 1 May, with a groin injury. He returned to the team two days later at Cradley. England won 62–46 and Ian Thomas & Richard Bott commented in their book *Speedway Grand Slam* that it was "Dave Jessup's match. He was by no means fit yet he turned on a display of courage and skill that was quite staggering. Seventeen points from the King's Lynn flier, beaten only by Bruce Penhall in heat seven." The report in the *Star* said that he was "in brilliant form" and "shook off the effects of recently suffered internal injuries to inspire England to a well-earned victory ..."

England then lost the third test four days later, which Dave missed through injury. He returned to the series a week later at Poole. The Americans won comfortably by 19 points, with Thomas and Bott saying that "Dave Jessup and Peter Collins grafted hard, but we had a few very disappointing performers." Dave top scored for England with 13+1 from his six rides. The *Star* said that "Dave Jessup, barely recovered from injury, bravely led England's challenge and he was the only rival rider to beat the highly impressive Penhall."

Before the final test at Swindon, the teams clashed again, with Australia and New Zealand, in the World Team Cup qualifying round at King's Lynn. England won the meeting with 42 points; the USA also qualified on 31. Australia and New Zealand could only muster 14 and nine respectively. The *Star* said that "Jessup continued his run of good form with another superb display culminating in a win in the second half individual battle." Dave contributed 11 from his four rides. The next round was the Inter-Continental Final in Vojens on 5 July.

The final test at Swindon, on 24 May, was an anti-climax for England's fans, with the team going down by 10 points. Curiously, they were allocated the away team facilities in the pits and dressing rooms by the Swindon management. Dave was top scorer for England with 12+1 from his six rides. Dave was third top scorer for England in the series, despite only riding in three of the five meetings. He did have the top average score, 14.07 (out of 18).

This was an incredibly busy period for Dave. Two days before the Swindon test match, his World Championship campaign started at Sheffield in a British Semi-Final. He won the meeting with 14 points to qualify for the British Final at Coventry. The *Star* reported that "Dave Jessup gave a superb performance to win the £200 first prize."

On bank holiday Monday, 26 May, Dave headed for Wimbledon for the Internationale meeting. This was one of the highlights of the British season, usually with a top-class field and well presented in one of the sport's famous venues.

World Team Cup qualifying round at King's Lynn: from left: Mitch Shirra, Dave, Shawn Moran and Phil Crump. (JSC)

England versus the USA at Cradley 3 May 1980, in front of a huge crowd. From left: Dennis Sigalos, Dave, Ron Preston and John Davis. (JSC)

1980 British Champion!

Left: With George Yule and John.

Middle: Dave (on right), fighting for every point.

Bottom: With the trophy (JSC)

The *Star's* report was headlined "Superb Jessup", and Dave won the meeting with a 15-point maximum. Philip Rising wrote that "The form book rarely means much in speedway, especially for meetings like the Embassy Internationale, but if ever a winner was predictable it was Dave Jessup on Monday.

The wee England and King's Lynn man has been in devastating form of late, for club and country, with consistently fast times up and down the country. Wimbledon is a track he likes and yet he had never won an Internationale. This particular event, unlike so many other individual meetings, tends to require a special kind of talent and a glance through previous winners suggests a top-class pedigree. Jessup is a world class performer and while riders like Bo Petersen made some early running the feeling was always that Jessup would ultimately come through. He did so magnificently, winning all five of his races in times of less than 60 seconds, including the fastest of the year, 59.1 in heat 13. He was never headed and didn't have a serious challenger."

Dave clinched the title in heat 18, and as well as the trophy took home a cheque for £1,250. Just over a week later, he returned to World Championship action in the British Final at Coventry. He continued his good form from the Internationale, winning the meeting with a 15-point maximum. He beat King's Lynn team-mate Michael Lee and Peter Collins in heat 20 to clinch the title for the first time. Dave says that "I was using an engine prepared nicely for me by Trevor hedge, a long-time friend and skilful engine tuner."

He was also chosen as the Coral Rider of the Month for May, for which he was given a prize of £200. He won it again in June, and received another £200 and a set of Waterford Crystal glasses. Kevin Brown interviewed Dave in the *Star* around this time. He said that Dave was convinced he is riding better now than at any time in his career: "It goes without saying that I am obviously delighted with the way things have turned out for me so far. I feel I am at my peak and that I am riding better now than I ever have done. I don't think there are any special reasons for my successes ... I am confident, my bikes are going nicely and that I have never been so set up so well off the track as I am this year I have always been consistent without actually winning the big meetings, although I have won my share as the trophies in my house prove." Dave also said that in 1979, he had had mechanical problems, but now the problems had been eliminated.

Four days after the British Final, Dave and Peter Collins represented England in the World Pairs semi-final in Czestochowa in Poland. The riders only took a bike each and a spare engine. However, disaster struck when Dave's bike broke down in the first heat. A replacement manifold, which supplies the fuel and air to the cylinders, was required. No other rider had a spare, so Eric Boocock 'borrowed' one from an old bike in a corner of the pits. For his second ride, Dave borrowed a bike from Rudy Muts, but finished last. However, by his third ride, Eric Boocock had completed the repairs, and Dave and Peter Collins ended up on 22 points to qualify for the Final in third place. Dave won his last four rides for 12 points and Collins contributed 10. However, they had needed a 4–2 against the Australian pair in their last race to secure a Final spot.

The Final was two weeks later. This time the British pair were better prepared, with Peter Collins's van taking the bikes and plenty of spare parts to the meeting. The final was on a 450-yard track at Krsko in Yugoslavia, near Zagreb. The inside gate was clearly going to be a big advantage. Dave was known as a very good starter, but Peter Collins was not. However, the British management team agreed with the riders that Collins would take the inside gate in each race. Ian Thomas wrote that "We banked on the fact that Dave Jessup's confidence was so high that he could make starts from anywhere. And we were dead right. The pair of them were in a class of their own."

Against a strong field, the English pair scored 29 out of a possible 30 points. Dave scored a 16+2 paid maximum and Collins contributed 13+3. The only point they dropped was in heat 19, when Jan Andersson beat Collins. The *Star* said that "Races were won or lost going into the first corner, but England's tactics worked with Jessup always getting alongside his partner. The two rode brilliantly together." The *1981 Speedway Yearbook* said that it was a "five-star performance" and "one of the most convincing displays of all time."

A week after the World Pairs Final, Dave returned to World Championship action with the Commonwealth Final at Wimbledon. Nine riders would go through to the Inter-Continental Final, the last meeting before the World Final in Gothenburg. Richard Bott wrote that Dave's "… 'purple patch' was getting bigger by the week. Jessup added the Commonwealth title to the British crown with another jet-propelled performance." Dave won the title with 14 points. The point he dropped was to John Louis. In the *Star*, Philip Rising commented that "The manner of Jessup's victories in both the British and Commonwealth Finals suggests he can go all the way this year. The Jessup of today is a far superior rider to the Jessup of yesteryear. The ability was always there, of course, plainly evident since he first rode for Eastbourne. What was a little suspect was his temperament on the big occasions when often nerves did more to wreck his chances than any opposing rider. Now Jessup appears able to master the tension and it reflects in his own performances. He is such an exceptional starter that he begins any meeting as a prime candidate for victory but consistency is his biggest asset at present. There ae those who wonder how long his golden run can continue. Certainly, his record over the past few weeks has been nothing less than phenomenal…"

One major meeting followed another, combined with his regular commitments for King's Lynn and other meetings. On Sunday 5 July, the England World Team Cup squad were in Vojens for the Inter-Continental Final of that competition. The top two teams qualified, and England went through in top spot with 33 points, one ahead of the USA, but crucially eight points clear of Denmark. Dave scored a 12-point maximum on a day when it poured with rain and the English riders felt that the meeting should not have gone ahead. Ian Thomas said that the meeting should have been postponed, but that "the Danes wanted it on at any price". The referee actually called the meeting off at 5.15pm, but was persuaded to reconsider. It eventually started at 8pm with a 35-minute parade! It did finish in the rain, and Dave beat Bruce Penhall in the last race to secure top place for England. The Final was not until September.

Four weeks later, the World Championship resumed with its Inter-Continental Final at White City. Ten riders would qualify for the World Final, and Dave finished in sixth place with nine points from his five rides, with an engine failure in his third. Four other English riders, Michael Lee, Peter Collins, Chris Morton and John Davis, also qualified for the Final. Surprisingly, Ivan Mauger and Ole Olsen both failed to qualify.

World Championship Commonwealth Final: Runner-up John Louis, winner Dave and third placed Ivan Mauger. (JSC)

World Final: Runner-up Dave, winner Michael Lee and third placed Bill Sanders. (JSC)

1980 World Team Cup winners: Back: Ian Thomas (manager), Michael Lee, Chris Morton, Eric Boocock (coach); front: John Davis, Peter Collins, Dave. (JSC)

The World Team Cup squad with Ivan Mauger at the RAC Club in London: Eric Boocock, Dave, Peter Collins, Ivan, Michael Lee, Chris Morton, Ian Thomas.

It is interesting to compare the records of Michael Lee and Dave in the qualifying campaign. From his four World Championship meetings, Dave scored 52 points from his 20 rides, with 15 wins. Michael Lee scored 41 points from his 20 rides, with nine heat wins. Had the competition been run on a Grand Prix cumulative basis, Dave would have taken an almost unassailable 11-point lead to Gothenburg.

Dave went to the Final as the 11-4 favourite to win the title. His first ride was in heat three, and he led all the way to beat Michael Lee and Peter Collins. However, that was the only point that Lee dropped all night to win the title with 14 points. In his second race, Dave was second to Finn Thomsen after both riders had overtaken John Davis. In heat 12 he was second again, this time to Billy Sanders. A win for Dave in heat 15 would have put more pressure on Michael Lee, but Jan Andersson led from the start. Dave overtook Zenon Plech and Petr Ondrasik but could not catch the Swede. In heat 17, Dave beat Bruce Penhall for a welcome three points to finish on 12, level with Billy Sanders. Dave won the run-off for second place, having made a good gate, and Sanders never challenged him. It was his best World Final place. In 1976, two British riders – Peter Collins and Malcolm Simmons – had finished first and second. However, before them the last time two British riders occupied the top two places was in 1953, when Freddie Williams won the title and Split Waterman was runner-up.

It is interesting to speculate if the World Final had been in July, after Dave had won the British Final, the Internationale and the Commonwealth title, as well as the World Pairs and scored a maximum for the England World Team Cup side, whether he would have won the title. By the time the World Final came in early September, his form had dropped very marginally, but enough to see him take second place, despite beating Michael Lee. Dave was one of the most consistent riders, and would have benefitted from the Grand Prix system of deciding the World title. As former World Champion Greg Hancock said in the *Star* (30 May 2020): "At a one-off World Final, you have to have everything right on the day – one broken chain, puncture, engine failure or knock-off and your day was done."

Anyway, 16 days after the World Final, Dave was in the England team to face the USA, Poland and Czechoslovakia in Wroclaw in Poland in the World Team Cup Final. England won comfortably, with 40 points, of which Dave scored eight from his four rides. The USA were runners-up with 29 and Poland third on 15. Chris Morton and Michael Lee top scored for England with 11 apiece, and Peter Collins got 10 points. England had the meeting won by heat 13, and each rider got a £500 bonus from the Speedway Control Board. They didn't actually get the trophy! New Zealand had won it in 1979, and it was at Trevor Redmond's house in England. He had been the Kiwis' team manager.

Dave had problems after the meeting. The English management team had been unable to book rooms in the Novotel, where the speedway reporters were based, because it was full. The English squad ended up in the same hotel as the Americans, which Ian Thomas described as "minus two stars". In the night after the meeting, Dave awoke to find someone in his room stealing his passport and wallet. Dave could not chase the man because he had no clothes on. Dave had to spend a day in Poland trying to get a replacement passport, and found it difficult to get somewhere to stay on the Sunday night. He had managed to fly to Warsaw, but could not get the international flight home.

He was disappointed that no one from the England management team stayed with him. When he got his replacement passport and visa, he was joined by the speedway journalists whose flight had been cancelled the night before. Dave remembers the incident well: "I got on fine with Ian Thomas, and knew Eric Boocock as a rider. I think someone should have stayed with me when I was stranded. My mechanic had come with me on the trip and we were sharing a room. I had gone up early and he was still in the bar. I couldn't lock the door and that's how the thief got in. I charged Ian a bit extra when I rode at open meetings for him after that. Also, he arranged a match race series with Ivan Mauger for me. The first Vicky knew that I was stuck in Poland was when Terry Russell, who lived near me, bought my suitcases round on the Monday."

In *Speedway Grand Slam*, Dave reflected that "... 1980 was my best ever season and I don't think there is any way I can hope to emulate it, even if I win the World Championship. It would have been great to cap it all with the world title, but I wouldn't have swapped everything else I achieved last season for the big one in Gothenburg. Michael Lee was a better man on the night and I know he would be the first to admit it was the only big individual honour he won last season. But what a meeting to win!"

Dave also pointed out that he had the difficult gate three twice in the World Final, and said that "I know I rode well. I passed six riders that night and that took some doing on that track." He said it was hard to explain his success in 1980, but said that "confidence breeds success and it all started going right for me when I came back from injury early last season [1980]." Dave also acknowledged the work that Ian Thomas and Eric Boocock had done for England, saying that he respected "their efforts in restoring England's pride. They took a lot of criticism but they proved themselves the right blokes for the job."

In their book, Ian Thomas and Richard Bott outlined the pay rates for the riders in the FIM competitions. They were not high. Dave received more for the 'Rider of the Month' award than for winning the World Team Cup. For winning the Internationale he received £1,250.

1980	FIM	Pay rates in £		
Round and competition	**Start**	**Point**	**Cash**	**prizes**	
			First	Second	Third
World Championship					
Semi-Finals	£6.51	£5.21	£0	£0	£0
Inter-continental/Continental	£6.51	£6.51	£0	£0	£0
World Final	£15.63	£19.53	£1,562.50	£625.00	£312.50
World Team Cup					
Qualifying rounds	£6.51	£3.91	£0	£0	£0
Semi-Finals	£6.51	£5.21	£0	£0	£0
World Final (Prize money per team)	£13.02	£10.42	£468.75	£312.50	£156.25
World Pairs					
Semi-Finals	£6.51	£10.42	£0	£0	£0
World Final (Prize money per pair)	£10.42	£10.42	£1,125	£562.50	£337.50

£1 in 1980 = £4.32 in 2020					
Above in 2020 prices:					
			Cash	prizes	
World Championship	Start	Point	First	Second	Third
Semi final	£28.13	£22.50	£0	£0	£0
Inter-continental/Continental	£28.13	£28.13	£0	£0	£0
World Final	£67.50	£84.38	£6,750	£2,700	£1,350
World Team Cup					
Qualifying rounds	£28.13	£16.88	£0	£0.00	£0
Semi-Finals	£28.13	£22.50	£0	£0.00	£0
World Final (Prize money per team)	£56.25	£45.00	£2,025	£1,350	£675
World Pairs					
Semi-Finals	£28.13	£45.00	£0	£0	£0
World Final (Prize money per pair)	£45.00	£45.00	£1,125	£562.50	£337.50

The start of heat 3 in the 1980 World Final. From left: Dave, Peter Collins, Michael Lee and Kai Niemi.

As well as all his international and World Championship commitments, Dave also had a busy season with King's Lynn. At the start of the year he had been interested in a trip to Australia to ride and run some training schools, but the plans fell through. The idea came up again later in the year, but again nothing materialised. In fact, Dave never rode in Australia, but did ride in South Africa for a couple of seasons, combining the racing with a winter break.

As well as his trials commitments, in January Dave had a go at go-kart riding on a track in Tilbury. He said it was "great fun", but did not pursue it further.

King's Lynn retained their top three riders from 1979. The long-serving Ian Turner moved to Boston, and Derek Harrison left the club early in the season. Bob Garrad was also no longer part of the Stars' line-up. New arrivals were Melvyn Taylor and Nigel Sparshott, who was recalled from a loan at Milton Keynes. The team looked strong enough to at least maintain their position of fourth in the league table, although Sparshott had limited experience and found British League racing a challenge at this stage of his career.

The home season opened with the Supporters Trophy. Dave was runner-up to Bo Petersen. The Spring Classic was again held in March, and Dave was again runner-up, this time to John Davis. However, in team speedway, Dave was unbeaten against Hackney in the Gauntlet Gold Cup, "in magnificent form against his old club" according to the *Star* in King's Lynn's win over Reading with 14 points from five rides, and then scored a maximum at Boston in an Inter-League four team tournament.

On Good Friday, the traditional clashes with Ipswich, this time in the Radio Orwell Cup, saw Dave get a 12-point maximum and a new track record at home, and then 10 from four rides in the return leg. For the rest of April, he scored double figures points in all six King's Lynn meetings, including three full maximums.

His good form continued in May, although he missed a couple of meetings for the Stars early in the month through the injury that kept him out of the first test against the USA. Dave rode four meetings for the Stars, scored three full maximums and 14 from five rides in the home Knock Out Cup win over Cradley, when he again broke the Saddlebow Road track record. He then broke it again three days later. At Halifax, where Dave scored 15 out of a King's Lynn total of 36, the *Star* said that they "owed much to the brilliance of Dave Jessup, who never looked like being caught." Dave's final meeting in May for the Stars was the Gauntlet Gold Cup Final first leg. King's Lynn drew 39–39 at Poole, with a "superb" 12-point maximum by Dave. He missed the second leg. King's Lynn won 41–36 to win the trophy.

Dave Lanning, writing in the *Star*, said that Dave's success was due to him having a settled house, and the installation of central heating in his workshop. Dave did agree that before he always seemed to be moving house. Whatever the reason, Dave's consistently high form continued in June. Dave says that they moved quite often because he saw a bigger house as a good investment.

A new Inter-League four team started in June. King's Lynn were in a group with Mildenhall, Ipswich and Leicester. The Stars dominated the group, winning three meetings and losing the other at Ipswich to the home team by three points. Dave won 15 of his 16 rides in the group, for 46 points out of 48. King's Lynn qualified for the Finals day at Wolverhampton on 20 July with 141 points, 16 clear of Ipswich on 125 who also qualified.

Top: The 1980 Internationale. The riders are Bruce Penhall (runner-up), Chris Morton (fourth), Dave (winner) and Hans Nielsen with the Penthouse Pets.

Left: Dave had a long-term sponsorship deal with R. White Lemonade. Part of the deal was a copious supply of soft drinks.

Riding in an international longtrack meeting at Haldon.

Ivan Mauger and Dave in a match race at Newcastle.

In the Semi-Finals, the Stars won a close clash with 28 points, including 12 from Dave, to reach the Final along with Cradley. Birmingham and Halifax qualified from the other semi-final. But in the Final, the Heathens finished a point clear of the Stars on 33. Dave scored eight from his four rides, including one retirement from an engine failure. In a four-team tournament where two teams dominate, as in this Final, that can make all the difference. He was still joint top scorer for the Stars with Melvyn Taylor.

Another individual competition which Dave was involved in was the Grand Prix. For the third season running, the format was changed. This time there were 16 'star' riders seeded, with 12 in each of four qualifying meetings. The numbers were made up with four riders from each track staging a qualifying meeting. Again, the competition points were awarded on where a rider finished in the meeting. Dave's first meeting was at Reading. He was runner-up to Dennis Sigalos. Dave then won the meeting at Eastbourne, and – a month later on 24 July – finished sixth at Sheffield.

The Final was at Wimbledon on 14 August. Dave had 24 competition points from the qualifying rounds. Michael Lee won the Final, which concluded in a downpour that would have stopped a league meeting. Dave finished third in the Final with 12 points, having been excluded after a fall in one race. He was a point behind Sigalos, who had gained a crucial point on the final lap of his last race when Alan Graeme fell. Sigalos won the competition – and the £1,000 prize money – with 69 points, five ahead of Dave on 64. Had their positions been reversed in the final, Dave would have had 69 points and Sigalos 64, because there was a five-point difference between finishing second and third in the final.

There were pros-and-cons to this format. It was not helped by some riders, including Ole Olsen and Ivan Mauger, withdrawing from the qualifying rounds. Also, Bruce Penhall, who had led the scores from the qualifying rounds missed the Final due to injury.

The competition was dropped from the 1981 speedway calendar, which in some ways was a pity. It rewarded consistency rather than one brilliant performance.

Dave continued to ride consistently for King's Lynn. At Saddlebow Road he was almost unbeatable. In August, in five meetings the only points he dropped were an engine failure in one race. This run included winning the Littlechild Trophy with a "highly polished display." He also had success in other individual meetings. At Hackney, the *Star* reported that "Mercurial gating was his main asset, but when he missed the start in heat nine he burst through the field to win in dramatic fashion." Dave took the Superama trophy with a 15-point maximum. Also, in August Dave won Poole's Blue Riband meeting with 13 points after a three-man run-off.

Another competition that Dave was involved in during August and September was the Golden Helmet. In August he beat Wolverhampton's Hans Nielsen 2–1 at Monmore Green. Ten days later, in front of a large bank holiday crowd at Saddlebow Road, Dave won 2–0. He was helped in the first race by Nielsen forgetting to turn his fuel taps on and coming to a halt. Dave received the trophy from Andrew Edwards, the editor of *Motorcycle News* editor who sponsored the competition. Dave was the first King's Lynn rider to win the trophy. However, he only held it for just over a month. Belle Vue's Chris Morton beat him 2–0 at Hyde Road and 2–1 at King's Lynn. Still, it was another first in this fantastic season.

One slight disappointment this season was that King's Lynn dropped two places in the league to sixth. They finished on 34 points from their 32 meetings, 15 behind the champions Reading. Remarkably, they lost eight league meetings by two points. Had the team had a little more strength at reserve, they could have challenged for the title.

In the Knock Out Cup, the Stars had been eliminated by Cradley Heath in the first round. In the Inter-League Cup, they had won comfortably at Rye House, then beat Hull and Cradley at home both by 20 points to reach the Final. King's Lynn travelled to Swindon at the end of September and won 41–37, with Dave contributing 11 points. The second leg was a month later, and King's Lynn won by six points to bring a second national trophy to Saddlebow Road. Dave's return in this meeting was a paid maximum.

Dave's good form continued to the end of the season. He won the Pride of the East Trophy with a full maximum. The *Star* said that "Dave Jessup climaxed a truly magnificent season by retaining the Norwich brewery Pride of the East title in scintillating fashion." King's Lynn also won the Anglia Cup against Ipswich. Dave scored full maximums in both meetings. His final meeting was a five-ride paid maximum against Cradley on the last day of the season. It was his 26th maximum of the year in all meetings. For King's Lynn in League and Knock Out Cup meetings he got 13 maximums, 12 full and one paid. He finished top of the King's Lynn averages on 10.39, about half a point better than 1979 and 0.25 clear of Michael Lee. However, Lee represented the Stars in the British League Riders Championship.

Dave's final honour for this season was winning the Speedway Writers and Photographers Association's Rider of the Year trophy. He was presented with the trophy, and a cheque for £500 at a dinner in Manchester. He beat Michael Lee by one vote to win the trophy. As well as receiving the trophy and cheque, Dave has another vivid memory of the event: "Vicky had gone up early to be with David. I was not back in the room and the fire alarm sounded. She went out into the corridor and the door slammed shut behind her.

She had to run downstairs in her nightie to get one of the hotel staff to open the door with a master key. There were around 500 guests downstairs, but she got a key and got David safely out of the room. It turned out to be a false alarm."

Dave had hoped to tour South Africa with a group of British riders, but it was reported that the trip fell through when the Speedway Control Board was not prepared to support it unless financial and other guarantees were given. Later they changed their minds, and Dave, Vicky and David did go to South Africa in January. This is covered in the next chapter. Dave played in a high-profile pro-am golf tournament in Spain. He and his partner finished as runners-up, winning £300 and several trophies. The report in the *Star* said that Dave was considering applying to join the Professional Golfers Association. More importantly for King's Lynn fans, it was reported in December that Dave would be staying with their team for the 1981 campaign.

Dave competing in the 1981 South African Indoor Championship.

13. England captain

Dave and Vicky, and their son David spent the first couple of months of 1981 in South Africa on a 'working holiday'. It was a chance to have a break in the sun, for Dave to play some golf, and ride in a few meetings. He rode three times for an 'Overseas' team against South Africa, and captained the side. The Overseas side won all three matches. The first was indoors at Milner Park in Johannesburg. Dave notched up 18 points for the Overseas side in a 60–48 win. Ten days later, the teams met at the Dunswart Raceway in Benoni. This time Overseas won 44–21; Dave scored nine points. Two weeks later, at the same venue, Dave's team won again, 38–33 and he got a 12-point maximum. He finished the series with 39 points from 13 rides. He missed the final match, which South Africa won 45–27.

At the start of the British season there was a positive outlook for the forthcoming campaign for both Dave and the King's Lynn Stars. Bent Rasmussen and Peter Smith had both left Saddlebow Road, and been replaced by Craig Featherby and Pierre Brannefors. David Gagen, who had ridden six times for the Stars in 1979 made 20 appearances in this campaign. At reserve, Nigel Sparshott had a season's British league experience under his belt. In the summer, Hasse Danielsson replaced Brannefors who returned to Sweden after he was injured. However, the Stars' campaign did not work out as hoped.

Dave could also look forward to a World Championship campaign with the Final at Wembley, and other international commitments for England. In early April, the new England manager Len Silver named Dave as the England captain for the forthcoming series against the USA. Dave Lanning reported that Dave was being managed by his father-in-law John Claridge, and would be sponsored by Massey Ferguson.

Dave started the season well, but then missed a League Cup meeting at Reading because of a disagreement with King's Lynn promoter Cyril Crane. This was the same day that his appointment as England skipper was announced. The day after the Reading meeting, Dave told the *Star's* Peter Oakes that he went out to play golf so that he could avoid "newspaper reporters … phoning me for my side of the sorry story and I knew that if I spoke to them on the phone I couldn't help but answer their questions honestly. I didn't want that sort of publicity for myself, for King's Lynn or for England … It was a pity it all blew up because I feel it could have been avoided. I don't really want to talk about it at all, but sometimes people don't realise the sort of pressure a rider feels having to go out in front of thousands of people. Of one thing I am certain – I wasn't in the right mental frame of mind to have done justice to myself or my club at Reading after what happened during the afternoon."

Oakes said that it was "an open secret that a very lengthy telephone call between DJ and his track chief Cyril Crane ended in harsh words and lost tempers." In another report in the same edition of the *Star*, Kevin Brown added that Dave was "in dispute over terms although neither Crane or the rider himself were prepared to confirm this or release any details". He quoted Cyril Crane as saying: "Jessup had no reason whatsoever not to go to Reading. His contract had been signed and had gone in. Team manager Alan Littlechild was very sick about the situation, but Jessup will definitely be riding … at Poole."

Keeping cool at the Tarlton Raceway in South Africa.

Riding for the Overseas team in South Africa.

Dave did ride at Poole, where the Stars went down by one point, and then scored a 15-point maximum in the return fixture. The *Star* reported that he "bounced back to top form after recent motor troubles and off the track problems with a superb maximum." The next day he "superbly led" the Stars to a 19-point win at Eastbourne with a five-ride paid maximum. Dave recalls that he got on with everybody at King's Lynn except Cyril Crane.

Peter Oakes also reported that Dave said how pleased he was to be made England skipper and how he was "very proud and determined to live up to the honour." Oakes also pointed out that Dave made his senior England debut in 1972, and had made at least one England appearance in every season since then.

Dave reflects that being England captain was "wonderful, excellent. I would do the coin toss, speak to the referee about any problems and see if the track was fit to race on. It was much easier than being England manager which I did later on."

The following week in the *Star*, Kevin Brown reported that Dave had helped "to destroy the [Poole] Pirates with a flawless five-ride maximum." Dave told him that "I've had problems with my bikes, blowing them up in the home match with Reading, but at least that showed there was something wrong with them and not me … The thing is that I have been using last year's Weslakes and although they have been done up during the winter, obviously something is still amiss … I was expecting delivery of a new engine last Saturday and that should get me really going." The dispute between him and the King's Lynn management seemed to have been resolved. Team manager Alan Littlechild commented that "There was nothing to it really, just that we read the contract different to what he did. But there is no trouble now and DJ is very happy…"

The Spring Classic at Wimbledon had been moved to a better date in April, rather than being held in March. The *Star's* preview said that Dave was a "rostrum specialist" for this meeting, with a win, two runners-up places and two thirds. Philip Rising's report said that there had been problems with the meeting, with accusations of cheating over the use of a new tyre, a 30-minute delay, the non-arrival of Michael Lee and the withdrawal after one race of John Davis, although he accepted that Davis's injury was genuine. Rising said that the sport's reputation with television and sponsors was damaged by meetings like this.

However, he did say that "At least there was a worthy winner in Dave Jessup who looks quite capable of dominating this season as he did last. At a time when the sport is fighting hard to increase its popularity, Jessup is a wonderful ambassador…" Dave won with 13 points, beating Gordon Kennett in a run-off for the top spot. The only points he had dropped were in heat 13, when Kennett and Bobby Schwartz beat him. However, Ole Olsen appealed against the referee's decision to disqualify him. The case was heard on 26 May, and his appeal was upheld. So Olsen was made joint winner with Dave, as he now had 13 points, although he did not claim any of the prize money he was due.

With the test series against the Americans about to start, Dave was interviewed by Bob Radford for the *Star*. He said that he was "very, very pleased" to be given the England captaincy. He said he was consulted by Len Silver about team selection. He added that the English fans should support England even if riding against some of the American riders who rode for their clubs.

Winning the 1981 *Daily Express* Spring Classic
and a bottle of Champagne for the celebration. (JSC)

Dave recalled how the Halifax announcer had wished him and Michael Lee good luck for the World Team Cup when King's Lynn were riding at The Shay in 1980. He said he expected a "tough and very exciting series."

The first test at Belle Vue took place in some "arctic" weather conditions, including driving sleet and bitterly cold winds. The *Star's* headline was "Jessup leads storm-troopers". Dave rode a Godden bike in the meeting, having switched from Weslake the previous week. Partnering Les Collins, Dave scored 12+2 from his five rides. England won 60–48 in front of a crowd of just over 4,000; less than had been anticipated because of the weather.

Three days later, England went 2–0 up in the series with a narrow two-point win at Poole. Dave was programmed to ride with Malcolm Simmons, but his Kent neighbour had bike problems, and was replaced by Gordon Kennett for four of his rides. Dave scored 11+1 from his six outings, which included a fall in heat nine. It was his win, with Kennett's third place that put England two points up in heat 17. Les Collins and Michael Lee followed Scott Autrey home for a 3–3 in the final heat to secure the win.

England won a sensational match at Swindon to clinch the series. Twelve points behind after four heats, they recovered to win 64–43. Michael Lee, Dave and Steve Bastable led the way. Dave scored 13+1 from his six rides. It was revenge for the Americans' win in 1980.

The Americans won the next match 52–44 at Ipswich. It was abandoned due to a thunderstorm with two heats left, but the team managers agreed that it would be awarded to the USA. Dave was joint top scorer with 11 from his five rides. Mike Horne's report in the *Star* said that Dave "wasn't his usual immaculate self at the tapes, rode well from the back ..." Horne did say that Dave could have been excluded following an incident when he overtook Dennis Sigalos in the last lap of heat eight, but that the referee allowed the result to stand.

Dave had his best meeting of the series in the fifth match at Cradley. Steve Johnson wrote in the *Star* that England were "brilliantly spearheaded by skipper Dave Jessup" in their 69–38 win. Dave scored 17 points and was only beaten by Bruce Penhall, who was riding on his home track.

Interviewed by Kevin Brown in the *Star* after England had won the first three tests, Dave said that "I'm very pleased and all the boys rode terrific. Our horses for courses ploy paid off, and a lot of effort was put in by everybody. A lot of people have said to me that being made captain would affect my own performance, but I think my showings on the track have dispelled that theory. I've waited a long while for this and I'm enjoying it immensely. I'm just happy that we have won the series." He also said that there had been a good relationship between the two sets of riders, and that he got on well with the Americans. He said that reports of him and Bruce Penhall "were at each other's throats" were incorrect and that he got on well with the American captain.

Another piece of good news for Dave was that he had been chosen as the Corals Rider of the Month for April. The SWAPA members had voted him into top place. The prize was the same as in 1980, a cheque for £200 and six more Waterford crystal glasses, meaning that he now had 18.

Dave continued to ride for King's Lynn in the middle of all his other meetings. The promoters did say that they had problems arranging meetings because of the other commitments of their three heat leaders. This was no fault of the riders involved, and was not helped by King's Lynn's regular meeting night being Saturday. In the League Cup, Dave scored 13+1 from five rides for the Stars in a narrow win at Plough Lane, and then a full five ride maximum in the return match against Wimbledon 10 days later. King's Lynn won 66–29 and the *Star* reported that Dave had "bounced back to peak form." Later the same week, Dave was "in supreme form" with a six-ride full maximum at Hackney in a 48–48 draw and then scored 17 points the next night as the Stars beat the east London side by eight points to reach the League Cup Final against Coventry. This was not staged until October.

Dave entered the World Championship at the semi-final stage. The British rounds had started in April with five qualifying rounds for National League and some British League riders. Sixteen qualified for the quarter-final, and the nine qualifiers from that meeting met the seeded British League riders in the semi-finals. Dave was drawn at Poole, and after scoring 13 points won a run-off with Steve Bastable to take top place. The British Final was three weeks later at Coventry. Dave qualified for the Overseas Final by finishing sixth with nine points. He won his last race to make sure of going through.

The World Team Cup also started in May, with a qualifying round at Reading. England faced the USA, Australia and New Zealand, and won the meeting with 36 points, four clear of the USA who also qualified for the next stage. The *Star* said that England won "more comfortably" than the four-point margin would suggest. The report also said that Dave and Michael Lee "were in superb form". Lee top scored for England with 11 points, followed by Dave with 10.

It was also announced that Dave would again represent England in the World Best Pairs. His partner would be Chris Morton. Peter Collins had opted out of British League speedway this season to concentrate on longtrack racing in Europe and therefore was not considered for selection for any England team.

In the same week as the World Team Cup meeting, King's Lynn visited Ipswich for the second leg of their Knock Out Cup tie. The Stars were in a weak position, having lost the home leg by two points. They went down by 10 to the Witches. Dave scored 16 from seven rides, and rode in three consecutive heats, fortunately a rare phenomenon. He won heat 11, was third in heat 12 and won heat 13. Dave and Michael Lee scored 34 points between them. Missing Richard Hellsen, the rest of the team managed just nine. A couple of weeks later, King's Lynn returned to Foxhall Heath for a League Cup meeting. Michael Lee was missing, and Dave again scored 16 from seven rides, but the Stars lost 65–31. With Hellsen also missing it really was an uphill struggle.

Dave was still riding in European longtrack meetings when time permitted. In May he scored 13 in the World Longtrack World Championship qualifying round at Marianske-lazne in Czechoslovakia to reach the semi-final stage.

In the second of week of June, England began a three-test series against Denmark at Hackney. It was the first time that a test series against the Danes had been staged in England, and it was closely fought. As skipper, Dave led the way at Waterden Road with 17 points from his six rides. Only Finn Thomsen in heat six stopped him getting a full maximum. The *Star* said that he was "consistently fast from the start" and "led his country by example". A particular highlight was his battle with Eric Gundersen in heat eight. The lead changed hands several times; Dave won the race on the last bend. England won the match 62–46.

As well as the test series, Dave was involved in the World Pairs. England were drawn in the Semi-Final at Norden in West Germany. The hosts, England and New Zealand all qualified for the final on 23 points. Chris Morton scored 12 for England and Dave got 11. A three-man run-off to decide the rostrum places was won by Egon Muller, Morton was second and Ivan Mauger third. The final was in Poland two weeks later. Dave told the *Star* that he was going to sleep on his passport, following the incident in Poland the previous year at the World Team Cup when it was stolen. The preview in the *Star* said that this was probably a tougher meeting for England to win than the World Team Cup. Far less strength in depth was required. For example, the Kiwis were represented by Ivan Mauger and Larry Ross, but had struggled in the World Team Cup where five riders were required.

On the day, England had a "disappointing afternoon" according to the *Star*. They finished joint fifth on 17 points. The USA won the meeting with 23 points, one clear of New Zealand. The *Star* said that Dave had machine problems and was below his best, and that Chris Morton found the going tough. He scored 10 points and Dave got seven, including two heat wins.

Two days after the World Pairs Final, Dave and Chris Morton were riding together again for England, this time in the second test against Denmark at Reading. England won 58–50 to take the series, with Dave scoring 12+3. Michael Lee and Kenny Carter both scored double figures as well, and England effectively had the meeting won by heat 16. The Star's report said that "Chris Morton and skipper Dave Jessup produced the goods at the right time" with a 5–1 in heat 10 that made the score 30–30.

Important meetings can thick and fast in this period. On Friday 26 June, England faced Denmark in a test match in Vojens. The Danes won 60–48, with Dave scoring one point. Two days later, on the Sunday, England faced a tough challenge in the World Team Cup Inter-Continental Final at King's Lynn. They were up against the USA, Denmark and Sweden. No rider scored double figures in a hard-fought contest. Denmark won the meeting with 31 points; England also qualified a point behind the Danes on 30. The Americans were eliminated with 26 and the Swedes finished last with 9. Dave scored eight points, and only won one heat. However, that heat 13 win over Eric Gundersen, with Dennis Sigalos in third place was key in the final reckoning.

Dave was top scorer with 12 points in the final test against the Danes at Coventry, but England lost 62–46. Of his 12 points, Dave scored 11 in his first four rides. England were never ahead in the match, and only won two heats in the second half of the meeting.

The next meeting on the World Championship road to Wembley was the Overseas Final at White City on 12 July. Before then, Dave rode twice for King's Lynn, scoring 12-point maximums in wins at Wimbledon and at home to Hull. His good form continued at White City. Philip Rising reported in the *Star* that Dave showed that "his failure to dominate the British Final ... was a mere hiccup by galloping away with this first ever Overseas Final." Rising said that Dave could have scored a maximum had he needed it. In fact, he had the meeting won with 12 points before coming third to Michael Lee and Ivan Mauger in the final heat. Rising said that "Jessup's magnificent gating and ability to control a race from the front had put him in an unassailable position. He shrugged off a challenge from Bruce Penhall in heat 12 but was never seriously in danger of losing until heat 20." Dave won £750 for finishing in first place.

Overseas Final: Runner-up Chris Morton, Dave and third-placed Bruce Penhall. (JSC)

Bruce Penhall and Dave inches apart at the Overseas Final.

Less than two weeks later, the Inter-Continental Final at Vojens was the final hurdle to overcome to secure a Wembley World Final place. Dave qualified in fifth place with 10 points. The lowest of the 11 qualifiers was Ole Olsen on six points. However, it was a difficult, fraught meeting. Philip Rising's report said that there was a "flood of controversy", initially over three poor decisions by the Polish referee in the first four heats. It then started raining, and 14 out of the 16 riders, and a lot of the officials wanted the meeting postponed for 24 hours. Rising said that there were "storms of protest, abuse and chaotic scenes" before the meeting got going again after a 95-minute delay. Jack Fearnley, the BSPA President, said that the meeting had become a lottery, with the riders unable to see properly where they were going. Fortunately, there were no serious crashes. Dave finished third in his first ride, then won heats eight and nine. Last place in heat 15 put him under pressure to score in his last ride, but he won heat 18, knocking out John Louis and Ivan Mauger in the process.

At this time, there were rumours that Dave was planning to leave King's Lynn. It was reported in the *Star* that he was upset by this talk, and Cyril Crane said that they would be talking to Dave, and wanted him to stay at the club. The King's Lynn management also had problems with Michael Lee at this time. Also, King's Lynn were losing money, and the local paper had said that they could not guarantee to keep their two leading riders. These matters would be resolved at the end of the season.

As well as challenging for the speedway world title, Dave had qualified for the longtrack World Championship Semi-Final. However, he was knocked out at the meeting in Herxheim in West Germany, with four points. Back on the speedway track, Dave defended his Internationale title at Wimbledon on 9 August. He finished fifth with nine points. Hans Nielsen won the meeting with a maximum.

The problems that the King's Lynn management team faced were exacerbated when Michael Lee was found guilty of possession of a small amount of cannabis in court. He had also been banned from driving for six weeks in a separate case. Cyril Crane admitted that he had not spoken to or seen Lee for ages. While this situation did not directly affect Dave, it did put more pressure on him when riding for King's Lynn.

On 16 August, the World Team Cup Final was held in Olching. Michael Lee withdrew from the England team through illness, so Dave lined up with Chris Morton, Kenny Carter, John Davis and Gordon Kennett at reserve. They were up against Denmark, West Germany and the Soviet Union. The Germans had won the Continental Final, but apart from Egon Muller did not look to be a great threat to England and Denmark.

Dave had an engine failure in the first heat, and it was not England's day. The Danes' Hans Nielsen won that heat, and they were top of the scores throughout the meeting. Dave finished on three points from three rides. He was replaced in heat 11 by Gordon Kennett. England finished on 29 points, one ahead of West Germany. They clearly missed Peter Collins and Michael Lee, who liked the Olching track. The meeting also showed that the Danes were going to be a strong force in the future, at least in the World Championship, World Pairs and World Team Cup. They maybe didn't yet have the depth that England and the USA had for a test series.

Despite all his speedway commitments, Dave still found some time for golf. Dave Lanning reported in the *Star* that he had spent three days playing in the BBC2 Pro-Celebrity tournament at the famous Gleneagles course. Some of celebrities included Jack Lemmon, George C. Scott, Terry Wogan, Sean Connery, James Hunt, Bruce Forsyth and Cliff Thorburn. Dave's partner was Lee Trevino. The event was going to be shown on BBC2 in the autumn.

As part of the *Star's* World Final preview, Martin Rogers contributed a feature on Dave. He said that "So the question to be resolved at Wembley ... is whether DJ can shake off the various crosses he has had to bear. He has beaten all of the best boys and done so consistently..." He wondered if Dave had "that indefinable extra ingredient which separates a world champion from the rest of the boys? Or is he now supremely ready to lift the title ... In so many ways he is reminiscent of Ivan, a ruthlessly effective starter, a less than flamboyant temperament and style, but a shrewdly analytical customer, all calculation and fine measurement, a mini-computer assessing all of the odds and options."

Rogers was also well aware of Dave's love for golf. He continued: "In attitude, application and approach, Jessup mirrors many of the characteristics of some of his sporting heroes, who just happen to be golfers rather than speedway riders. DJ has a consuming appetite for that challenging game, and is described by Peter Allis as 'a bit of a bandit off a handicap of 12'". Rogers pointed out that Dave was very close to the standard that warranted playing off scratch. He concluded by saying that he believed there would be a new world champion, and it would either be Dave or Bruce Penhall.

In his preview of the big night, Ivan Mauger said he thought that Dave had "gone off the boil recently." In the last week of August, Dave had a rare "disastrous night" at Hull, scoring two from four rides, including a two-minutes time exclusion. Two days later, he scored 13 from five rides at Swindon, and 11 from five rides, including an engine failure, when Swindon won the return match. However, two days before Wembley, Dave got a 15-point maximum at Ipswich, and was said to be "razor sharp".

Martin Rogers was correct in his prediction, but sadly for King's Lynn and England fans, it was Bruce Penhall who won the last-ever World Final at Wembley, although no one knew this at the time. A 90,000 crowd saw Dave win his first two races, heat four and heat eight. Robert Bamford and Glynn Shailes, in their history of the World Championship, said of Dave's win that "It was a popular victory and many in the crowd had their fingers crossed that the diminutive 'DJ' could at last slay his World Final ghosts of the past."

Out again in heat nine, Penhall led from the outside gate, with Dave close behind him. On the final bend, Penhall locked up, and Dave's engine failed. A clip on the carburettor had snapped. He pulled up sharply on the inside and Plech and Jancraz went past him. In heat 15, Dave suffered an engine failure while leading. If he had finished both races, he would have gone into his final race, heat 18, on 11 points. As it was, with only six points to his name, he finished third behind Tommy Knudsen and Egon Muller to finish on seven points, Penhall won the meeting with 14, but knew in his last ride he only needed one point to take the title. Philip Rising pointed out that Dave was still younger than Ivan Mauger when the Kiwi legend won his first title, "but he needs better luck when it matters most".

After the World Final, Dave's form was uneven for the rest of the season. In a disastrous 20-point home defeat by Belle Vue, Dave scored six points from five rides for King's Lynn. The report said that he was "dogged by mechanical problems", including an engine failure in heat 12 when he was "yards from the line".

In the pits at the 1981 World Final. Edward Jancraz is the rider in the background. (JSC)

At Cradley three days later, Dave scored seven from four rides for the Stars, and was "a shadow of his real self". Things improved at Sheffield the next night; King's Lynn lost by two points and Dave scored 10+1 from his five rides.

In October, King's Lynn faced Coventry in the Final of the League Cup. They were missing Michael Lee, who was reported to have flu. At Brandon in the first leg, the Stars lost by 40 points, 68–28, with Dave scoring just five from seven rides. Only Richard Hellsen, with 16, challenged the home side. The second leg was the next day. Although King's Lynn did better, with Dave scoring 15 points, they still lost 54–42 to make the aggregate score 122–70.

Dave represented King's Lynn in the British League Riders Championship, and finished fifth with nine points from his five rides. The next day he secured a 15-point maximum as King's Lynn lost at home to Leicester. Things did pick up a bit towards the end of the season. Dave and Mel Taylor won the Anglican Pairs at Saddlebow Road; the next week Dave was runner-up to Michael Lee in the Pride of the East meeting and on 6 November, Dave won the Vic Harding Memorial Trophy at Hackney with 14 points. He beat John Louis in a run-off.

At the end of October, it was reported that the Speedway Control Board had banned a proposed private tour by a group of riders to South Africa. Dick Bracher, the SCB manager, said that "... we felt we could not give permission until the situation over sporting links with South Africa has been clarified." However, George Barclay from the Speedway Riders

Association said that he had originally been against any riders going to South Africa after the United Nations had issued a blacklist of sporting personalities who had visited the country. However, since then several sportsmen had visited, including some road racers. The 1977 Gleneagles Agreement had committed Commonwealth countries to discourage sporting contacts with South Africa.

In December, it was confirmed that the riders could not tour. Bracher commented that "We are not prepared to run the risk of British teams in international competitions being excluded for the sake of about half a dozen riders going to South Africa in our off season." However, Dave did the chance to ride again in South Africa in the future. He had already sent a bike to South Africa and Dave had been in talks with the South African promoters since the end of the British season. Dave and Vicky and their son David still had a holiday in South Africa.

As the season came to a close, it became clear that King's Lynn faced major financial problems. The team had struggled. Instead of moving up the table, they had sunk to 14th place, just two from the bottom, with 22 league points. Only seven league meetings at Saddlebow Road had been won. After a successful League Cup campaign, the Stars' fortunes had declined. Michael Lee had faced problems for much of the campaign, and missed 11 of the Stars' 48 league and cup meetings. His average actually increased marginally compared to 1980, but too often he pulled out of meetings at short notice. Richard Hellsen also saw his average drop by 1.6, and he also missed 13 meetings, mainly due to international commitments. Dave rode in 44 of the Stars' official team meetings, but his average fell by just under a point to 9.57 compared to 1980. Melvyn Taylor improved his scores, and Craig Featherby had a reasonable first season with the Stars. But Pierre Brannefors and Hasse Danielsson made little impact, and both had averages below four points

In the *Star's* review of the season, Eric Linden said that Lee's "absences and the up and downers with the management must have had an effect on the rest of the team." Linden says that Dave was "invaluable" to the side, but also commented that the team's tail was too long. He did point out that they took 18 league points from their first 15 matches, but only four – two wins – from their last 15.

The *Star's* 'end of term' report said that "The problems with Michael Lee had an adverse effect, but Mel Taylor has yet to realise his full potential and Richard Hellsen was short of his best. The reserves were weak too, leaving Dave Jessup as the one plus factor."

In October it had been reported that team manager Alan Littlechild was considering leaving the club. Later the same month, it was revealed that the promotion had lost £80,000 in three years, and would have to cut costs. In December, Dave said in the *Star* that he would not take the captain's role at the club if Michael Lee was still there. He said that "...there is no way it will work. Michael is only human after all and I feel that he will resent the change."

Looking back, Dave said that Michael Lee "had a troubled career and went off the rails. It was a great pity because he was very talented. He socialised with some of the American riders who maybe weren't a good influence. Maybe he had too much money too quickly. When I was King's Lynn manager, I worked with him to get his licence back, but he only rode a few meetings for us and never really changed."

Dave featured on the cover of the *Speedway Star* over 20 times in his career, here shown riding a Godden bike.

Dave did say that he would like the captaincy role, and did not think that it would put any extra pressure on him. However, he said that he had turned down the three deals that King's Lynn had offered him to stay at the club. He said that "It is not purely the figure that I don't go along with, but the way they want to pay it to me."

Dave also said that he had been depressed after the World Final, saying that "You work all year towards that one vital meeting and it all went wrong in a few seconds". Kevin Brown concluded his report by saying that "... Jessup did a grand job for his club in often difficult circumstances with fellow heat leaders Richard Hellsen and Lee frequently not around to assist him. One of Jessup's biggest assets though is his dependability and throughout Lynn's trouble-torn campaign he stood firm as a rock."

The King's Lynn club history by Martin Rogers and Chris Hornby says that Michael Lee missing meetings and him being in the headlines for the wrong reasons saw an "uncertain atmosphere [which] had an adverse effect throughout the club." They also point out that

Richard Hellsen "missed many important matches because of increased international calls". However, they also say that "Dave Jessup did not always relish the additional weight of responsibility which came his way." At times he was the only one of the team's three heat leaders who was available. Particularly for a short period after the disappointment of the World Final he did have some low scores, but there is no record of him refusing to take extra rides, and usually he was one of the top two scorers for the side.

Despite his international commitments for England, Dave only missed four league or cup meetings for the Stars. One was at Halifax when all three King's Lynn heat leaders were at a longtrack World Championship meeting, another was when he had had the bust-up with Cyril Crane early in the season. He missed the evening league meeting at Coventry due to a longtrack qualifying round in Czechoslovakia the next afternoon. The other meeting he missed was on 1 August, a league match at home to Reading when Michael Lee was also absent. Dave scored 11 maximums – nine full, two paid – in his 44 meetings for King's Lynn. During his three years at Saddlebow Road he missed 10 official league or cup meetings, and generally was very consistent. The problems at King's Lynn were not his responsibility to try to resolve.

There had been talk of King's Lynn closing because of their financial problems, but things looked more optimistic towards the end of the year. Whether Dave would be part of the club in 1982 remained to be seen.

14. Wimbledon

The new year opened with good news for Dave and Vicky. Vicky's grandfather had won a substantial amount on the football pools. Dave said that it did not affect him in the short term, but could have long-term implications for the family.

In mid-January it was announced that the ban on British riders racing in South Africa had been lifted by the Speedway Control Board. SCB manager Dick Bracher said that the lack of support for the anti-apartheid campaign SANROC's (South African Non-Racial Olympic Committee) "black list" at the United Nations, and a speech by Sports Minister Neil McFarlane had prompted their change of heart. Dave and Vicky were already in South Africa, so this meant that Dave could compete there before they returned home in March, in time for the British season.

Dave's future was still up in the air. He agreed with Jawa to become one of their works riders in 1982 both for speedway and longtrack. Dave switched to Jawa because "I had been waiting for a Jawa works contract and couldn't turn it down. It was a very good deal. It had a double overhead cam engine, so it was fast but could be difficult to ride. It was more suited to King's Lynn than Wimbledon, but I thought I could get by on it. I was altering stuff in the first half of the season to get it right. It could be inconsistent. Ivan and Ole were moving from Jawa to Weslake and Godden at this time."

Jawa's British base was near King's Lynn, so this led to speculation that he may stay with the Stars. Dave Lanning reported that Dave had been offered a new deal at King's Lynn including a 'testimonial', although he had only been with the club for three years. Lanning said that the clause was "frowned upon" by the speedway authorities. Dave was entering his 14th season in British speedway, but had never stayed more than four years with any team. Lanning felt that it was unlikely that Dave would commit to a long-term deal with the Stars.

The issue had still not been resolved at the end of January. King's Lynn were now interested in bringing former Ipswich star Billy Sanders back to East Anglia after Hull had closed. In the *Star* at the beginning of February, Cyril Crane said that he had to make plans assuming that Dave would not continue at Saddlebow Road. He also, rather unfairly, implicitly blamed Dave for the promotion's financial problems, saying: "After buying Jessup three years ago when Terry Betts left, we have lost money since that time but up until then we had never lost money..." The reasons for King's Lynn's problems were discussed in the last chapter. Dave comments that "King's Lynn had the number one and number two English riders riding for an English club. If they couldn't get the finances right that isn't my fault."

However, it was clear that a parting of the ways could be best for both sides. The following week, it was reported that Crane had agreed terms with Wimbledon for Dave to move there, with Colin Richardson moving to Norfolk in part-exchange.

In the *Speedway Diary* in the *Star* on 27 February, it was reported that "Cyril Crane, a promoter who doesn't mince his words, has let rip at Dave Jessup who is hoping to sign for Wimbledon later this week. Crane claims that Jessup approached a number of tracks before leaving for a holiday in South Africa and that the England skipper had no intention of riding for King's Lynn in 1982." Dave's contract was for three years at Saddlebow Road. It could be argued that he had every right to talk to other promotions to see what they could offer.

In the end, the deal went through at the beginning of March, with Colin Richardson leaving Wimbledon for King's Lynn. Billy Sanders spent a year at King's Lynn before returning to Ipswich. At the end of 1982, Martin Rogers returned to King's Lynn to take over as promoter.

In moving to Plough Lane, Dave was joining one of the most prestigious clubs in British speedway, albeit one that had hit hard times on the track. They had a well-appointed stadium at Plough Lane, and some of the great names of the sport, including Ronnie Moore, Barry Briggs and a young Ivan Mauger had all worn their colours.

For the first time since 1949, Wimbledon had finished bottom of the league in 1981, with just 17 league points from their 30 meetings. Dave's friend and neighbour, Malcolm Simmons, had been their leading rider in 1981, and he stayed on for the new campaign. Polish star Edward Jancraz had also filled a heat leader slot, but only for 17 meetings. No other rider averaged over seven points a meeting. As well as Dave, Wimbledon manager Cyril Maidment had also signed Finnish star Kai Niemi. Brad Oxley and Anders Eriksson had second string slots, while Jancraz also rode for 14 meetings, but averaging less than six points. At least now the Plough Lane fans had a heat leader trio worthy of the name.

Dave said that he was "very pleased" to be joining Wimbledon, and said that "I like all the boys in the team, and that is important. It will be the first time that I have ridden for a local team." The *Star* reported that he was pleased to no longer have the "extensive travelling" to King's Lynn, and that his scoring power together with his influence on those around him should ensure that Wimbledon would be stronger than in 1981.

Wimbledon's first match was against Ipswich in the League Cup. Dave scored just 5+1 from his four rides, and it was his heat 12 engine failure that cost the Dons a win. He was using a new bike that stopped after two laps. However, two days later, the Dons won by six points at Saddlebow Road, with Dave scoring eight from four rides, including another engine failure. A week after that win, The Dons lost by 19 points at Cradley, and Dave was taken to hospital for x-rays after a heat 11 crash.

The *Star* reported that Dave was having teething problems with his switch to Jawa after 10 years on Weslakes. His accident at Cradley had not helped matters. He expected to be back to his best within a couple of weeks. Things started to improve. A "trouble free" 15-point maximum in an inter-league meeting at Crayford was followed by 10 in a challenge match against Belle Vue, and a five-ride paid maximum at Hackney. On Easter Monday, he scored "an immaculate maximum" against Sheffield at Plough Lane, followed by another at Swindon in a six point away win for Wimbledon.

Dave was also reappointed as England captain for the forthcoming test series against the USA. Philip Rising wrote in the *Star* that "Skipper Dave Jessup is still experiencing a few mechanical gremlins but generally his riding has looked world class of late and he is a man for the big occasion."

The test series opened at Plough Lane with a comfortable win for the home team. Dave contributed 6+2 from five rides. Three days later, the USA won the second test at Swindon. Dave was England's top scorer with 12+1 from six rides. The Americans got off to a 5–0 start as both England riders fell in the first heat, and were never behind. The Americans went 2–

1 ahead in the third test, with Dave scoring eight from six rides. Mike Horne said in the *Star* that "skipper Dave Jessup was a shadow of his usual self until the second half of the meeting. He bounced back with two heat wins, but by then the Americans had the match in their pockets."

England recovered in the fourth test at Belle Vue to win by 14 points. However, Dave was off form and scored 2+2 from his three first half rides before being replaced by reserve Alan Grahame in the second half. The series concluded 10 days later at Poole. The third test had originally been scheduled for the south coast track, but had been postponed because of bad weather.

Dave had a stomach upset before the match and was switched to reserve. He rode once, in heat 10, scoring one point as England went down 69–39. Despite only having one ride in that meeting, Dave still finished as third highest points scorer for England in the series, behind Kenny Carter and Chris Morton. Dave and John Davis had both supported American skipper Bruce Penhall's demand for appearance money for the riders in the test series.

Speedway was regularly covered by ITV at this time. Dave Lanning reported that Dave had spent a day with an ITV crew, including riding with a camera on his shoulder to give the viewers a rider's view of a speedway race.

Between the fourth and fifth tests, the World Team Cup qualifying round was staged at King's Lynn. The *Star* previewed the meeting and said that "Dave Jessup has run into more problems and just doesn't look the same rider on a Jawa as he did on a Weslake. [Eric] Boocock says Dave did a real captain's job at Belle Vue. He worked hard, rallied around everyone and helped knit the team together, but on Sunday his contribution must come on the track."

England and the USA dominated the World Team Cup meeting, scoring 39 points each to qualify for the next round at Vojens at the end of June. Dave and Michael Lee both scored 11 points. England won the meeting when Peter Collins beat Kelly Moran in a run-off.

The World Championships in speedway and longtrack both started in May. In the former, Dave qualified for the British Final by finishing third in the Semi-Final at Hackney with 11 points. Things looked uncertain after two third places in his first two rides, but then he won his last three races. In longtrack, he rode in a qualifying round at Schessel, but only scored eight points to qualify as reserve in the Semi-Final.

Dave was not usually involved in controversy. If he was, it was often around track conditions and rider safety. It is important to remember that this was a different era from today in terms of safety provision for riders. There were no air fences, and generally some aspects of track safety and design then would not be acceptable today. It is significant that while researching this book I noted that usually two or three riders were killed in track accidents each season. To be fair, some of these were in training events, but riders still had to try to ensure that it was safe to ride. Some of the promoters had ridden in the 1950s and 1960s, when safety standards were even worse, and based their views of what was safe on their riding experiences.

On 3 May, the bank holiday Monday saw Reading and Wimbledon scheduled to meet twice. Reading won the first encounter, but at Plough Lane in the evening, the match was called off. Referee Reg Trott, a former team mate of Dave's from his Eastbourne days, said that the track was fit to ride, as did the two team managers. However, all 14 riders said it was not, and the meeting was called off. Trott fined all the riders £50 each for refusing to race and the meeting was abandoned. Five days later, Wimbledon were beaten 56–22 at Halifax. Gordon Sampson's report in the *Star* said that the Dons "put their worst British League performance at Halifax down to the track, which they claimed had been over-watered and was rough." Dave withdrew from the meeting after his third ride, having scored six points, including winning heat 11. Dave says that "I loved riding at Halifax usually, it was a big track with banking." The *Star* also reported that Cyril Maidment was unhappy with the state of the track.

On 30 May, Wimbledon travelled to Eastbourne for a League Cup match. One of Eastbourne's heat leaders was the American, Kelly Moran. He had flown in overnight to Gatwick Airport, arriving earlier that day. Dave Jessup and the other Wimbledon riders believed he was not fit to race when he fell twice in his first two rides. He was excluded in his first ride, the referee put all four riders back in the race after another first bend fall in heat five. Moran then fell again in the rerun, but the referee excluded Wimbledon's Brad Oxley. Moran trailed in third in that race, won heat nine and was then last in heat 13 when Dave and Kai Niemi took a 5–1 to secure a 39–39 draw.

Years later, and with Moran having sadly died in 2010, Dave is still indignant about the incident. He believes that Moran was not fit to ride, and was putting other riders in danger. The Wimbledon captain, Malcom Simmons, asked that Moran take a fitness test to see if he was fit to be in the meeting. Simmons says in his autobiography that Moran was a "notoriously big drinker" and that he "turned up for the meeting pissed". Simmons also says that Moran's breath "stunk of whisky". The referee asked the track doctor to give Moran a breathalyser test, but this was not done, and the doctor said that Moran was fit to ride.

In his biography of Moran, Brian Burford says that Tony Millard, Eastbourne's announcer that day, recalls arranging for someone to collect Moran from the airport, and that on the way to the meeting, Moran smoked some cannabis joints in the car. Eastbourne promoter Bobby Dugard said the incident was "a serious matter", and according to the report in the *Star* was considering taking legal action. This effectively stopped further reporting of the incident or debate on it. There is the wider issue of some American riders and the use of 'soft' drugs. Certainly, Dave believes that some of them were using cannabis regularly, which he was concerned about, although it is not clear what influence this had on British riders.

There are stories of professional footballers in the 1950s and early 1960s bring drunk or heavily hangover in the Christmas fixtures when teams had to play twice in two days, and often had lengthy travelling between the games. Certainly, county cricket also has stories of players who were not sober on the pitch. But the potential for serious harm in a sport like speedway is far greater than in football or cricket. Fortunately, Dave never came across another incident like this during his time as a speedway rider. He says that he didn't drink alcohol until he was 30 years old.

It is interesting to note that in July, the referee at Belle Vue refused to let Moran ride for Eastbourne because he had a hangover. He was fined £10 and the incident was referred to the Speedway Control Board.

There was further controversy about the Eastbourne meeting. The next week, the *Star* reported that Eastbourne were planning to protest about the re-running of the first heat, because the green light failed to operate. The report quoted Dave saying: "The green light didn't come on and when the tapes went up, I was left there. I moved off the track, waited until the race was over, attracted the referee's attention and asked that he test the light. It didn't come on and it was found that the bulb had gone. The meeting was held up while the bulb was changed and then the heat was re-run."

Meanwhile, Dave's next step in the World Championship was the British Final. Peter Oakes's preview questioned whether Dave's move to riding Jawa bikes was working. He said "... there' still a nagging doubt about his Jawa equipment. Will it be good enough to get him into the first turn as quickly as he has in the past? Aboard a Weslake DJ would be almost certain of a top three placing and his skill and experience should still see him through." In fact, it was a close-run thing. Dave finished eighth, the final qualification place, with eight points. He had won his last two races to qualify for the Overseas Final in July at White City.

Dave Lanning reported that Dave was going to act as an 'adviser' to the Crayford National League team. This was the track where he had his first big pile up – with Laurie Etheridge – back in his Eastbourne days in the Second Division. How much time Dave would have for this role remained to be seen.

Dave was justifying his place as Wimbledon's number one, but was experiencing some frustrating bike problems. Full maximums at home to Reading and Poole showed what was possible. The report on the latter meeting said that he "showed his best form yet in Wimbledon colours – including two superb wins from the back against Davis." But the report in the *Star* on Wimbledon's home meeting with Halifax said that "Another Dave Jessup engine failure didn't help and England will be hoping that DJ has a trouble-free night in Vojens on Saturday." The preview of the World Team Cup Inter-Continental Final, which the writer was referring to, said that "Jessup goes into the round with a background of mechanical problems clouding his own form."

England were knocked out of the World Team Cup. The USA won the round with 34 points, Denmark were second on 28, three clear of England. Dave scored four points with two second places, a last and an engine failure – "a ridiculous electrical fault" – according to Philip Rising in the *Star*. Kenny Carter scored a 12-point maximum, but Chris Morton with six points and Peter Collins with three were also responsible for England's defeat on the Danes' home track.

Away from speedway, Dave was making a good impression on the golf course. The *Star* received a letter from Peter Brown of the Hollingbury Park Golf Club: "'... I feel your readers would like to know if a rider who projects a first-class image and does a fantastic PR job for the sport' wrote golf pro Peter. 'I have played in several Pro-Am tournaments in which Dave Jessup has taken part and I can assure all speedway fans that he is a first-class advert for the sport as well as being a very capable and competitive golfer. I also know that he has succeeded in bringing some newcomers through the turnstiles due to the impression he has created and his support of charity events is very much appreciated by everyone in the golf game.'"

The next round of the World Championship was the Overseas Final at White City on 4 July. The top 10 riders would go through to the Inter-Continental Final. It was a controversial meeting, but Dave was not directly involved in the controversy; in fact, he gained from it.

Dave won the title with 13 points. After a second place in his first heat, three straight wins not only ensured qualification, but put him in line for a place on the rostrum. In heat 18 he finished second to Kenny Carter to finish on 13 points. He was one point clear of Carter, and two ahead of Bruce Penhall who was 11 points, having been beaten by Dave in heat 10, when Philip Rising said that Dave "produced the ride of the day in passing Penhall from the back."

In heat 19, Penhall faced three other Americans who all needed points to qualify for the next round. Instead of going for the win that would have given him the £1,000 winner's cheque, he stayed at the back, knowing that he had qualified, and did wheelies while his compatriots competed ahead of him. His blatant behaviour in not competing and helping the American riders stunned the fans and damaged his reputation.

The World Championship rounds when a large number of riders went through to the next round were always open to this sort of occurrence. When riding for Reading, Dave had been accused by Hackney promoter Len Silver of 'team riding' Bernie Leigh home in a qualifying round at Hackney leading to Silver's rider being knocked out.

But Penhall's antics should not take away from an excellent performance by Dave. Rising said that "given a trouble-free run with his Jawas, [Dave] proved that he is still a world-class performer and capable of rising to the big occasion." Dave had also used the wet condition of the back straight, which had been flooded earlier in the afternoon when a water main burst, to his advantage when beating Bruce Penhall.

Six days after the White City meeting, Dave returned to King's Lynn. Wimbledon lost by 14 points, and the *Star* reported that "Dave Jessup played down his problems at King's Lynn where his former boss Cyril Crane made life difficult for the Wimbledon number one. Jessup wanted to change a tyre after puncturing, but Crane insisted that he fit a new tube instead and DJ eventually found himself excluded under the two-minute rule. Jessup publicly said nothing, but was obviously unhappy about the incident which killed off Wimbledon's lingering hopes of a good result."

Next up in the World Championship was the Inter-Continental Final in Vetlanda in Sweden. The *Star's* preview said about Dave: "Of all the 16 finalists he is the one rider you should never write off – no matter how badly things appear to be going. Has the priceless ability to win a vital race against all the odds and is still one of the quickest starters in the game. Aiming for a sixth World Final."

Eleven riders qualified for the World Final from the meeting, and although Dave probably wasn't happy with eight points from his five rides, he qualified comfortably in seventh place. Peter Collins was the lowest qualifier with six points after winning a three-man run-off. The *Star* reported that "Overseas Champion Dave Jessup lost to Moran in heat four but reared at the start of heat eight and lost ground that he could never make up. But DJ had no time to think about it, being out again in the following race and his impressive win against Nielsen calmed his nerves."

Left: Wimbledon press day 1982 – Dave as a Jawa works rider.

Bottom: Winner of the 1982 World Championship Overseas Final at White City. Runner-up Kenny Carter on left, Bruce Penhall (third) on right. (JSC)

In early August, Dave was diagnosed with tic-bite fever, and had to pull out of Wimbledon's match against Leicester. He thought he picked it up on a trip to South Africa some time ago, and had been told that it could reoccur at times until it cleared up naturally. He also missed the World longtrack Championship semi-final. Apparently, the virus could leave someone without a sense of balance, which is not good for a speedway rider.

Dave missed the Dons' Knock Out Cup match at Eastbourne, and pulled out of the London Riders Championship after falling in his second ride. However, despite having been ill for three weeks, and with a long journey to Los Angeles, he was never going to miss the World Championship Final. Dave did ride for Wimbledon against Eastbourne in the return leg of the Knock Out Cup tie, and scored nine from four rides. He also rode at Leicester in the Golden Gauntlets meeting, which was abandoned through rain after 12 heats.

In the *Star*, Ivan Mauger gave his predictions for the big meeting. He said that Dave was "not quite as consistent this year on the Jawa as he has been in the past on the Wessies. Whether that is a change of engines or change of clubs I'm not quite sure but the track is big and fast and Jawas have always had top speed. I'm not one of those people who are prepared to write him off. He gates well enough and he has enough class to still finish very high up."

Dave was interviewed by Philip Rising in the *Star*. Rising wrote that the illness had taken Dave out of the spotlight for the meeting. Dave said he preferred being one of the favourites, but on this occasion had been keeping a low profile. He said that he had been looking forward to the final since it was agreed in 1980 that it would be in America. He said that "I've never been to America but it's one place I always wanted to go to. There has been a lot of talk about how expensive it is for the riders and that's true." He said it would cost £1,000 to take Vicky with him, compared to £200 to go to Sweden. He said that apart from the Friday before the Final he would be treating the trip as a holiday, and planned to visit some of the tourist attractions.

Rising commented that "Jessup's image over the years has tended to misrepresent the man. He is not at all the staid, humourless, monotone rider some appear to think. He has a studious look about him, a textbook riding style and a meticulous attention to detail. But that is the professional racer in him." He said that Dave was easy to interview and always gave a good impression of himself and speedway. Rising believed that Dave could overcome his health problems and win the title, and that Dave would make a good world champion.

It was not quite to be. Dave won heat three from the gate, and then was second to Wimbledon colleague Kai Niemi in heat six. But in heat 12 he was third to Bruce Penhall and Dennis Sigalos when his bike packed up 40 yards from the tapes. Dave won heat 15, but last place in heat 17 saw him finish in sixth place with eight points. Dave and Vicky did stay on for a few days in the USA after the final.

The rest of the season saw Dave riding regularly, but in September failing to score double figures in any meeting. A couple of injuries and bike problems did not help matters. In a double header at Plough Lane in early October he scored 11 points against both Poole and Reading, but a couple of weeks later he struggled in the British League Riders Championship, scoring just three points from five rides.

Left: Dave with John in the pits at the 1982 World Final in Los Angeles.

In the *Star*, he reflected on his bike problems, which were getting him down: "'It's a long, lonely walk back to the pits when you stop out there on the track,' he says. Jessup's transfer from King's Lynn to Wimbledon hasn't bought about the expected results for the England skipper and he has finished the year with his lowest average for some time. Injuries and illness have also plagued him and it is just as well that he still thinks his move to Plough Lane was a wise decision. Jessup spent another week trying to cure his problems prior to Wimbledon's double header with Poole and Reading and was a much happier man after going through eight races without any bother."

A couple of weeks later, a report in the *Star* said that "he still refuses to put this drop in scoring down to a switch from Weslake to Jawa, but there are many good judges around who feel that the sooner Dave gets back on a Weslake the better for him, Wimbledon and, indeed, England. There are times when DJ also appears to have lost some of his appetite for the sport, but a winter's break and a new start in 1983 should see this rider of proven ability and class re-establish his place among the top riders."

At the Wimbledon Supporters Club dinner, Dave said that he had tried Weslakes, Goddens and Jawas, and was now thinking about a Honda 50. He said that he had given his speedway future serious consideration and had been close to hanging up his leathers and looking towards a track promotion. But now he promised the Wimbledon fans a much better year in 1983. In his last meeting of the season at Plough Lane, Dave finished fourth in The Laurels with 11 points.

For the Dons, he rode in 35 official meetings and finished top of the averages with a CMA of 8.77, 0.8 below his figure the previous season at King's Lynn. More worryingly, it was his worst average since his second season at Wembley in 1971. However, Dave would just be turning 30 at the start of the 1983 season, certainly not old for a speedway rider, although he had just completed his fourteenth season as a full-time rider. The *Star* commented that Wimbledon's hopes for 1983 – they had finished 11th in the league table – depended on Dave "re-finding his golden touch, but at this stage that looks a fairly good bet."

In early December, it was announced that Dave, Malcolm Simmons and Kai Niemi would be staying at Plough Lane for 1983. That at least gave the club a good basis to build on. Eric Linden's review of the Dons' season in the *Star* said that Dave managed to keep Malcolm Simmons in second place in the Wimbledon averages, despite "two injuries, plus a bout of tic fever and a heap of mechanical problems" which showed how good a rider Dave was. Looking at the Wimbledon scorers for 1982, they lacked a second string who would average over six points, and were also weak at reserve, where Alan Mogridge was probably not experienced enough for the British League.

As Eric Linden concluded, the Dons had improved, but still had a long way to climb to be challenging at the top of the table. A winter break in South Africa, and some golf as well as some speedway could help recharge Dave's batteries after what had at times been a difficult campaign.

15. "The ultimate professional"

The first edition in the new year of the *Speedway Star* carried a major interview with Dave by Russell Lanning. He said that Dave was "... the ultimate professional. He is a business-conscious rider who's always in the limelight." Much of the interview covered Dave's career up to 1982. Reflecting on the previous year, Dave said that he had enjoyed the 1982 campaign because he had cut his travelling in half. He said that "My average has dropped a little from the previous year but that in no way means I am going downhill. I feel I have the opportunity to win the world title. If I didn't, I wouldn't be competing in top class speedway."

He said that he had plans to have less bike problems in 1983. He also said that he would be writing to the BSPA to say that he wanted to continue as the England captain, and would be "honoured" to do so. There was a new England manager, Wally Mawdsley, who needed to rebuild the team to challenge the USA and Denmark.

Before Dave and Vicky left for South Africa, the *Star* reported that he had agreed a new two-year deal with Wimbledon. The report also said that Dave would be riding new bikes in 1983, and was "keen to re-establish himself as one of the country's top scorers" after the mechanical problems and health issues had caused his average to drop below 10 in 1982.

South African speedway seemed to be doing well. Dave had been told that 15,000 people had watched a meeting in Durban. He was also hoping to ride in indoor meetings being organised by former Wimbledon rider Peter Murray. Dave had bookings to ride in Johannesburg and Tarlton. Dave finished fourth in an Open Championship meeting at Tarlton on 22 January. The meeting was won by the Zimbabwean rider Peter Prinsloo, who had been at Wembley with Dave in 1971. Five other riders with British speedway experience took part in the meeting.

He also captained an Overseas side against South Africa in two test matches at the indoor arena in Milner Park in Johannesburg. In the first he scored 5+1 from his four rides. The next day he scored 10 points. The Overseas team, which was mainly British riders, won both meetings. Dave also won the Indoor Open Championship at the same venue with a five-ride maximum, "five brilliant rides" according to the report in the *Star*.

Dave was clearly the best rider in the South African meetings: "I would often agree with the promoters that I would miss the start and work my way through from the back in some races. It made for a better show for the crowd. Peter Prinsloo was the only one riding there who could really challenge me."

Andy Campbell, who had been one of the British riders in South Africa, wrote to the *Star* about his experience of the indoor meetings. He said that everything the British riders had been promised they had received, and said that they were "treated superbly". He said that the meetings had not been a financial success, with "small but enthusiastic" crowds, but it has been "professional and well run". The venue was a huge show jumping arena and the grandstands and track had been built from scratch in three days.

In February, Peter Oakes in the *Star* reviewed the possible choices for the England captaincy. He made Peter Collins the favourite, ahead of Dave, Kenny Carter, Michael Lee and Chris Morton. He said that Dave had been through "a barren spell by his own high standards" in 1982, but was the most reliable rider with the possible exception of Kenny Carter. Oakes said that Eric Boocock said about Dave: "If you had to pick one rider to win a race for you it would be Jessup." Oakes also said that Dave was "far more articulate than many folk realise and if Mawdsley is looking for a diplomat to lead his international hopes then he could not pick a better man. DJ can mix easily with the blazer brigade of world speedway and you can rest assured that he would never say anything to embarrass British speedway."

Things looked promising for Wimbledon. New arrivals included Finland's number two, Ari Koponen, and Mike Ferreira, a South African rider who Dave knew from his visits there. Another new recruit was a young Kelvin Tatum. Roger Johns also hoped to improve on a disappointing 1982 campaign. Cyril Maidment confirmed that Dave would be the team's captain, and said that "I feel last year he was on equipment that didn't suit him, but he is terrific to have around and such a good man in the team."

Interviewed by Philip Rising in the *Star* when he had just returned from South Africa, Dave showed his determination to have a better season than 1982. He told Rising "Just sit tight and watch me this year. I have got something to prove and, if I don't do it, this year will be my last in speedway." Dave also said that he had bought five acres of land just outside Johannesburg, and planned to build a house there next winter. It was conveniently next to a country club golf course. However, he did assure the Wimbledon fans that he was enthusiastic about the new season.

Dave was named as England vice-captain for the 1983 season, with Peter Collins being the new skipper. Mawdsley told the press: "In no way does that tend to reflect on the performances of Dave Jessup. He has got a lot to offer. He ... fully endorses anything I have got to do. The object is to win right from the word go – not just qualify." Dave was certainly in demand by the media at this time. He was interviewed by a BBC television crew for the *Superstore* programme to be shown on Saturday morning.

In an interview with Bob Radford in the *Star*, Dave said that speedway was no longer his main source of income, but he was "still hungry for success". He added that for the first time since 1974 he was not a works rider, and was paying for his own equipment. He didn't feel under pressure to win the World Championship, but said he might be a "surprise packet" if he reached the Final. He said that he wasn't pleased to lose the England captaincy, but confirmed that Peter Collins would "have my full support in all he does. I want to be an important part of the team because I'm English and proud of it."

As far as Wimbledon was concerned, he said that with the sponsorship of Chalfont Coaches, "we have a formidable seven." The team were to be called the Chalfont Dons and the company's owner, Chris Shears, would be working with Cyril Maidment on the management side. Dave added that both Koponen and Ferreira were good signings. He also said he enjoyed riding with his old friend Malcolm Simmons, who lived a mile away from him, although he did say that Simmo was "a fair bit older".

Dave and Wimbledon started the season well in the League Cup, beating Ipswich 51–27 at Plough Lane, with Dave scoring 10+1 from four rides. The *Star* said that he looked "much more at ease back on Weslakes" and that the bikes suited Dave's style. Further wins followed at Reading, at home to Eastbourne and then at home to Hackney in the London Cup.

Dave riding a bike with a GM engine. (JSC)

Dave was also playing golf. On Easter Sunday he played at Silvermere in Cobham with Simmo. They had a distinguished caddie for a few rounds – Barry Briggs, who had turned up to watch. Briggs did admit that he would have preferred to be playing.

Wimbledon's good form continued. The *Star* reported that "Jessup has been showing tremendous form of late. It's not just that he is scoring points, that's taken for granted. But his team work, tenacity and attitude were particularly evident against Poole when the going was tough and the side trailed by 10 points. 'It's taken time to settle down on Weslakes again' said Jessup, 'but I'm happy with the way things are going for me and the team.'" Dave was waiting for a consignment of equipment from Weslake, and was using a bike that he thought was over 10 years old.

The season's international action started with a five match test series against the USA. Although missing Bruce Penhall, who had retired after winning the world title in 1982, and Scott Autrey, the Americans could still field a strong team of riders with experience of British conditions, including Bobby Schwartz, Dennis Sigalos, John Cook and the Moran brothers. They won the first test at Wimbledon 64–43, with Dave scoring four from six rides, including an engine failure and retiring in one race. England bounced back three days later at Swindon. Partnering Gordon Kennett, Dave won three heats to score 12+1 as England levelled the series with a six-point win. Ten days later, England won the third test at Poole. Dave rode with Michael Lee. He won the opening heat, but ended up with six points from five rides. The next night at Ipswich, the home track of Sigalos and Cook, the Americans won comfortably, with Dave contributing seven points from six rides.

Curiously, the World Championship semi-final at Eastbourne clashed with the final test at Sheffield. England won 58–50 to take the series. Dave, of course, had to ride in the World Championship meeting, and comfortably qualified for the British Final at Coventry with 10 points from his five rides. He beat Malcolm Simmons and Gordon Kennett in a run-off for third place.

In mid-May, Dave Lanning reported that Dave was the first British rider to use the Italian GM engine, which had been "inspired by Giuseppe Marzotto" supported by the well-known engine tuner Otto Lantenhammer. The problem Dave had was that the instruction books were in Italian. Lanning said that Dave was considering taking them to an Italian restaurant near Plough Lane if he needed any translations.

Dave had used the GM engine for the first time in the test series against the USA. In an article about Giuseppe Marzotto and the development of the engine in the *Star* (8 August 2020), Brian Burford said that "… during the England versus USA test series in 1983, England's Dave Jessup wheeled a GM into the pits and impressed." Burford quotes Marzotto saying: "At first, few believed in the Italian engine. It was through Otto Lantenhammer and his involvement with Trevor Hedge who convinced Dave Jessup to try the GM."

A week after the test series had finished, England's World Team Cup campaign started. Dave's form for Wimbledon had been slightly inconsistent, reflected in his average so far of 8.41. He was chosen as reserve for the World Team Cup meeting, with Simon Wigg taking his place. The USA won the meeting at Reading, with England also qualifying, seven points clear of New Zealand. Dave had one ride, replacing Wigg who had been last in his first outing. However, a stone flew up ff the track and hit Dave in the eye, forcing him to retire.

Dave scored his first paid maximum of the season at Hackney, and was said to be "back to his very best". Two days later he scored a full "untroubled" maximum at Eastbourne. Wimbledon won both meetings comfortably. He followed this up with 11 against Swindon at Plough Lane.

Peter Oakes's preview of the British Final said that Dave "seems to have found more confidence since switching to the expensive Giuseppe Marzotto made-in-Italy engine, but there always remains that question mark about the efficiency of his equipment. Often it's not the engine that lets down DJ – but the equipment that surrounds the focal point of any racing machine." It was Dave's 11th British Final. He had won the title in 1980, been runner-up twice and third twice. As usual, the meeting was at Coventry.

Philip Rising saw Dave eliminated from the World Championship after a disastrous third ride: "If Dave Jessup stood in a crowd of 100,000 and a single drop of rain fell, he would get soaked. The little Wimbledon skipper is cursed by misfortune and it is amazing how often it manifests itself during World Championship meetings. Coventry was a prime example. After two stylish wins, one setting a new track record, DJ was well on course for the Overseas Final when he clashed with Peter Collins.

Some claim it was a reckless, unnecessary tactic to dive inside Peter Collins when the race was young and time on Jessup's side. He could have settled for a safe second place and still led the field at the interval. With hindsight Jessup might even agree. But his smooth-running GM motor appeared to have speed on Collins and Jessup was sucked into a passing attempt that rebounded with horrible consequences for his world title aspirations."

Dave went to hospital for a check-up, and with just six points was two points short of the qualifying places. Malcolm Simmons also failed to qualify, and with Kai Niemi also eliminated in his qualifying meeting, Wimbledon had no representatives in the World Championship left.

Dave told Dave Lanning that he was "sick about the accident. I won't even watch a video of it." However, Dave said that he still had a lot to race for in 1983, and hoped to force his way into the £5000 British Open at Wimbledon in September, concluding that "... I want to prove this year, on the GM motor maintained by Trevor Hedge, I'm as good as anyone in the world."

Dave recalls that "I was going so well, so fast, but I should have waited to pass Peter Collins. The GM engine was better than the others, it was a rider error. I didn't break my shoulder, the handlebars hit me in the stomach and I couldn't move." His recovery from the injury was also unusual: "After a week at home I still couldn't move. I was shuffling around, but there were no marks on me. I was very frustrated, so I contacted a local osteopath to see if she could help. I went to see her, paid her £20 and lay on the bed. She seemed very tense, and put her hands on my head, and then rubbed my temple and ears. She was above me and I could feel her tears dripping onto my face. She did not go near my stomach. She said that that was all she could do today, so I got up and shuffled away to go home. I lay on the sofa watching television and then got up to go to the toilet. From my hips to my knees I was black and blue. Whatever she had done had brought the bruising out, and I rode the next day. She had absorbed the tension that was screwing up my guts."

Dave also had a nerve-wracking race at Wimbledon, although he was not riding. He lent the 19-year-old Kelvin Tatum his "super-fast" GM bike. Tatum initially declined the offer, then changed his mind. Jessup watched the youngster's four laps when he looked "decidedly out of control" according to Dave Lanning. It is only fair to point out that Tatum went on to have a distinguished career in the sport and in longtrack, as well as becoming a successful broadcaster when he retired from racing.

When Dave was riding the GM bike, particularly at Plough Lane, his form had improved. So, it was surprising that he was again chosen only at reserve for the World Team Cup Intern-Continental Final at Wimbledon. England faced a strong Danish team, the USA and Sweden. Hans Nielsen and Erik Gundersen both scored maximums for the Danes, who won the meeting with 35 points. They were four clear of the USA, who were five ahead of England. Dave ended up as England's joint top scorer with Chris Morton on eight points from four rides. They were also England's only heat winners. Philip Rising reported that "England skipper Peter Collins had only one ride before Dave Jessup was drafted in. Jessup, bitterly upset at being left out of the original team and dropped from the test side at Coventry on Wednesday, responded with a hard earned eight points."

However, England would have another chance. The team who finished third would be included in the Continental Final at Abensberg in West Germany on 10 July. Before then, Wimbledon were in the League Cup semi-final, where they faced Belle Vue. The first leg at Hyde Road saw them lose 50–28. Dave had a bad night, with just five points from his five rides. He had carburettor problems, which caused engine failures in his first two rides. A week later, the Dons won the second leg at Plough Lane, but only by seven points, so missed out on the Final.

Dave was not selected for the first two tests against Denmark. He was recalled for the third test at Hackney, two days before the World Team Cup meeting. England won 65–43 to take a 2–1 lead in the series, with Dave contributing 10+2 from his six rides.

At Abensberg, Dave was back in the team. Not surprisingly, England dominated the meeting, scoring 40 points, 13 clear of Czechoslovakia, who also qualified for the Final. Dave dropped just one point, when he was beaten by Jiri Stancl. The England riders had missed out on practice because the van bringing their bikes had broken down. They were offered a special dispensation to practice at 6am on the day of the meeting, but turned this down.

It was unusual for Dave to have problems with a referee. However, after the first heat of Wimbledon's home match with Poole, he was fined by Frank Ebdon after going to the referee's box to argue his case over a first-bend tussle with Michael Lee. Dave had pulled out of the race, but the Dons did go on to win the meeting.

Meanwhile, there were problems at Wimbledon. The management team held a meeting with the riders to find out what was going wrong. This came after they had lost both legs of the Knock Out Cup tie against Coventry, and been beaten in the League Cup semi-final by Belle Vue. A two-point defeat at home was followed by a 10-point loss at Brandon. Coventry were a good team, who went on to reach the Final, and finished above Wimbledon in the league. But the Dons had been doing well at Plough Lane, and the tie was effectively over after the first leg. For the away match, they had switched Dave to number three, but he didn't like waiting until the fourth heat for his first ride. The report in the *Star* said that the "...man who really pleased Shears over the two legs was Dave Jessup. 'He deserves praise because he's carrying the team again. He's taken some stick earlier in the year but you couldn't fault him against Coventry." Chris Shears was mainly concerned about the form of Malcolm Simmons and Kai Niemi.

The report of the Dons' comfortable home win against Belle Vue said that they showed "more determination. This was followed by a 15-point home win against Leicester. But then further problems developed. The *Star* reported that Dave "had asked for a meeting with the Plough Lane management to clear the air following a team talk held at the stadium two weeks ago that the England international missed. At the meeting, the riders asked that Malcolm Simmons take over from Jessup as captain...". Dave was told of the decision a few days after the meeting by Cyril Maidment and was understandably unhappy about it. Malcolm Simmons did offer to stand down as captain, but it is difficult to see how Dave could have continued in the position. Dave did not ride in the Dons' fixture at Halifax, and would not be riding in the next Wimbledon home meeting because of a clash with the World Team Cup Final.

Dave did return to the Wimbledon line-up at Swindon, and scored 9+2 from his four rides in a 43–35 win. The *Star* said that the Dons "were boosted by the arrival of former skipper Dave Jessup after his recent dispute with the club and it was he more than anyone who proved the inspiration..." Chris Shears said that he "would like to thank Dave for sticking by his word and for turning up with immaculate machinery and riding as he did." There was an embarrassing moment when the two captains were asked to toss a coin and no one from the Wimbledon side stepped forward.

Chris Shears said that he was "very critical of the way the management have handled the affair", but he was part of the management team and had been at the meeting when the riders made their decision. A couple of weeks later, Dave Lanning reported in the *Star* that Dave "... was certainly all stitched up about the recent backroom backbiting at Wim that sought to dispose his captaincy of the Dons. 'I've been amazed by the attitude of my team-mates' said Dave. 'This kind of criticism is something new to me. There is even one bloke who refuses to ride as my partner because he says I'm consistently too quick at the start.'" Two weeks later, the *Star* reported that Chris Shears was bidding to become the Hackney promoter, and said that Shears "also criticised the handling of the Dave Jessup affair which, he feels, has never been satisfactorily settled."

In the middle of all this turmoil at Wimbledon, Dave was chosen to represent England in the World Team Cup Final. He was winning heat three when the engine blew up on his GM bike on the last corner. Philip Rising said that a win then would have put England four points clear of the USA and six ahead of Denmark. Rising did say that this was conjecture, but also said that the Danes were better prepared. Dave, Chris Morton and Michael Lee had one bike each at the meeting. The Danes between them had 13. However, to be fair to the English riders, the meeting was on a Friday evening, and all of them had meetings for their clubs back in England on the Saturday. As it was, Denmark won the meeting with 37 points. Michael Lee rode well for England to score 11, and they were runners-up on 29, two points clear of the USA, with Czechoslovakia scoring three points. Dave scored two from two rides, and was replaced twice by Peter Collins who captained the side from reserve.

In September, Dave rode three times for England in a three team inter-nations tournament. He scored 13+5 in the meetings; England lost the tournament by one point to the Rest of the World team. Denmark finished third.

Dave rode consistently well for Wimbledon for the rest of the season, only twice failing to score or be paid for double figure points. Highlights included a paid maximum against Sheffield, and a 15-point maximum against Hackney at Plough Lane on a wet track. The Dons lost the meeting, but won the return match at Waterden Road the next day. Dave also scored a 15-point maximum at Poole. This was the day after Wimbledon had gone down 59–19 at Cradley. Dave scored five points and was their only heat winner. Chris Shears said that Dave looked "despondent" after the meeting.

In individual meetings, Dave won the Final of the Favre Leuba WJ Cearns Memorial Shield at Plough Lane, taking home a £300 wrist watch as the first prize. However, he missed the British League Riders Championship because of a burglary at his Kent home.

Dave was runner-up in the London Riders Championship. He won the first leg with a 15-point maximum. However, the second leg was abandoned after heat 17, when he was the top aggregate scorer on 25 points. Heat 19 of the meeting was run after the London Cup meeting the following week. That led to a run-off with Bo Petersen which Dave lost. However, the Dons did win the London Cup over two legs against their local rivals.

Winning Fabre Leuvre watches with Vicky at Wimbledon in 1983.

As always, there was speculation about Dave's future at the end of the season. The new regulation on team strengths, with a 48-point limit, could be an issue. A report in the *Star* said that for Wimbledon "Some adjustments will have to be made to conform with the 48 points regulations but they are unlikely to involve Dave Jessup despite some internal problems at the club a few weeks ago. Jessup, top of the averages for the second successive season, hopes to tie up a sponsorship with GM and that in itself could be good news for the Dons. Jessup rode a single GM engine virtually throughout the season and the lessons learned from a range of experiments will undoubtedly pay off. Although still upset at some of the comments of his team mates, Jessup is happy to stay with Wimbledon if they want him and is not seeking a move. ... Wimbledon can look forward to 1984 with a certain amount of optimism if Jessup does stay."

Dave finished the season top of the Wimbledon averages on 9.25, around half a point up on the previous season. In official fixtures he scored six full maximums and two paid. In the league, Wimbledon had climbed the table to sixth place, with 31 points from their 28 meetings. Cradley dominated the league, only losing two matches all season, but the Dons were 14 points behind runners-up Ipswich. It was an improvement, but there was still work to do for them to be challenging at the top of the table.

In his review of the Dons' season, Eric Linden pointed out that they had a very successful League Cup campaign, but then lost their first two league matches at home – admittedly against Cradley and Ipswich. He said that Dave was "the only one of the top three to better his average, but his season was soured by an internal wrangle which had many folks waiting for a transfer request that, all credit to Jessup, never came."

Dave was planning to ride in South Africa after Christmas. At the end of December, the *Star* speculated on a possible exchange deal for Dave to move back to King's Lynn and Gordon Kennett to move the other way. However, Dave had moved from King's Lynn because of the travelling. Martin Rogers was now the promoter there. All would be resolved in the new year.

16. Return to Saddlebow Road

As had been suggested in the *Star* just after Christmas, the rider-exchange involving King's Lynn's Gordon Kennett and Dave duly took place. On 14 January, the *Star* reported that Wimbledon wanted a cash adjustment for the exchange because Dave had a higher average than Kennett. The report, from the magazine's Wimbledon correspondent, said that "A change could be good for Jessup as well. The former England captain wasn't too happy when his Wimbledon team-mates voted against his continuing as club skipper during the 1983 campaign. He joined the Dons from King's Lynn for £20,000 in 1982, but despite being the undisputed number one, didn't reach the heights expected."

Bob Radford commented that: "The arrival of Jessup and [Steve] Regeling adds top end strength to the Stars side. So, what prompted the move to bring Dave back to Saddlebow Road?" King's Lynn promoter Martin Rogers said to Radford: "I signed Dave for King's Lynn during my time as manager there, and many felt he possibly shouldn't have left. I wasn't there, so it isn't for me to say. There were known elements of uncertainty at Wimbledon, and he has a popular following at Saddlebow Road. Dave's record as a Lynn rider is unsurpassed, even exceeding the likes of Michael Lee and Terry Betts. He's an accomplished top line rider with that extra something with which the team and supporters can identify. I've known him since he was a 14-year-old at West Ham, we get on well, and the Abbeygate Group of Companies have re-entered the sponsorship fold to back him. Effectively, He'll be the first works GM rider in 1984."

Looking back, Dave says that he would have been happy to stay at Wimbledon, and that he was approached to return to King's Lynn. The captaincy issue was not the reason for the move. He was happy to work with Martin Rogers again, and was pleased to be supported by Peter Thurlow again. Dave says that "Peter was a great supporter of King's Lynn and the sport overall. I remember once that we were on the ferry to Denmark for the World Championship Overseas Final and Peter bought dinner for all the riders. He gave me a lot of support over the years."

Dave certainly had a good record while he was with the Stars, although Terry Betts was still – and always will be – a legend in East Anglian speedway, first with Norwich and then King's Lynn. It was reported that John Louis, who had joined the Stars in 1983, would continue as team captain. There was also the possibility that Trevor Hedge could work for Dave on his GM engines.

Dave and Vicky were away in South Africa for the first couple of months of the year. He rode in five matches between South Africa and an Overseas team. The Overseas team won the series 5–2, with meetings being held in Benoni and Bloemfontein. Dave missed the first test because he had not yet arrived in the country, and – along with Phil Kynman – missed the sixth in Durban because he could not agree terms with the promoter. Dave scored maximums in the third, fourth and seventh meetings. In the seventh match he broke the Bloemfontein track record three times. He also retained the South African Open Championship which he had won in 1983, and scored a maximum in the South African best Pairs at the Dunswart Raceway in Benoni, riding with one of the locals, Flippie Blignaut. Sarl

Kotze's report in the *Star* was headed 'Jessup Top Man in South Africa.' In reality, Dave was a class above the local riders and British tourists. The one rider who may have challenged him, Peter Prinsloo, pulled out of the series after the first meeting, unable to agree terms with the promoters. The trip was a holiday for Dave and Vicky, and a chance for Dave to do some competitive riding in the British speedway off-season. Undoubtedly there was some golf as well.

On 27 January, Dave and Peter Collins were part of a Speed on Wheels team, coached by Stirling Moss, who played a Rugby Union team in the BBC1 programme *Super teams*. The Union team included several internationals and won the event. It must have been pre-recorded because Dave was thousands of miles away when it was shown.

There had been considerable changes at King's Lynn since Dave had left. Martin and Linn Rogers had returned to the club in 1983, as promoters. They were also running Leicester, which closed unexpectedly at the end of the 1983 season when the stadium site was sold for housing. It had proved impossible to find an alternative site in the city, and the sport did not return to Leicester for over 30 years. Only Richard Hellsen from the 1981 Stars team was still at the club. Michael Lee had left to join Poole. John Louis was still a heat leader at the age of 42, and had probably had a boost to his career by not having to travel to Halifax every week from his Ipswich base. In fact, this season turned out to be his last season in the sport as a rider.

Australian Steve Regeling, who had originally been signed for Leicester, came to Saddlebow Road. Kevin Jolly, Martin Dixon and Keith Bloxsome made up the rest of the team. Colin Richardson and Melvyn Taylor both moved on. The Stars had finished eighth in the league in 1983, and had been strong at home, but weak away, with just one draw to show from 14 away trips.

There were changes in the British League as well. Birmingham had closed, and Hackney had dropped into the National League. Three 'new' teams returned to the British League: Exeter, Newcastle and Oxford.

The season started with the League Cup, and the Stars' first fixture, maybe inevitably, was at Wimbledon. Martin Rogers told the *Star* that it was a "difficult opener with a few personal considerations", clearly referring to Dave and Gordon Kennett. Wimbledon won by six points, with Dave scoring 10 from five rides. He was better off than Gordon Kennett, who was one of three riders who had to withdraw from the meeting through injury after five reruns in the first three heats. Two days later, another of Dave's former teams, Reading, came to Saddlebow Road. The Stars won by nine points, with Dave's return drawing a "healthy" crowd. After being on the receiving end of a first heat 5–1, Dave won his next three races and the second half.

Dave continued to score double figures consistently, and except for a poor night against Oxford, the Stars were winning at home and being competitive away. International action for the season began in April, with a five match test series against the USA. Dave was chosen for the first test at Swindon. The Americans won by eight points, but the match was close to the end, with six of their points advantage coming in the last two heats. Dave scored 12+1 from his six rides, and was second highest scorer. The meeting was started at 2pm at

Swindon. Dave managed to get to King's Lynn in time to ride for the Stars, and not surprisingly only scored 5+1 from his four rides.

The next test was at Sheffield, 15 days later. Dave had a full schedule, with four meetings over the Easter weekend. He rode well against Ipswich in home and away clashes on Good Friday, despite blowing up a new GM engine in the second half. However, on the Saturday, he scored an uncharacteristic three points from five rides, including a tapes exclusion, at Coventry. Dave had got up at dawn, gone to Trevor Hedge's workshop and fitted a new engine. He then headed off to Coventry, but –understandably – was "a bit blitzed" as Martin Rogers put it.

Dave took over the England captaincy for the second test. A 6,500 crowd saw England win by eight points, with Dave scoring 10+1 from his six rides. He was clearly having some bike problems at this time. He had engine failures at Wolverhampton in a challenge match, and a League Cup match at Oxford, where he scored just four points from three rides. The night before the Sheffield test match, Wimbledon won 53–25 at Saddlebow Road. Dave just scored a point from his three rides.

The third and fourth tests were disasters for England. At Cradley, the Americans won by 10 points. Dave did not score, and only took two rides. The *Star* reported that "Skipper Dave Jessup broke the tapes in his first race and after finishing last next time out took no further part in the meeting as a new engine let him down." Two days later, on the May Bank Holiday Monday at Ipswich, the Americans won the match 72–36 and the series. England's cause was not helped by Michael Lee being excluded for touching the tapes in his first ride, and then failing to finish in his next two. England team manager Carl Glover had already decided to pull Lee out of his second half rides when he quit anyway. Dave scored just three points. The *Star* reported after the fifth test at Poole, which England lost by eight points, that "Dave Jessup, for so long our most consistent performer at international level, was way below par at Cradley Heath and Ipswich – so much so that he then asked to be rested at Poole."

The World Team Cup qualifying round was the following Saturday at King's Lynn. Dave was captaining the side, but after finishing third in his first race to Shawn Moran and Phil Crump, was replaced by John Louis for his next three rides. England qualified for the Inter-Continental Finals, and eventually reached the final, to finish second – by 20 points – to a dominant Denmark side. Dave was not selected for any of the World Team Cup meetings.

For King's Lynn, Dave was also having a run of low scores. One better meeting was the World Championship semi-final at Poole. Dave qualified for the British Final with nine points from his five rides. Dave's average at the end of May was 7.31, low by his high standards. He had even stopped playing golf because he couldn't relax on the golf course because of his 'low key' period on the track. Things did pick up at the start of June, with nine points at Swindon and 10 at Eastbourne in a six-point King's Lynn win.

Despite his poor run, he was selected for two of the test matches against Denmark, at Reading and Wimbledon. In a 54–54 draw at Reading, Dave was joint top scorer with 11+1 from his six rides. His win in heat 17 preserved England's two-point lead going into the final heat, but John Louis was excluded, and Peter Ravn beat Chris Morton with Bo Petersen third to secure a draw for the Danes.

1984 World Team Cup qualifying round at King's Lynn: Back: John Louis (reserve), Dave (captain), Chris Morton; front: Simon Wigg, Michael Lee. (JSC).

However, it was a different story three days later at Wimbledon. England went behind from the second heat, and lost by 18 points. Dave was top scorer with 9+2 from his six rides. Alan and Andy Graeme came into the team for the last two tests, replacing Dave and John Davis. England won both to take the series 2–1.

Things improved for Dave in June after the test matches. King's Lynn comfortably beat Newcastle in the Knock Out Cup, winning by 20 points at home and 13 on Tyneside. Dave scored his first full maximum of the season in the away match. However, Dave Lanning reported that Dave had "tennis elbow", and missed the King's Lynn fixture on 23 June with an arm injury.

Three days before, he had safely qualified from the British Final. He finished third on 11 points, one behind Andy Graeme and two behind Kenny Carter. It was a controversial meeting. There had been heavy rain in the afternoon, and after three heats, several riders wanted to abandon the meeting. Carter won riding with a broken leg, and had won the second heat. The more experienced riders were the ones who were unhappy with the conditions, and the dispute almost came to blows. Peter Collins only qualified as reserve at the Overseas Final. The riders who were knocked out included Gordon Kennett, Chris Morton, John Louis and John Davis.

At the end of June, King's Lynn had a good win at Oxford. *The Star* reported that "The Stars were well served by England veteran Dave Jessup and it was his timely victory over home skipper Hans Nielsen in the penultimate heat that more or less confirmed their victory." *The Star's* preview of the Overseas Final said that Dave had been DJ "Plagued by mechanical problems during the early part of the season but recently showing signs of the old consistent Jessup. Quietly went about his business at the British Final and over the years a regular World Final qualifier. Slick starter and that is a valuable asset in the World Championship."

The meeting was at Belle Vue on 15 July. Dave "never looked comfortable" according to the report in the *Star,* and was eliminated with three points, three away from qualifying. His best result was a second place in heat six, but that came after Shawn Moran's bike had packed up.

Dave's form continued to be uneven. One better meeting was at Plough Lane. The Dons beat the Stars by 10 points, but Dave beat Malcolm Simmons twice towards the end of the meeting. A week later, he was involved in a 57–21 defeat at Eastbourne in the Knock Out

Cup. He scored six from five rides, including one retirement, and the King's Lynn management conceded the tie, but later changed their minds.

On 18 August, Dave fell out with Martin Rogers over the Stars meeting at Swindon. The Star's report said that "Nothing went right for King's Lynn in this match. With John Louis suffering concussion in the opening race, the last thing they wanted was to see Dave Jessup walking out. Jessup was unhappy at the start of Heat three when he was left for dead at the tapes." The *Star* reported, under the headline 'Jessup Banned': "... Dave Jessup was suspended by King's Lynn after walking out of British League match at Swindon. Jessup stormed over to see the referee after what he claimed was an unsatisfactory start to heat three. Back in the pits Jessup also complained about track conditions and said he was going home. Lynn promoter Martin Rogers then told him not to bother turning up for the following day's home meeting.

Rogers said after the match: 'I am suspending Jessup indefinitely. He will not be racing for us tomorrow (Sunday). Jessup subsequently talked to Rogers, apologised and accepted that he was in the wrong and was reinstated for Lynn's visit to Reading last Monday.' Dave did miss the King's Lynn home fixture, but was back in action at Reading. Kevin Brown commented in the Star the following week: "Jessup and Lynn promoter Martin Rogers have settled their differences and no doubt the former world number two will be trying to recapture his old sparkling form. Indeed, Jessup's returns have generally been disappointing by his own high standards and the sooner he gets back to his past winning ways the better for both the rider and his side. Jessup's displays of late have smacked of inconsistency as indeed have Lynn's overall recent performances."

Dave was then involved in one of the more remarkable recoveries in the sport's history. The King's Lynn management did stage the second leg of the Knock Out Cup tie with Eastbourne, and won it 57–21. Dave and Steve Regeling scored a 5–1 in the final heat. A week later, the Stars won the first leg of the replayed tie 51–27, with Dave contributing 11 from four rides. An eight-point defeat in the second leg saw the Stars progress to the Semi-Final, where they would meet Ipswich. King's Lynn won the first leg by 10 points, with Dave being their top scorer with 11 points and "produced vintage efforts" after being beaten in his first race by John Cook. However, the Witches were too strong at home, and won 57–21 to reach the Final.

Dave and John Louis represented the Stars in the British Open Pairs meeting at Wolverhampton. They finished runners-up in Group A with 15 points, but only the group winners went through to the Semi-Finals.

After the defeat at Ipswich, Cradley won at Saddlebow Road by 20 points. The Star then reported that "Veteran Dave Jessup has ridden is last race of the 1984 season. The 31-year old England international is due to go into hospital this week for an elbow operation. He first damaged the ligaments and tendons last May but has insisted on carrying on riding ever since. However, the heavier late season tracks have taken their toll and specialists have now advised that he should have an operation.

He missed the Stars' last race defeat against Oxford on Saturday night and is due to go into hospital earlier this week. It will be eight weeks before he is able to consider racing again but should have plenty of time to recuperate during the winter. King's Lynn promoter

Martin Rogers admitted 'He will miss a few matches but it was a case of having an operation the sooner the better.'"

In early November, the *Star* reported that Dave was "on the road to recovery following an operation for an injury to his right arm which has been likened to an acute form of tennis elbow." On 1 December, the Star carried a detailed report on Dave's operation. It showed how it had blighted his season. He had sustained the injury at Oxford at the end of April, and then aggravated it soon afterwards. In June he had been told that "he would benefit from an eight-week stint in a plaster cast, but Jessup bravely would not entertain such a suggestion and continued to ride despite being in pain and some discomfort."

The report also said that Dave "found the going extremely tough at times" and that he "lost some of the old zest and sharpness … [he] persevered with the aid of a series of painkilling injections which is the long term he admitted did him no good at all." He said that he was on the way back to full fitness, but could not lift anything. He had not been able to do any training or physio work, but was due to see his specialist in early December.

He was planning to go to South Africa when he got clearance from his specialist, and said that the King's Lynn fans had not seen the best of him. He concluded "When the weather was good, I was getting away with the injury, but on a bumpy track it was murder."

Dave recollects that "My elbow was very painful. I was having weekly Cortisone injections. I had the operation near the end of the season, which reattached the muscles. If I had had it during the season I would have been under pressure to come back before I was properly fit. This way I had four months to recover."

Just before Christmas, there was speculation in the *Star* about whether Dave would be staying at King's Lynn. The article said that Martin Rogers may want to build a team around younger riders. The article said that if King's Lynn did decide to not renew his contract, there would be a "winter change" for him and signing him would be "a major coup for any club seeking to boost its top end strength."

That would all be resolved in the new year. Meanwhile, the Stars could reflect on a season that had seen them move two places higher in the league; finishing with 30 points from 30 league meetings. John Louis finished his last campaign as a rider top of the King's Lynn averages with 8.29. Dave's was 7.42, his lowest for some time. He scored two full maximums and one paid in King's Lynn official fixtures. However, given the injury problems that became public knowledge at the end of September, he had ridden for over half the season less than fully fit. He would be 32 years old in March 1985, not old for a speedway rider.

Dave recalls that King's Lynn had faced some financial problems during the season, and he had agreed with Martin Rogers to take a pay cut about halfway through the season. Dave was told that the promotion was under threat and wanted the team to survive.

In Eric Linden's review of King's Lynn's campaign, he said that Dave's return "must be ranked as terribly disappointing" and that "A string of double figure scores in the League Cup suddenly ended as April went out and that consistency never returned. Whether it was an elbow injury, about which he made no fuss but which eventually led to him closing his season slightly early to have an operation; or whether it was equipment problems; or both; or both plus other factors, was never really aired." It should be pointed out that Dave's elbow happened at the end of April. Hopefully better times would come in 1985.

17. Finale at King's Lynn

The 1985 campaign saw a major restructuring of British club speedway. The original British League had started in 1965 with 18 teams, and since then the competition stayed around that size, fluctuating between 19 and 15 teams. Suddenly, for 1985 it was reduced to 11. Writing in *Backtrack*, Martin Rogers said that Coventry promoter Charles Ochiltree "was the most consistent advocate of a 'super league' and eventually got his way in 1985." The season was to consist of 20 League Cup matches and then 20 British League matches, so each team met the others home and away twice. Rogers says that there were some advantages to the idea – some teams were not a draw and bought little away support. However, it produced a surfeit of British League level riders, so standards went up. King's Lynn were struggling financially at this time, and were now in a more competitive league. Riders 'doubling up' as British speedway fans are familiar with today was very limited.

Rogers continued in *Backtrack:* "At a stroke, a lot of riders who had been heat leaders now were only good enough for a second string or maybe even reserve role. None of them volunteered to take a pay cut to reflect their diminished status, of course. Riders designated as heat leaders and capable of remaining so wanted to receive more to reflect the increased difficulty of the smaller competition." He said that they spent more on the riders in 1985 than the previous year, and were rewarded with bottom place in both competitions.

The changes saw Wimbledon, Eastbourne, Poole and Exeter join the National League. Speedway did not run in Newcastle in 1985. With Hackney having joined the National League the previous year, for the first time ever in the sport's history, the top league did not include a team from London.

Dave and Vicky had their usual break in South Africa, and returned home in mid-February. Dave had a long meeting with Martin Rogers, who was hopeful that he would stay at Saddlebow Road. However, the next week the *Star* reported that Rogers was "trying to sort out the Dave Jessup situation, and "The England international said he was unhappy with the terms Lynn offered him and was waiting for Rogers to get back with a better offer. Said Jessup: 'The deal nowhere near met my expectations and I'm waiting for Mr Rogers to come back with a better deal or in a revised form.' DJ stressed though that he would dearly like to stay at Saddlebow Road saying that he has done enough moving about in his career. Rogers said: 'I would like to get the Jessup situation resolved as quickly as possible. However, the stature of the rider I am presently chasing is such that it might put the Jessup matter in a different light.'"

Rogers then signed Paul Woods from Eastbourne, who had moved to the National League. The transfer fee was £18,000. Rogers said that this had "thrown the Dave Jessup position into the melting pot a bit". Dave was now on a golfing holiday in Spain.

The next week, Kevin Brown reported that Dave had been put on the transfer list by King's Lynn at £12,000 – 25 per cent less than they had paid for him. Rogers told the *Star*: "Jessup's name has been circulated and hopefully I will be able to get him fixed up quickly. Obviously, it's disappointing because DJ has had two enjoyable stints here but it's just the way it has gone. Dave feels quite confident he can do a job for somebody and I'm certain he is right." It was also reported that King's Lynn had signed Eastbourne's 23-year-old Finn Olli Tyrvainen, although in fact he never rode for the Stars because he could not get a work permit.

However, on 23 March, the *Star* reported that Dave had signed up for another season with King's Lynn. Rogers commented that "Dave has agreed on a deal on his ability to prove his case and he has still got ambitions ... He remains in the team on terms like those comparable with other team members. The days of guaranteed monies seem to be disappearing but if DJ does the business, he will be okay."

Dave signed for the Stars the day after their press day, but was in the line-up for their first meeting of the season, a 48–30 League Cup defeat at Coventry. In the close season, John Louis had retired. Martin Rogers had signed Mark Courtney and Paul Woods. Steve Regeling, Kevin Jolly and the long-serving Richard Hellsen all stayed with the Stars from the 1984 line-up. Michael Lee was still suspended, but did return to the club in May when his suspension from British speedway was completed. Mick Poole rode in 10 meetings for the team, and a variety of others filled gaps.

Interviewed in the *Star* at the beginning of April, Dave said that he "never ever wanted to leave King's Lynn and I was quite happy to be reinstated. The article said that he was "in the twilight of a highly successful career but he remained hungry for points and success." He said that he was only interested in winning when he was riding, and there was "no pleasure in ... trailing in last." He said that he was also considering various business opportunities in the future. However, he said that his elbow was fine for everything except riding a speedway bike, and was still causing him problems, which he found very disappointing.

It became clear early on that the Stars were relying on Dave. Their season started with a run of seven defeats in the League Cup. Dave was top scorer with 11 points at Swindon, and at Ipswich on Good Friday. In the return match later in the day, he scored 13 points, but could not stop the Witches winning at Saddlebow Road. The *Star* commented that "The Stars relied heavily upon old guard members Dave Jessup and Richard Hellsen."

The team's first win was at home to Reading on 20 April. A 5–1 from Dave and Richard Hellsen in the last heat earned the Stars a League Cup bonus point. Dave scored his first maximum of the season at Canterbury in an inter-league challenge match. The Stars won 57–21, which showed the gulf between the leagues, although Canterbury were not one of the stronger National League sides.

Michael Lee returned to the team for the home League Cup fixture with Halifax. The Stars won, and then beat Cradley the next week. The League Cup campaign continued until June. The only away point the Stars collected was at Wolverhampton. Dave contributed 11 points to their 39–39 draw and was said to be "back to something like his best." But three days later they went down 61–17 at Sheffield. The *Star* reported that "the visitors put on a sorry show with only Dave Jessup battling to stem the tide." The Stars finished bottom of the table with 10 points from their 20 fixtures.

In the World Championship, Dave was seeded to the British Semi-Final at Cradley. He qualified for the British Final in eighth place with seven points. He beat Steve Bastable to secure the final qualifying place.

Eric Linden's preview of the British Final said that "Dave Jessup went like the clappers in last year's final for 11 points and third place. If he had a tail, he'd wag it to get anything like that this time round. He needs a big 'un to help pull himself out of the relatively low scoring rut." The meeting was postponed due to rain. When it did happen, Dave scored four points and was eliminated, as was his old rival and World Pairs partner Peter Collins.

A rare highlight for King's Lynn was beating the old enemy, Ipswich, 45–33 in the Anglican Cup. Dave scored a four-ride paid maximum. However, the trophy went back to Foxhall Heath as the Witches had won the first leg 49–29. In the Knock Out Cup, the Stars drew 39–39 with Cradley at home, but lost the away leg heavily to go out of the competition.

The international action in England that summer was test series against Australasia and the USA. Dave was selected for the first match against the Australasia side. The match was at King's Lynn, and he added some experience to a relatively young side selected by England team manager John Berry. Dave was winning his 106th cap; the rest of the team had 31 between them. The Australasian side were missing Billy Sanders, who sadly had taken his own life in April. Dave scored 15 from his six rides, contributing to a 71–37 England win. In the *Star*, Philip Rising said that he "displayed real class". Dave was not selected for the second test, which England won comfortably; or the third at Halifax in September, when the Australasians won by two points.

Dave was also selected for the second test at Ipswich of a three-match series against the USA. The Americans won the first test at Belle Vue by 10 points. Dave scored a very respectable 12+2 from his six rides, and was joint top scorer with Jeremy Doncaster. However, the USA won 58–50, and took the series 3–0 with a very comfortable win three days later at Swindon.

England had reached the World Team Cup Final on 10 August. John Berry had problems putting a team together. Kenny Carter was injured, Chris Morton had fallen out with Berry and refused to ride for England while he was team manager. Malcolm Simmons and Simon Wigg were suspended from international speedway. Philip Rising wrote that Dave "was ruled out through lack of available equipment as much as anything else." The five who represented England – Phil Collins, Kelvin Tatum, Jeremy Doncaster, John Davis and Richard Knight had two World Team Cup Final appearances between them. The meeting was at Long Beach in California. Denmark won; two points clear of the USA. England finished third on 13 points, three ahead of Sweden. Had he been available, Dave would have added some experience to the squad. Two days before the World Team Cup Final, Dave missed a King's Lynn challenge match at Middlesbrough. Martin Rogers said that this was because he did not have a working bike available, and said this was why he had turned down the World Team Cup opportunity.

At the beginning of August, Dave was involved in a controversial incident at Reading. The dispute was over the track conditions. There had been a heavy storm in the afternoon. Dave Wright reported in the *Star* that Dave "... pulled out of heat one after just two laps but left his bike on the side of the track. Caked in dirt, Dave made his way up to the officials' box to confront referee Barry Richardson." Dave was suspended for the rest of the meeting for "ungentlemanly conduct" and fined £50. His bike had been quickly removed from the track by one of the track staff.

Dave and King's Lynn team-mate Richard Hellsen (JSC).

King's Lynn withdrew from heats two and three, but, "advised" by Martin Rogers, did complete the rest of the meeting. The report says that the track improved, and the home side won 54-22.

In October, the *Star* reported that Dave "was fined £500 and given a six months ban, suspended for two years, after being found guilty on three charges of misconduct during King's Lynn's visit to Reading in August ... Former England skipper Jessup was charged with foul and dangerous riding, disorderly and ungentlemanly conduct and conduct prejudicial to the sport. The Control Board hearing found him guilty on all counts and also ordered him to pay £350 towards the costs. And only Jessup's previous record of good behaviour saved him from being banned immediately." Looking back, Dave says that "I had fallen out with Barry Richardson again. I do not see how there was any 'foul and dangerous riding' when I parked the bike at the side of the track, not on the racing line and certainly not across the track. I didn't agree with Mr Richardson's version of events. The SCB panel should be neutral, but in my experience, I thought that they tended to believe the referees. The whole thing was disappointing. Around the same time there was a rider who threw his helmet at the referee's box and broke the window, with glass flying everywhere. He got fined less than me! I just wanted to talk to the referee."

In the league, King's Lynn continued to struggle. The team just wasn't strong enough. Particularly away from home, Dave was at times the only real force against the home side. At Cradley in July, he was "the only visiting rider to win a race and he fought a lone battle as Cradley controlled the match from start to finish." At Ipswich in August, where the Stars lost by two points, the *Star* reported that "Dave Jessup, riding as well as ever, inspired a

Lynn fightback which saw them pull level with three races to go...". In the return match with Cradley, Dave "was best for Lynn who battled gamely but ran out of steam." The Stars has beaten Sheffield 52–26 at Saddlebow Road. In the return at Owlerton, on a poor night for the Stars, "Dave Jessup stood alone against Sheffield achieving maximum points in all 13 heats against a weakened King's Lynn".

Dave qualified for the British League Riders Championship at Belle Vue. Eric Linden wrote that Dave had the "lowest average among the qualifiers, even lower than the reserves. That tells the story that wee Dave has not regained the old golden touch. Yet a fearsome gater on big occasions, and not one, therefore, to be taken lightly. I still remember how close he came to winning the world title not all that long back." He had scored 71 points from eight British League Riders Championship meetings, including 12 in 1974 when he finished third. It was not to be this time, he scored three points from four rides.

The end of season statistics tell the tale of a season when King's Lynn finished bottom in both the League and League Cup. Dave was top of the averages with 7.8, a slight increase on 1984. Michael Lee averaged 7.2, but only rode in 19 meetings, and was suspended near the end of the season when Martin Rogers ran out of patience with his failures to appear at meetings. Steve Regeling and Kevin Jolly maintained their form from 1984, but with Lee absent were the second and third highest scorers with averages of just over six points. Mark Courtney and Paul Woods both saw their scores decline from 1984, Woods quite dramatically. Dave says that "Paul Woods had ridden for his whole career at Eastbourne and Crayford, which were both small tracks. Maybe he had problems adjusting to King's Lynn. In those days, unless someone was injured, promoters didn't change teams that much. It was quite different to today, when it seems to me that one bad run can see a rider being dropped."

Richard Hellsen, who had a testimonial at the end of the season, averaged less than six points a meeting in his last season at Saddlebow Road.

Looking back, Dave says that "Everyone gets confidence from being in a winning team. There is no extra pressure. When a team is struggling, the top riders get asked to do more rides, which is nice, but it does have an effect. You are rushing to get ready at very little notice. Also, the more you ride, the more your tyres become worn. I may have done six rides against someone who has done three and has more tread left in their tyres. Also, the bike wears out more quickly."

Curiously, the attendances at Saddlebow Road were up compared to 1984. However, reinforcements were clearly needed and whether Dave would be part of the King's Lynn set-up in 1986 remained to be seen.

Dave and Vicky looking smart for a night out.

18. Mildenhall

Martin Rogers clearly had some serious thinking to do about how to rebuild the King's Lynn team for 1986. He was also operating on a limited budget. In his book, *In my view*, he says that "Jessup and perhaps [Kevin] Jolly could still do a job, but the indications were that the value they placed upon their services might not coincide with mine." He then signed Bobby Schwartz, one of the leading American riders, as his number one for the forthcoming campaign.

In early February, the *Star* reported that Dave wanted to stay with King's Lynn, but that he was yet to agree terms with Rogers. Dave said that "Nothing is definite at the moment and I don't want to jump the gun. Unfortunately, the financial situation isn't what I am looking for. I've got to be fair because in previous years I've been to South Africa during the close-season and it's been my fault that we haven't come to an arrangement earlier. But I've been at home all this winter and we're no further advanced and I would like to know where I am riding." Dave added that "I held the side together through thick-and-thin last year and I think I deserve a better deal. I was quite happy with my performances last season. I didn't start very well, but rallied in the middle of the season and towards the end. I'm not happy with an eight point average but then again racing becomes more competitive as you get older and life becomes harder... I feel I have several more years to offer speedway. I just want to be happy in my mind that I'm getting a fair return for my efforts." Dave didn't rule out riding in the National League, and concluded that "... I want to carry on riding and earning as much as I can. But the money comes through winning points and the more points you get the more happy you are."

It was also reported that Dave was running a new Jawa agency in Kent. The importers, Skoda, had wanted more outlets. Peter Collins had set one up in the north of England. A couple of weeks later, ambitious National League side Mildenhall confirmed Mel Taylor would ride for them in 1986, and would not comment on rumours that Dave was the main target for them. The next week it was reported that Michael Lee and Kevin Jolly were targets for the West Row side. Jolly did sign for them, but then was loaned to Boston for the season after a financial dispute.

As the start of the season approached, Dave was still on the King's Lynn retained list. Martin Rogers says that Dave said four days before the opening meeting that he wanted an extra £4,000. With King's Lynn reported to be £64,000 in the red, he decided to let Dave go to Mildenhall, and received a transfer fee. Only two riders from the 1985 line-up stayed at King's Lynn, including Michael Lee who only rode in 15 meetings before not turning up for a meeting and being suspended by the club. Despite the changes, the Stars again finished bottom of both the League and League Cup tables.

At the end of March, Randall Butt reported in the *Star* that "Mildenhall have got the star man they have been searching for to launch their new promotion." He said that Dave had signed for the 'new-look' Fen Tigers for a £12,500 transfer fee. Dave said that "I'm all set up and ready for the off. There were other National League tracks interested, but Mildenhall were top of my list." He said that there was a good team spirit at the club, and that there was a "family atmosphere" at their Sunday afternoon meetings. He hoped to be able to help the younger riders in the team, and that he "wanted to put his knowledge to good use." Dave was given a "huge" average of 11.60 for the National League. Skid Parish, one of the team's promoters, commented that "We were very impressed when we spoke to Dave. He was genuinely keen to join us. He even went out and bought a pair of mudguards in Mildenhall colours before he had finished negotiating and little things like that show you how a rider is thinking. Dave is 32 now [actually 33], but still one of the best riders in the country, and obviously, he will be a top man in the National League."

Dave was not the only former British League star who had switched to the National League. Malcolm Simmons was at Hackney, along with Barry Thomas, and Gordon Kennett had rejoined Eastbourne in 1985 when they moved to the National League. Les Collins and Doug Wyer were at Edinburgh. It was a 20-team league, and 11 of the other teams were in the southern half of the country, so Dave would also have less travelling. However, there were three teams in Scotland, and two in the north-east.

Mildenhall had originally been set up as a training track in 1974. Local residents had objected to the noise, but when the local council's inspector came to check, a large plane was landing at the American Air Force base nearby. It was so loud he couldn't hear the speedway bikes. The team had joined the New National League in 1975. There had been a change in ownership before the new season, and a consortium had taken control. Skid Parish, a former rider, and Barry Klatt were responsible for the day-to-day running of the club.

Dave recalls that "I did think about retiring, particularly after the hearing at the end of the 1985 season. But then I thought that I can still ride, and could drop down to the National League and still enjoy riding. The other team interested in signing me was Exeter. They had a plan to fly me down from Rochester Airport for home meetings. I came close to joining them. The advantage for the home riders at that track was fantastic. There was the steel fence, and you knew that apart from the top two riders, the away team wouldn't fancy it. But in the end, I chose Mildenhall. I did say to the consortium that I wanted one person to deal with and that worked out ok. I still got some sponsorship from Peter Thurlow and the Abbeygate Group."

However, Dave's debut for Mildenhall in a challenge match against Arena Essex was not a great success. In arctic conditions, he was excluded for breaking the tapes in his first race, and then missed the start in his second and said that he "went through all his goggles and flickers, but there was flying mud everywhere." He won his last two rides.

Things looked up three days later when Dave won his World Championship qualifying round with a 15-point full maximum. The *Star* reported that "Former World No. 2 Dave Jessup got the ball rolling in the British rounds with an immaculate display, including a superb win from the back over Kevin Smith. Competition was fierce, and although the top three qualifying places were virtually secure, Jessup, home skipper Roger Johns and the lively Andrew Silver clashed in Heat 19, all in with a chance of top spot. Jessup's renowned gating ability didn't let him down, though, as he led all the way in the decider."

In early May, Peter Oakes looked at the possible composition of the England team. He said that there were only 38 riders in British speedway who had worn the England race jacket, and 18 were not in the British League.

Left: Dave on parade for the CRM meeting at Mildenhall on his works Jawa.

Below: winning the CRM Champions Chase in 1986: riders from left: Paul Thorp (third), Dave and Eric Monaghan (runner-up)

He said that Dave, Malcolm Simmons and Gordon Kennett had a wealth of experience "that appears lost to the England management team." But it was not be, there was no recall to international speedway for Dave.

Dave notched his first maximum of the season for Mildenhall at home to Exeter. He followed this with another 15-point full maximum at Boston. He was favourite for the World Cup Quarter Final at King's Lynn, and had set his sights on reaching another British Final. However, he scored eight points, and lost a run-off with Neil Middleditch for the reserve place in the semi-finals. A broken wire in the magneto meant that he could not start in heat 10, and that was decisive.

Not surprisingly, Dave continued to regularly score double figures for Mildenhall. At home to Milton Keynes, he scored a 12-point maximum, but lost to Kevin Smart in the match-race Silver Helmet. He accidentally pulled his cut-off switch while leading and could not make up the lost ground. A couple of weeks later, he rode for the 'Ex-Dons' in a four-team tournament for the Vic Harding Memorial Trophy at Hackney. He scored 10 points and beat British League heat leaders Phil Crump and Kelly Moran. In June, he rode for an Ex-Stars side at King's Lynn in a challenge match and scored 11 points from five rides. His races with Michael Lee were the highlight of the meeting.

Dave was not officially a 'rider-coach' but says that "I did support the other riders with information and passing on my experience. I talked to them about preparation, arriving on time and generally set a good example. Some of them were astounded at how easily I could ride a new track, such as when we went to Glasgow. There was a gap between the British League and the National League, and there were very few national League riders who could challenge me. Most of them were youngsters on their way up."

Many of the away meetings for Mildenhall were at tracks Dave had never ridden, or not ridden for a long time. One was Long Eaton, and on 21 June, Dave was part of the Mildenhall team that refused to ride on a track they considered unfit for racing after a mid-afternoon downpour. Rob Henry was the Mildenhall captain, and spoke on behalf of the team, saying that they were adamant that the track was not fit for racing. Each rider was fined £100 by the referee and a further £50 by their own promoters. Dave was not mentioned by name in the report in the *Star*, and had a suspended sentence hanging over him from the previous season. The matter went to a Speedway Control Board hearing in September. Dave and three other riders were fined £250, of which £50 was for leaving the meeting without permission, and the other three £200. The riders were also given six-month bans, suspended for two years. However, the Board did decide not to implement Dave's suspended sentence from the previous season. Speaking on behalf of the riders, Rob Henry said that Long Eaton had admitted breaches of track safety regulations on four occasions, but this was ignored.

In June, Mildenhall did a 'Scottish tour', riding at Glasgow and then Berwick. In the two meetings, Dave scored 29 points from 10 rides. At Glasgow, the *Star* said he was "ultra-professional" and at Berwick, he scored "a superb 15-point maximum on his first visit to Berrington Lough." Dave says that he did fit in a round of golf on his trips to Scotland.

In July, he returned to Eastbourne for the first time as a National League rider. In a top-of-the-table clash, Dave scored 13 points. The Tigers lost, but had beaten the Eagles at few days before at West Row. Dave had scored double figures in every away meeting. He says it was "great to be back winning races."

In the National League Best Pairs, Dave and Eric Monaghan finished joint top of their group, but lost in the semi-final when Monaghan fell and was excluded. Mildenhall started as favourites in the National League Fours the next month. They won through to the Final, but finished fourth, with Mel Taylor and Eric Monaghan having mechanical troubles. Dave was top of the National League averages with a CMA of 10.8. He qualified for the National League Riders Final at Coventry, but after scoring four points from his first three rides, had an engine failure and did not take his last ride.

Towards the end of August, Dave signed for Swindon as their 'number eight', to cover for Kai Niemi who was unavailable. He rode three meetings for the Robins in September, at Bradford and Oxford, and at home to Cradley Heath. He scored 15+2 points from the three meetings. His Mildenhall commitments had to take priority. He also rode once for Ipswich, scoring 6+2 from his four rides.

Since they joined the Second Division in 1975, Mildenhall had never reached the final of the Knock Out Cup. Dave scored a 12-point maximum at home to Milton Keynes in the second round and added a 15-point maximum in the away leg. The Tigers won that match by eight points, but their 20-point win in the first match saw them safely through to the last eight. Middlesbrough were potentially tougher opposition. Dave scored an "immaculate" 12-point maximum in a 43–35 win in the first leg. He dropped a point in the second leg, but the Tigers won by six points on Teeside, Middlesbrough's only home defeat in 1986.

The semi-final was in September. Dave scored 12 points from five rides at Lakeside as Arena Essex won 43–35. The second leg was 10 days later at West Row. The Tigers won 44–34 to take the tie on aggregate by two points. Dave scored 10+1 from his four rides. The *Star* said that "The bruised and battered Fen Tigers fought their way through to their first Cup Final in one of the most thrilling meetings ever staged at West Row." There was a crowd of over 2,000.

There they faced Eastbourne, the National League Champions, with the first leg at Arlington. The Tigers were missing Rob Henry and Richard Green, and could not contain the Eagles who won 51–25. Any hopes Mildenhall had of a miracle in the second leg – as King's Lynn had once memorably done to Eastbourne a few years before – disappeared when Dave was involved in a nasty freak accident in the final heat.

Dave recalls that: "The rear wheel seized. It was not done up correctly, so the chain came off and the bike stopped dead. I never turned a race down, but we were hurrying to get the bike ready, and two bolts that stop the wheel moving weren't adjusted properly." Dave was thrown forward and landed on his face. He was carried unconscious from the track, and took an hour to come round. He was kept overnight in Eastbourne District Hospital. He had broken a bone in his neck, suffered facial injuries and had concussion. Dave recalls that his teeth had been forced into his top lip by the crash. His lip was hanging off and had to be stitched. He still has the scar, but didn't lose a tooth.

Mildenhall recovered some pride in the second leg, securing a 39–39 draw, using rider-replacement to cover for Dave.

In the National League, Mildenhall finished seventh, 14 points behind Eastbourne. It was their away form that let them down, with only three wins and a draw on the road. Dave finished with a 10.69 average, and secured 19 maximums, 16 full and three paid.

The only meeting he missed was the second leg of the Knock Out Cup Final. And for Mildenhall, with a new promotion team who only took control of the club just before the start of the season, it had been a successful campaign. Dave could look forward to coming back in 1987 once he had recovered from his crash at Arlington.

19. Finale at Mildenhall

The new year opened for Dave with success on the golf course. On New Year's Day he managed his first 'hole in one' on the 181 yards 11th hole at Rochester & Cobham Park. Dave Lanning reported in the *Star* that Dave was "recalculating his 1987 contract payment" after having to buy everyone at the club a drink to celebrate the achievement.

Negotiations over both Dave's contract and most of the other riders dragged on from January to March. The *Star* reported at the end of January that Dave wanted to stay at Mildenhall. He said that I've only had one brief conversation with the Mildenhall consortium so far. When I didn't agree at that stage to sign, I was asked if I wanted a transfer, but there's no way I want to ride for another track. I enjoyed myself at West Row last summer. It has a marvellous family atmosphere. After taking the difficult decision to drop down from the British League, I don't want to go chopping and changing teams in the National League at this stage of my career. We have a few things to sort out at Mildenhall, but it's no big drama."

In the first week of March, only Rob Parish, Skid Parish's son, had actually signed for the team. The next week, the *Star* said that Dave was close to signing a three-year deal with Mildenhall at the team's press day. Dave commented that: "There are one or two little things to sort out but it looks as though I will be signing a contract to keep me at Mildenhall until I retire from the sport. I was very happy at West Row last season and I wouldn't want to move to another track at this stage of my career. It's a pity we weren't able to arrive at this sort of agreement earlier in the year. I'm probably not as well set up for the season as I would have been because of that, but I'll be a Jawa works rider again." Skid Parish said that it was a very fair deal.

Both Melvyn Taylor and Eric Monaghan also stayed at West Row. There had been speculation that Monaghan would leave because of the amount of travelling from his Cheshire home. There were changes in the second strings and reserves. Only Richard Green remained from 1986. Rob Parish was also retained, but only rode seven meetings. Robert Henry had retired due to injuries in a crash in 1986.

Dave missed an opening challenge match with Cradley Heath because he was playing golf in Portugal, a trip he won through his 'hole in one'. He was due to ride in the World Championship Qualifying Round at Mildenhall on 5 April, and said how much he was looking forward to competing with some of the 'up and coming' stars, and show them what an 'old has been' could do.

Sadly, Dave broke his shoulder in the second leg of the early season 'Grudge Cup' at Arena Essex three days before the World Championship meeting. The doctor said he would be out for eight weeks. He returned to action after a month, riding in the Grand Slam individual tournament qualifying rounds, but aggravated the injury and had to sit out a couple more meetings. An eight-point score in the meeting at Arena Essex meant that Dave did not reach the final. Each rider rode in three qualifying rounds. Dave had scored 13 at Mildenhall and 11 at Wimbledon. His overall total of 32 was not enough to reach the final.

Mildenhall 1987: Dave, Glen Baxter, Richard Green, Maurice Everett, Paul Blackbird, Mel Taylor, Dave Jackson, Eric Monaghan (on bike). (JSC)

He then returned to action on 20 May in a narrow home win against Stoke, and said that "The bike was not quite right and neither was I" after scoring 10+1 from five rides. Mildenhall had used rider-replacement to cover for him.

A season that had started so inauspiciously turned into one of the most successful at club level that Dave ever had. After the Stoke meeting, he scored two full maximums in his next three outings, including an 18-point haul at home to Rye House in the Challenge Cup.

In June, the qualifying rounds for the National League four team tournament started. Mildenhall faced Boston, Stoke and Peterborough. The top two teams would qualify for the finals day. Mildenhall dominated the first meeting, at West Row. Dave scored a 12-point full maximum and with Mel Taylor "outclassed the opposition." Mildenhall drew the round at Peterborough with the hosts, both teams ending on 31 points. At Boston, Dave scored another maximum as Mildenhall won comfortably with 42 points out of a possible 48. Stoke won their home meeting, but by then Mildenhall and Peterborough had comfortably qualified for the finals day, at Peterborough on 9 August.

Before then, Dave and Mel Taylor represented Mildenhall in the National League Best Pairs at Poole on a Sunday afternoon. The night before, they had been at Berwick, helping the Tigers win a crucial Knock Out Cup match. They had a 400 mile journey through the night to get to Poole.

The meeting used the 4-3-2-0 scoring system to reward team riding. Dave scored 10 and Mel Taylor seven to see them through to the semi-finals in fourth place. It had been close following Taylor's exclusion in heat 12. Fortunately, in their last race, they faced the Berwick Bandits pair of Rob Woffinden and Sean Courtney, who had also made the long overnight trek to the meeting. Dave and Mel Taylor secured the 7–2 win they needed to reach the Semi-Finals.

There, they beat Eastbourne 6–3, with Dave winning and Taylor third. They repeated this result in the final against Peterborough. It was the first time that Mildenhall had won the event. The report in the *Star* said that Mildenhall "fully deserved their success."

However, both riders were surprised to find deductions from their pay for the meeting of £50 for Dave and £25 for Mel Taylor. They had been fined for protesting at the exclusion of Taylor in heat 12 of the qualifying races, but not told about this on the day.

The Fours Final at Peterborough was scheduled for 9 August. In the *Star*, Dave admitted that it was not a day he particularly looked forward to: "We are there all day and that's what I don't like about it. I'm being honest although it's probably a very good meeting to watch." He suggested two smaller meetings for the semi-finals, then a separate final.

In fact, that was what happened. Mildenhall won the first Semi-Final with 18 points, but then the meeting was abandoned due to rain after seven heats of the second. The final qualifying heat was run at Milton Keynes in September, and then the four finalists had a meeting at Hackney on 30 October over 16 heats. It had originally been scheduled for a week earlier, but was postponed due to bad weather. Mildenhall won the meeting by a point, scoring 31 against Arena Essex's 30. Eastbourne came third on 27, and Wimbledon struggled, scoring just seven. Dave only scored six points from his four rides, but it was his third place ahead of Arena Essex's Mark Chessell in the last heat that gave his team the title. Arena Essex had challenged the West Row side in the latter half of the meeting, and even were in the lead at one stage. But in heat 15, Eric Monaghan secured second place, meaning that Dave knew that he only had to finish ahead of Arena Essex's Mark Chessell to win the title.

In the *Star*, Andrew Skeels said that "For a fraction of a second at the start, it looked as though the Hammer [Chessell] was going to produce the ride of the season at the very death as he jumped out of the gate. But by the first corner, Eastbourne's Dean Standing and Neville Tatum of Wimbledon were in the clear and Jessup was settling into third. The veteran Fen Tiger knew that he only had to keep Chessell in check at the back and the title belonged to Mildenhall. Game Chessell gave it all he had but, by the finish, it was Jessup who was posing more of a threat to second placed Tatum as young Mark's hopes of an East End fairy-tale vanished."

As well as being only the second time that Mildenhall had won the title, it was the first time that any team had won both the National League Best Pairs and Four Team Tournament in the same season. The Pairs competition had started in 1975 and the Four Team Tournament a year later. Dave had been at the centre of both victories.

In the League and the Knock Out Cup, Mildenhall fell just short, being runners-up in both competitions to Eastbourne. In the Knock Out Cup, after beating Rye House in the preliminary round, the Fen Tigers lost by six points at Exeter, but won the second leg by 33, with Dave scoring 12 from five rides. Two weeks later, Dave secured a five-ride paid maximum as the Fen Tigers again topped 60 points, winning 61–35. The second league was scheduled for 18 July, but was rained off. It was put back a week, to the eve of the National League Best Pairs meeting. Dave contributed another five ride maximum, this time a full one, as the Fen Tigers won the second leg by four points.

The Semi-Final at the end of August was against opponents nearer home – Arena Essex. The Fen Tigers went to Lakeside for the first leg, and lost by six points. After the second leg was rained off, Mildenhall then won it by 24 points to reach the Final on aggregate.

In the Final, Mildenhall faced the Eastbourne Eagles, a repeat of their 1986 clash. The first leg was at West Row, and a crowd of 3,000 saw the home team win by just four points. Dave scored 11+1 from his five rides. Once again, scheduling hit the Fen Tigers' chances – they had a league match at Berwick the night before, which included a punch up in heat 12. At one stage Mildenhall were eight points up, but that allowed the Eagles to use a tactical substitute which produced a 5–1, cutting the lead to four. The report in the *Star* said that it was the Eagles "best performance of the season."

A week later, a 4,500 crowd saw the Eagles win 54–41 to take the Cup with a nine point aggregate win. The *Star* said that Dave, Mel Taylor and David Jackson "ensured Mildenhall went down with all guns blazing." Dave scored 11 from six rides. At one time, use of a tactical substitute reined in the Eagles' lead to two points, but the Mildenhall second strings and reserves were not strong enough to cause an upset.

The National League was hit by two teams dropping out mid-season, Mildenhall's local rivals Boston and Glasgow, who had transferred their operation to Workington. Mildenhall finished as runners-up to Eastbourne. The Fen Tigers' record of just one home defeat – by two points to Milton Keynes – and six away wins and an away draw was not quite good enough. Eastbourne won the league by three points.

On 30 August, Dave won the Central Riders Championship at Mildenhall with 14 points, his last win in an individual event. He ended the season with a 9.93 average, 0.8 below his 1986 figure. Mel Taylor pipped him for the top spot at Mildenhall with an average of 10.38.

Interviewed in the *Star* in early December, Dave was uncertain about his future and said that he had no concrete plans for the 1988 season. He was going with Vicky to South Africa for a holiday. He felt at the end of season that he was going to hang up his leathers, but now some enthusiasm was coming back: "I do feel better about it than I did a month ago. I'll have a good break in South Africa, then talk to the Mildenhall consortium when I come back. I have a contract with them for the next two seasons but there is an agreement that it would be waived either if I want to retire, or they have problems with the points limit. Whenever I was in a race last season I felt as enthusiastic as ever but as the seasons go on, it's the business of travelling and preparation which makes things more difficult. It was another good season for me and very nice to finish off by winning the National Fours. I felt we blew our chances in the league though. We were pretty well placed on the run-in but then had a couple of riders who experienced their bad spell in the season at the wrong time. I could well have another season but I don't want anyone jumping to conclusions at the moment because it depends on so many things. I haven't mapped out what I would do if I finished racing. It's something I'll have to face but its' the sort of thing you keep putting off until you have to make the decision."

Winning the 1987 National League Pairs at Poole with Mel Taylor.

In fact, Dave did decide to retire. Dave had agreed with Mildenhall to "tear up" his contract without dispute. However, he had said that if they were in serious trouble with injuries, he would help them out. Eight months after what he thought was his last speedway meeting, he was asked to help out the team in the second leg of a Knock Out Cup match at Wimbledon. He reluctantly agreed because he knew that the track had a good reputation and a smooth surface.

Dave recalled in *Backtrack* that he was "unfit, two stones overweight and my bike hadn't been touched since the end of the previous season." Dave recalls that he went to Hackney on the way to Plough Lane to have a practice, but there was a greyhound meeting going on, so he could not get on the track. When he arrived at Wimbledon, he was so apprehensive he threw up in the car park. The Wimbledon management, including John Berry, pointed out that he did not have a racing licence, and were told that 'it was in the post' by the Mildenhall officials.

Dave rode in seven races and scored 12 valuable points for Mildenhall. He crashed in his fifth ride, and said that the next day he was "black and blue". The teams ended up tying on aggregate, but Wimbledon won both legs of the replay to go through to the semi-finals. The Mildenhall management did ask Dave to ride again for them, but he refused. It had taken him some time to recover from his Plough Lane outing, and his future involvement in speedway was as a team manager, machine examiner and running the spare parts business he set up with Vicky and initially Malcolm Simmons. However, that one outing at Wimbledon did mean that he was involved as a professional speedway rider for 20 years, a notable landmark.

Accompanying the interview Dave did with *Backtrack* in 2007 was an assessment of his career by John Berry. He does recall how annoyed, as the Wimbledon promoter, he was when Dave rode against his team in 1988, saying it was "a cynical exercise in expediency by the men from the Fens" and was surprised that Dave had got involved.

Dave never rode for John Berry as his club promoter. So, there is no 'bias' when he pays him compliment after compliment, about his demeanour, his professionalism, his commitment, reliability and loyalty. He was "a team manager's dream" according to Berry. On Dave's international performances, he says that "I had the pleasure of working with the man quite a lot in his top international days and my job was always made easy by his sheer professionalism and desire to give of his best. There was no dragging him out of night clubs the night before racing, or any excess celebration of successes, of which there were many."

20. Management

In 1987, Dave and Vicky started a speedway parts business, *Shorne Speed Racing*, with Malcolm Simmons. Dave says that "It was Malcolm's idea. We sold parts and tyres at meetings in the south east. We covered Hackney, Wimbledon, Rye House, Arena Essex, Eastbourne and later Sittingbourne. We had a mobile van. Vicky did most of the work, especially when I was managing King's Lynn and later England. I also had golf commitments. However, it did keep us involved in speedway. I also did some engine tuning." After a couple of years, Malcolm Simmons left the business, ending a long-term friendship. Dave and Vicky sold the business as a going concern in 2015.

Meanwhile, in 1988, Bill Barker, a Kent businessman, had become the King's Lynn promoter, buying the club from Martin and Linn Rogers. Barker had little background in speedway, but was a friend of Malcolm Simmons, who became a partner in the business, and ran the speedway side of the operation. Barker managed the financial side. However, in February 1989, the two fell out, and Simmons left the club.

In March Dave joined the club as team manager, although he was also 'co-promoter' so he could attend the BSPA meetings. Although not publicised at the time, Dave did invest in the company and became a minor shareholder. Dave says that "I was the go-between with the riders and the management. I enjoyed the role, although King's Lynn was always run on a tight budget. I did some coaching with the juniors, not with the senior riders." The promotion had been committed to buying the company from Martin and Linn Rogers, and there was an historic overdraft with the bank. Also, they did not own the stadium and had to pay rent to use it, a common problem for British speedway. Dave says that "I got on well with Bill. He was very down to earth, and I remember that he helped me on some work I was doing on one of my houses. Barker also recognises the contribution Dave made, commenting in *Forty Years On*, the history of King's Lynn speedway: "It was nice to be able to leave everything to Dave ... I have complete and utter faith in him. He is magic and his personality is brilliant. Dave's wicked sense of humour kept my spirits high during the darkest moments."

The team struggled, finishing bottom of the league table in 1989 and 1990. In *Forty Years On*, Martin Rogers and Chris Hornby say that "DJ did not have the resources to make a huge name for himself because he was in charge of a couple of not especially accomplished teams...".

In 1989, Richard Knight and Lance King were the top riders, but both averaged less than eight points a meeting. In July, John Davis left to join Swindon, and although Dave signed Dennis Lofqvist – son of former West Ham star Christer Lofqvist – as a replacement, the team won only three meetings after Davis left.

One event that Dave did enjoy organising was the sport's first combined speedway and golf tournament. Bill Barker did various fundraising initiatives, and did secure a major sponsorship for the 1990 season by Zetor Tracks, a local company that was part of the Skoda group.

A major signing for 1990 was National League Riders Champion Mark Loram, one of the best young British riders. He had cost £20,000, but showed he was good value by becoming the team's number one in his first season. Lofqvist also improved on his first season's figures, and reached the World Final as a reserve. Another good recruit towards the end of the season was Swedish star Henrik Gustafsson, who finished fifth in the 1990 World Final at Odsal. Gustafsson topped the King's Lynn averages from 1991 to 1993, consistently averaging over nine points, and was the first Stars rider to do that since Bobby Schwartz in 1986. Dennis Lofqvist was also a successful recruit, and gradually improved until he left the club after the 1992 season. He rode for Sweden and also represented his country in the World Team Cup.

While two of his Swedish recruits were successful, Dave did miss out on another Swedish rider: "Tony Rickardsson came to King's Lynn for the club's practice day, probably in 1990. I didn't think he was good enough. His bikes were poor and we didn't sign him. We needed someone who could get points straightaway, and we had signed Dennis Lofqvist. If we had been stronger, we could have signed Tony as a more long-term prospect. I think at the time he went to some other tracks as well, but did not join a British team that year." Rickardsson joined Ipswich in 1991, and went on to win the World Championship five times.

At times, Dave found the job frustrating. He recalls one of his top riders refusing to take a tactical substitute rider when the team needed him in a close match, and then complaining about not been given an extra ride when the team were winning comfortably the next evening.

The story of King's Lynn in the 1980s and 1990s is inseparable from that of Michael Lee. Dave had been involved as a rider in 1985, when Lee had returned from a one-year suspension to ride for King's Lynn against Halifax and beat Kenny Carter in his first race back. He rode for the club for parts of that season, and again in 1986 until he failed to turn up for a meeting at Sheffield in June. In March 1988, Bill Barker and Malcolm Simmons considered signing him, but with his historic average could not fit him into the team.

In March 1990, Lee was refused an ACU licence because of an unpaid £50 fine from almost four years earlier for not turning up at the Sheffield meeting. Dave recalls: "I moved heaven and earth to try to get Michael's licence back. I went to the Speedway Control Board, the ACU and tribunals to get him back on a bike." In November, he was granted a licence to ride for King's Lynn.

Lee went to Australia early in 1991 to ride some meetings to get fit. King's Lynn had already had problems fitting the riders they wanted for 1991 into the British League points limit, and Richard Knight had left to join Berwick because of the problem.

However, further problems arose on the composition of the team when Michael Lee returned. Tony Macdonald says in his authorised biography of Lee: "But the [King's Lynn] promotion, with Dave Jessup as team manager, did suffer a setback when they realised there was not going to be a reduced average for Lee on his return to the sport, despite having a verbal agreement for a reduction at the BSPA Conference...". Lee's average of 7.74 meant that King's Lynn made changes in the reserve positions. The top five were Lee, Henrik Gustafsson, Mark Loram, Bohumil Brhel and Dennis Lofqvist. These riders left 5.80 points to be used for the two reserves. Dave recruited Paul Fry to fill one of the slots, and Roger

Horspool took the other. Horspool was replaced by Kevin Brice before the season started and later Nigel Leaver was also recruited.

There was a good crowd for Lee's return on the opening night of the season. Lee won the first race, but the meeting was abandoned after eight heats due to bad weather. Dave remembers saying to Michael's dad, Andy Lee, that it might be wise to not pay Michael all his earnings, but just to give him £200 and put the rest out of temptation's way in the bank. But his dad said to pay him the full amount.

The team's form was erratic in the first couple of months of the season. Dave had told Bill Barker that if they lost at home to Oxford in the second meeting of the season, he would walk home. Oxford proved to be stronger than Dave had expected and won by four points. Bill Barker did not keep Dave to his promise!

By the end of April, Michael Lee's form had declined. He was out of the World Championship. Dave had arranged a midweek team practice, and Lee crashed in that and was taken to hospital. He was struggling for fitness after two bad crashes. In early May, King's Lynn lost at home to Coventry 60–29. The Star reported that the fans were unhappy and were demanding changes. Dave recalls that at one meeting a plane flew over the King's Lynn stadium with a banner saying 'Barker and Jessup must go'. It may have been around this time. After this defeat and a home loss to Wimbledon, Dave warned four riders that their places were under threat. This produced a better performance against Poole in the Spring Gold Cup.

Dave says that after a poor away meeting, he offered Michael the chance to practice. He asked Richard Knight to come and ride with him. But that ended in a disaster, with Michael crashing through the fence. Dave had to call an ambulance, and the crew, after speaking to Michael, felt that he was not fit to be riding. His final meeting for the Stars was at Cradley in early June, where he scored 2+1 in a 57–32 defeat. His average for the season was 5.52, far below what he had achieved in the past. He only rode four league meetings for the Stars, but in the Spring Gold Cup he rode 10 meetings, with a highest score of nine points. He made a brief comeback attempt in August 1991 and planned to ride for Poole. but was injured, and never rode speedway again.

After a dispute over a drugs test after the Commonwealth Final at King's Lynn, Michael Lee had been cleared to ride for King's Lynn. However, the club had signed the Italian rider Armando del Chiele to replace Lee, although he only stayed for a few weeks because he was homesick. However, in July Dave told the *Star* that Lee did not figure in King's Lynn's immediate plans. Dave said that he would only consider Lee only when he saw him practicing and riding well enough to maintain a spot in the team. He added: "Michael Lee has the potential to get points but I have to try someone else for the sake of the team. I am not prepared to take a risk with Michael Lee at the moment."

In mid-September, Dave left King's Lynn. Chris Hornby reported in the *Star* under the headline *Jessup Out – Betts In:* "Dave Jessup has resigned as King's Lynn team manager after a personality clash with top rider Henka Gustafsson. The shock moves came last week and the Stars moved in quickly to appoint former rider and England international Terry Betts as caretaker manager for the remainder of the season ... Jessup has been in the hot seat since 1989 and club promoter Bill Barker commented at the weekend: "I have a lot of respect for what Dave has done over the last three years. We are still good friends and remain so. I am still very upset about the whole matter and I make no bones about that. It is true to say there was a clash of personalities between Henka and Dave but, at the end of the day, it was Dave's decision to resign, he was not forced into it."

Dave told the *Star*: "I am very disappointed this has happened because I think we were getting towards the sort of team that could challenge for honours. My reasons are due greatly to what appears to be a personality clash between myself and Henka and one or two others over team differences.

In particular, there was a situation that Henka said he would not go to Middlesbrough for a challenge match unless he was offered more money. All the other riders are contracted to ride in challenge matches but that is not in Henka's contract. With the knowledge that Henka was threatening to stay in Sweden and would tender a transfer request, for my own loyalty and regard for King's Lynn Speedway, I had little alternative but to relinquish my job as team manager. Even so, I think this is a situation of the tail wagging the dog.

I understand that there was a meeting between some of the riders and Bill Barker. I am disappointed that I was not present to deny or comment on what they said. I wish they could have said things to my face. This seems to be rider power and I hope that it is not something that is coming into speedway. I wish my good friend Bill Barker the greatest success in the future and to the tremendous fans at King's Lynn who have given me personally so much support in the past three years. Good luck also to my junior team in the Knock Out Cup Final. They have ridden exceptionally well all season and I hope the fans will keep behind them."

Dave said that, as far as his immediate plans, he would now have more time to spend on his speedway business, Shorne Speed, and on engine tuning. "I certainly want to stay in speedway but I am not planning on taking another team manager's job at the moment. I will also be able to devote more time to my family, especially my son David, who has ambitions to become a professional golfer."

Dave recalls that: "I was in my workshop when Bill came round. He said that the supporters were asking what was happening. I said that I would leave. He did offer to buy my shares, but I said I would keep them. In May 1992, the takings from the Commonwealth Final at King's Lynn, £26,000, were stolen from Bill Barker's house, and the company went into liquidation." Buster Chapman took over the promotion, and still runs it today.

Looking back, Dave says that he was never involved in the financial side: "I remember that one of the riders had a very good night at an away meeting, and there wasn't enough cash to pay him. The debts had been turned round, and I do feel now that a lot of the work that had been done to stabilise the club was wasted. I didn't look at promoting again. I lost the money I had invested."

Dave had taken over a team that had consistently finished near or at the bottom of the league, although to be fair this reflected the promotion's financial restraints in a smaller, more competitive league, as much as the riders' ability. However, things had improved in 1991, with a respectable eighth place in a 13 team league. Dave had been able to recruit better riders and developed more of a team. The reserve team finished fourth out of 13 teams in their league, and reached the reserve's Knock Out Cup Final. His work with them had paid dividends.

So, Dave could reflect on a relatively successful final season with King's Lynn. It is interesting to note that there are similarities – riders calling a meeting about his management without him there – to what happened at Wimbledon in 1983 when he lost the captaincy in a similar situation. Maybe in both cases, the high standards that Dave had as a rider and manager were not being reached and accepted by others.

Dave did not take another management post in club speedway, but his next manager role was far more high profile.

England

One of the great differences between speedway today and the era when Dave was riding is the lack of international fixtures. In the 1970s and 1980s, test matches were a regular occurrence, along with the World Team Cup and the World Best Pairs. Today, there is just the Speedway of Nations – a best pairs competition featuring three riders from each country. While the Speedway Grand Prix offers top class international individual meetings, test matches are very rare. There is now a Great Britain academy for younger riders, and opportunities for under-21 riders. However, the chance for most riders to represent their country – the pinnacle of a career in most sports – is now very limited.

In most team sports, certainly all the football codes and cricket, the coach or manager is the main spokesperson on behalf of the club. The club chair or chief executive are more in the background, although some football and rugby (both codes) club chairs in some cases have a higher public profile.

In speedway, the main person at a club has always been the promoter. The team manager is literally that – organising the team, deciding on riding positions, usually having a role in transfers or changes to the line-up, and making decisions about substitutions or tactical rides during a meeting. The hectic international schedules for the top riders and 'doubling up' between leagues in Britain allow almost no opportunity for coaching, or team meetings. Most team managers are former riders, and can give advice, but the role has its limitations.

Similarly, the England team manager role in speedway is not a high profile one. It only seems to have become a post in its own right in the early 1970s. Before then, the promoter or team manager from the home track where a test match was being staged would often carry out the role, and there would be a rider-manager for British Lions tours to Australia and New Zealand.

And when a manager was appointed, it was usually someone who was already a promoter or manager of one of the British League teams. People such as Len Silver, John Berry, Colin Pratt, Eric Boocock and Wally Mawdsley all had the job before John Louis was appointed in 1993. He held the post, initially with support from James Easter, and then with support from former referee Graham Reeve, for four years. John says in his autobiography that he had doubts about taking the post because "running Ipswich was a full-time job on its own."

John Louis stood down at the end of 1997, and Dave was asked to become the England manager. He recalls that Terry Russell was the chair of the BSPA then, and believes that he canvassed for Dave to be taken on. Dave says that the role "was mainly about the test matches and the Speedway World Cup. I organised a pre-season get together at Dunlop

Tyres, who were supplying tyres to the British League clubs at the time. It was a team-building exercise, and I thought the riders would find it interesting to see how the tyres were made. I particularly wanted to involve the younger riders, such as Carl Stonehewer, Scott Nicholls and Joe Screen."

However, Dave soon hit a problem with his choice of captain: "I wanted to change the captaincy. I didn't think Gary Havelock was riding very well, and said to him that he was probably good enough to be in the team, but was not necessarily my first choice. I thought not having the pressure of the England job would help him, so he could get back in the team on a regular basis. I felt Chris Louis would be the best captain." However, *The People* newspaper carried a two-page interview with Gary by Russell Lanning about changing the captaincy. Dave says that "Gary said he wouldn't ride for me, so I didn't pick him. Even today he is stand-offish towards me."

Dave wanted a better identity for the England team: "I wanted the riders to have a smart uniform, black shoes, socks, trousers with patch pockets and a white shirt with a collar. The BSPA paid for this and liked it. It linked in with Dunlop and the promotional work we were doing. It helped promote the sport. The riders wore it for the first test, but after that they didn't bother. Only Chris Louis made an effort. I don't think its professional for a rider to be representing England and be wearing flip-flops, a t-shirt and shorts. They got an appearance fee to ride for England. I raised this with the BSPA and they said 'don't upset the riders'. The same happened when I got England anoraks for the riders. We got team leathers as well, and they did wear those, although I remember once allowing Chris Louis to wear his own as the team ones were too tight for him.

It could be frustrating at times. One of the leading English riders told me that his priority was to earn as much money from speedway as he could, and then retire. I went to meet him at his home track to try to persuade him to ride in one of the test series. Another rider wanted one more free tyre than his team-mates. I didn't want to do it, but to drop him and bring in the reserve just before the meeting would have done more damage. In the end someone bought him a tyre. I know that we did not have a budget to spend on the team as other countries did; I couldn't take them out for a meal with the BSPA paying, for example.

Sometimes I thought the riders were petty. At one international meeting, there was a lot of shale on the track. It was inches deep. But two of our riders, who were not great starters, didn't want to put on new tyres unless the BSPA paid for them. One of the established riders who had come along to support the team, but was not well enough to ride, backed me up. They nearly came to blows. Needless to say, we did not win the meeting.

In another meeting, one of our riders knocked off a Danish rider. It wasn't intentional, these things happen in racing. But his promoter, who was English and prominent in the BSPA, started having a go at my rider. I almost ended up pushing him out of the pits."

Overall, Dave's record in test matches was won five, drawn one and lost two. His England team faced Australia in two series, winning both of them. In a series against the USA, the teams tied one all. The third match was scheduled for Ipswich but was rained off.

Dave's first match against the Australians was at Wolverhampton on 6 July 1998. England won the 16-heat match 55–41. Chris Louis, Martin Dugard, Mark Loram and Joe Screen were all kept from the 1997 side. Scott Nicholls moved up into the main body of the team, while

Andy Smith and Paul Hurry were the reserves. The Australians were missing Jason Crump, and Todd Wiltshire was also not selected, having arrived in the UK only a week earlier to join Oxford. Peter Foster, in his *History of the Speedway Ashes*, says that "England had one of their better nights, with youngsters Nicholls and Hurry being especially impressive."

Just under a month later, the teams met again at Eastbourne. Dave Norris replaced Andy Smith and Glen Cunningham, the National League Riders Champion, was given a chance at reserve. England again won comfortably. Jason Crump was back for the Australians, but he was the only one of their riders to score double figures. For England, Martin Dugard, riding on his home track, top scored with 13. Screen and Hurry also reached double figures.

The series finished the next day at King's Lynn. Maybe the larger King's Lynn track suited the Australians better than Eastbourne. England lost Mark Loram in a heat three crash, and the Australians dominated the meeting. For England, only Chris Louis reached double figures, and the visitors had the match won by heat 13.

The teams met again in 1999. The Australians now had Todd Wiltshire, and looked stronger than in 1998. The whole series took place in a week, with meetings at Belle Vue, Hull and Oxford. Dave selected an experienced team for the first test. A bike failure for Martin Dugard in heat 14 saw a 4–2 for England reversed, and in the final heat, a win for Jason Crump saw the visitors secure a 45–45 draw. After heat nine England had been eight points up, and the Australians were never winning.

For the match at Hull, five days later, Dave chose National League rider Carl Stonehewer at reserve, replacing Dave Norris. The match was very close, and the Australians suffered a blow when Jason Crump crashed in heat 13 and was taken to hospital with a suspected broken collarbone. Dave used Stonehewer with Martin Dugard in heat 14, and their 5–1 levelled the scores. Dave nominated Stonehewer for the final heat with Chris Louis. The England captain led from the tapes, and Stonehewer managed to split the Australians to give England a narrow 46–44 victory.

Two days later, England won comfortably, 60–30 against an Australian side missing Jason Crump. The Australians only provided four heat winners, and every England rider was paid for at least nine points.

In September and October, England faced the USA. The first match was at Eastbourne. The Americans had a strong side, including Sam Ermolenko, Ronnie Correy, John Cook, Greg Hancock and Billy Hamill. For England, Dave chose Joe Screen, Chris Louis, David Norris and Paul Hurry in both matches; Mark Loram, Dean Barker, Martin Dugard and Lee Richardson rode in one match.

The first eight heats of the first test were fairly even, but the Americans provided every heat winner from heat nine, and won the match 51–39. A month later, the teams met again at Wolverhampton. This time, England came out on top. Louis and Hurry secured a 4–2 in the first race, and from then on England were always ahead, at times by 10 points. The Americans narrowed the gap towards the end of the meeting, but England won 48–42. The third match, scheduled for Ipswich, was rained off twice. It was the last test series to date between the two countries.

Left: Dave and Chris Louis at Belle Vue – England versus Australia on 11 June 1999. (JSC)

Middle: Chris Louis and Dave after winning the World Team Cup semi-final at Poole in August 1999. (JSC)

Bottom: Joe Screen, Dave and Dean Barker at Eastbourne – England versus USA 18 September 1999. (JSC)

World Team Cup 2000 at Coventry

Left: Dave looking concerned. (JSC)

Bottom: Dave with Mark Loram, Chris Louis, Carl Stonehewer and Joe Screen. (JSC)

Having not entered the World Team Cup, along with Australia, in 1998, England were back in the tournament in 1999. The formula had changed since Dave had ridden in it. The World Best Pairs had finished in 1993, and merged with the World Team Cup.

Each team now had four riders – two pairs – and a reserve. There were four teams in each meeting, over 24 heats. However, it was the conventional 3-2-1-0 speedway scoring, with no reward for team riding. England entered the competition in the Semi-Final at Poole, with the winner qualifying for the Final. England won comfortably, with 53 points, eight clear of Denmark. Chris Louis scored a paid maximum from his six rides, Joe Screen and Mark Loram just dropped a point each.

However, the Final was a disappointment. Australia won the meeting with 51 points, 16 clear of Czechoslovakia, who had qualified as the hosts. The USA and England finished on 29 points, and Sam Ermolenko beat Joe Screen in a run-off for third place. Chris Louis and mark Loram topped the scores for England with 12 points each. But Joe Screen, Carl Stonehewer and reserve Andy Smith made little impact.

Interviewed in the *Star*, Dave said that the referee had refused to extend the time limit so that Chris Louis could ride as a tactical substitute in heat 19. He would have replaced Andy Smith, and may have taken the extra point that would have put England into third place overall. However, to be fair the Americans were also treated harshly by the referee's interpretation of the two-minute rule.

Dave also said that Chris Louis was "brilliant" to win two races after an unavoidable collision with Carl Stonehewer. He also explained that he had chosen Joe Screen for the run-off against Sam Ermolenko because Louis was still feeling the effects of his fall, while Mark Loram felt he was not "100 per cent on the pace." Screen had ridden well to win heat 24, after having bike problems earlier in the meeting. However, overall, Dave said "It was very, very disappointing and I was absolutely gutted that we finished last. It was a very bad day; it just didn't go for us." He praised the Australians, and added that for the Lions: "We have got a lot to put right, and rebuilding will take place immediately. The riders were equally disappointed with the result. I can't say it was lack of effort, it was just a lack of points. Everyone was trying. I can't say we weren't prepared. Now we've got to make sure we get back to the top. I'd like to see us have a test match series to get the side up and ready for the World Team Cup. I think the tests against the Americans were planned too close to the Team Cup this year. If we're going to take the Americans and Australians on, they've got to be programmed from March and early enough to see who's going and who's not."

However, in 2000, Dave didn't get his wish for some preparation for the World Cup. There were no test matches scheduled. There was a Young England versus Young Australia series, which Dave was not involved in. England qualified as hosts for the World Team Cup Final, which was held at Coventry on 17 September in front of a disappointing 2,500 crowd. There they faced Sweden and the USA who had qualified by winning the semi-finals, and Australia who were the holders.

The formula was the same as in 1999. Dave chose Mark Loram and Chris Louis as one pair, Joe Screen and Martin Dugard as the other with Carl Stonehewer as reserve. Dugard fell twice, and Dave replaced him with Stonehewer for his last two rides. The England riders did well. They only lost one heat, a 4–2 in heat two to the Swedes when Dugard fell.

However, that result was important for what happened later in the meeting. England provided seven heat winners and, after securing a 5–1 in heat 23 against the USA, had a final total of 40 points. The Americans finished on 35 points.

Going into the final heat, Sweden had 35 points and Australia 28. Sweden needed a 5–1 against Australia to reach 40 points and tie with England. If this happened there would be a run-off for first place. Henrik Gustafsson and Peter Karlsson were riding for the Swedes, Jason Crump and Leigh Adams represented Australia. Both Australians had scored double figures, and Crump had finished first or second in each of his heats except one where he had an engine failure.

However, the Swedes secured the 5–1 they needed to force the run-off. Tony Rickardsson faced Mark Loram to decide the title, but Loram fell and was excluded, so the Swedes won the World Team Cup. Even to this day, Dave will not publicly comment now on what he thought about the race, but did tell Tony Macdonald in a feature for *Backtrack* in 2007 that he was "absolutely disgusted" with what he saw.

The *Star's* report of the meeting said that "The England camp felt the Aussies had done the Swedes a favour." Their reporter Mike Berry interviewed Dave, who said: "It appeared a couple of the Australian bikes had brakes on. We should be pleased that we finished second but at the death we feel like we have been robbed. I think there is a rule in the rulebook saying that you must have a bona-fide attempt to race and I wasn't sure they were doing that in heat 24." Dave concluded that "Last year we finished fourth and it was an abysmal attempt. This year we nearly did it, and I feel we would have been deserved winners. But the record books will show that we finished second behind Sweden."

In Mike Berry's report, he said that "The grievous sense of anti-climax was bad enough for England's Lionhearts. To have the World Team Cup torn from your grasp in the cruellest possible way was one thing. To lose with an undercurrent of injustice made it an especially painful pill to swallow ... it will also be remembered with a large dose of bitterness by England, who were left aggrieved by what they perceived as a palpably below-par display from Australia in a crucial heat 24. The Aussies pleaded their innocence against any accusation of subterfuge, but the chorus of jeers that greeted Jason Crump and Leigh Adams as they returned to the pits told their own story."

It turned out that the meeting marked the end of his stint as England team manager. He submitted a basic report on the meeting to the BSPA, most of whose members had been at the meeting anyway. He then got a phone call from the BSPA chairman, Chris Van Straaten, saying that his report was inadequate, and that they had decided to make a change. Dave reflects that maybe he should have been more critical of the conduct of that last race.

Van Straaten said that Colin Pratt and Eric Boocock would be taking over the England role. Dave has never received a letter telling him this officially, or any thanks for what was a largely successful spell as England manager. It was a post he was honoured to have held, despite all the frustrations and problems that went with it.

Apart from in 2004, when they were within one point of Sweden, neither England or Great Britain ever came close to winning the Speedway World Cup, as it became, again. In 2018, in the Speedway of Nations, a pairs competition, Great Britain topped the aggregate scores after two days of racing, but in the final drew 3-3 with Russia, who were deemed to be the winners by taking the second and third places.

Finally, it is worth noting that the structure for the World Team Cup was changed for 2001, to an event with qualifying meetings, and five rider races representing the different teams in the race-off meeting for places in the final, and the final itself. England missed out on the final by losing a run-off. One wonders if some lessons were learnt by the organisers following the 2000 tournament.

Looking back, it is worth considering whether the BSPA missed an opportunity when they terminated Dave's role as England manager. This is not to criticise the people who have held the post since then, but to have a widely respected former British rider, with no other responsibilities in the sport, could have developed the England team manager role further. As well as managing the senior team, Dave could have played a coach/mentor role for the under-21 British riders and helped develop new talent. Looking at the shortage of British riders now capable of competing at Grand Prix level shows what an opportunity was missed. The sport now has an apprenticeship scheme, and a better management structure for the Great Britain set up. But British speedway is now far behind both Poland and Sweden. One post on its own would not have solved the problems, but it could have played a part in starting to put a better structure in place earlier.

The next generation: Dave and Vicky's grandson Jensen on his motorbike.

21. Playing golf for England

For any sportsman, representing one's country is one of the greatest honours they can achieve. Certainly, in a team sport, it is the ultimate achievement. In a sport like speedway that is both a team and individual sport, it is still a major achievement. And in the individual competitions, such as the World Championship in Dave's time as a rider and the Grand Prix today, there is still an element of representing one's country. How often are questions posed such as "How many American riders have been World Champion?" or "Who was the first New Zealander to win the World title?" [Five and Ronnie Moore in 1954 to save you looking it up.]

Only a small minority in any sport reach the level of being an 'international'. So, to be a 'dual-international' – to represent your country at two sports is very rare indeed. This is particularly true over the last 60 years or so. Professionalism has grown, seasons have become longer, and the clubs who employ the players have asserted more control about what they do away from their main sport. A study of 'dual internationals' by Jeremy Malies, *Sporting Doubles*, looks at the careers of 17 of them. Twelve were born in the nineteenth century and another in 1902. The youngest was born in 1918. Twelve played cricket, eight rugby union and five association football, although two of those only represented England in war-time internationals. Surprisingly, golf was only played by two of Malies's selection, both women.

One area where dual-internationals are common is in the two rugby codes – league and union. Although the rules are different, the basic skill set for both codes is similar. Playing association football or rugby union and cricket at international level was rare, but not unheard of, particularly when the players were amateurs, even if they were playing with professionals in football. But in these examples, the sporting careers ran in parallel – a winter sport and a summer sport.

There are also people who are natural sportsmen – who have the hand-eye co-ordination, sense of balance, courage and ability to perform under pressure or in front of a crowd. As well as speedway and golf, Dave was successful in motorbike trials riding, football as a youngster and cross-country running at school.

To spend almost 20 years as a professional in one sport, and then to play another having retired from their first, is arguably more unusual. This is partly because there are far fewer opportunities for international representation as players get older. However, senior amateur golf is one such area, and this is where Dave became a dual international, adding golf to speedway in sports where he represented his country. Interestingly, footballer Alan Hansen played for Scotland at golf and football, but he played for a Scottish Boys team, and had to make the choice at a young age of which sport he was going to concentrate on.

It is interesting to note that, in Dave and Vicky's living room, the trophies and photographs on display are almost all from Dave's golf career, rather than his speedway one. Maybe this reflects that he was a speedway rider for around 20 years, compared to 47 years on the golf course. He still plays at his local club, Rochester & Cobham Park, two or three times a week. He also plays in South Africa when he and Vicky are on holiday there.

After Dave injured his knee in 1973, his doctor said he needed to walk to get fit. He recommended that Dave play golf and suggested he play at Deangate Ridge, a local public course. He said it would be a seven-mile walk. "How far???" was Dave's response. But he followed the doctor's advice, who was a member of the Rochester & Cobham Park Golf Club.

Dave recalls that: "I went there and bought a second hand club. I knocked the ball around and went back the next week. I bought another club, and by the time I had finished rehab, I had a bag full. Malcolm Simmons started playing as well. We played quite regularly. As well as Deangate Ridge, we played a couple of times at Rochester & Cobham Park, a local private members golf club.

After one of the games, I went back to my Dad's garage and put my golf clubs on the floor. One of my Dad's customers, Vic Chance, asked me 'Do you play golf?' I said 'Not really, I'm just trying to keep fit'. He asked if I had a handicap and I said 'no'. He asked what I scored at Deansgate Ridge and I said '82'. That was 10 over par, so my handicap would have been 10."

Mr Chance asked Dave if he would like to join the Rochester & Cobham Park club. Dave said that he would love to, he knew the course, but didn't know the club. Mr Chance replied "Fine, I'm the chairman." It turned out that Dave's doctor, Doctor Cornell, was on the club committee. Dave was given an application form, completed it and was asked to come to a committee meeting for an interview.

This was a few months after Dave had started playing. He explained that he could not attend the meeting because he was riding for England in a test match against Sweden. The committee meeting went ahead anyway, and accepted Dave as a member. Dave says that "They rang me and told me to pay my subscription and I would be in. It was not easy to join, you needed the support of an established member."

Dave played regularly, fitting in golf around his speedway commitments. He says that "I could not play at weekends, so often played with some of the 'old boys' in midweek. They knew about speedway and had watched it in London in the 1950s. It was very convenient, we lived close to the club. Sometimes I would be working in my workshop, and they would ring me, saying they needed one more player to make up a fourball. It was friendly, there was banter and rivalry, but it had a nice atmosphere."

Soon, Dave was playing in Celebrity Amateur tournaments, which raised considerable sums for different charities: "It was Peter Brown, a golf professional who was also involved in speedway who got me started. He was part of my move from King's Lynn to Wimbledon. He got me the invitation to play in a tournament in Woking in Surrey. I joined the Variety Club, and the SPARKS charity, which had a lot of different sports personalities involved. Jimmy Hill, the football television presenter, and former manager and player, was one of the leading lights in SPARKS. Lots of people from different walks of life were involved. For me, it was a free round of golf, usually a free shirt or some golf balls, and the chance to play on different courses, all in a good cause."

As well as playing in Britain, Dave played overseas: "The comedian Jimmy Tarbuck organised a golf week in San Lorenzo in Portugal. Henry Cooper had one at the Penina Golf Club in Portugal. I won the tournament twice in fourball team events, and the individual tournament several times. By then I was playing off a three handicap."

One of the people who got Dave involved with SPARKS, which funds medical research into rare conditions that affect children, and the Variety Club, was actor Garfield Morgan, best known for his role in *The Sweeney* and many other successful television programmes. Dave remembers that "Golf charity days were booming in the 1980s. One year I was invited to 135 events, and played in 50. From March to October, there was something going on almost every day. Over the years, I helped raise £40 to £50 million for good causes. Companies would bring their clients and the celebrities would be allocated to different teams.

They weren't always good players, but it didn't matter as long as people enjoyed it and we were raising money. Overall, I had a wonderful time. I still play occasionally in these events today, but there are far fewer than there used to be."

From 1980, Dave started to take his golf more seriously. He was involved in the 1981 Marley pro-celebrity event for a week that was televised. It started on a Tuesday morning, and Dave had to drive there from a speedway meeting at Birmingham on the Monday, arriving at the hotel in Gleneagles around 2am. Dave's televised game was on the Thursday morning. He recalls that some international stars from show business and sport were involved: "There were people like Jack Lemon, Jack Palance, Christopher Lee, James Hunt, Sean Connery and Bruce Forsyth. I played with some of them when we were practicing. There was a special room in the hotel which had food and drink for the golfers, and we could watch the tournament live." It was shown on television later in the year. After the tournament, Dave flew from Edinburgh to a speedway meeting in Europe.

Another event that Dave enjoyed was the Vodaphone tournament at Wentworth for the top 50 celebrity players. Again, a wide variety of sports were represented: "There were snooker players, like Willie Thorne, Dennis Taylor and Cliff Thorburn, footballers including Gary Lineker, Alan Hansen – who was a very good golfer – and Glen Hoddle, racing driver Nigel Mansell, boxers Henry Cooper and John Conteh, cricketers Graham Gooch and Pat Pocock, Alan Wells the sprinter and from show business Mike Reid, Garfield Morgan, Eric Sykes, Bernard Cribbins, Tim Brooke Taylor, Rick Wakeman, John Lodge from *Yes,* Stan Boardman, Kenny Lynch, Jess Conrad, Kevin Whately and Russ Abbott. On the first day we played in teams, and carried our scores over to the second day. I finished second in the tournament five times, then finally won it, just beating Glen Hoddle. The winner was given a green jacket, just like the Masters tournament in America."

At club level Dave's golf also improved, particularly after he had retired from speedway in 1987. He played for his club in 'scratch' matches, which was the level established professionals were meant to play at. He won his club championship five times, including three in a row. However, he was not selected for the Kent county team, although he did play once when someone didn't turn up. Dave was on the Kent committee for 10 years, and was the team manager for the under-18 Boys team.

Things changed for his prospects of playing representative golf when he turned 55 in 2008. He was now eligible for the Kent Senior Amateurs team, and was chosen for them straightaway. He played for Kent for 10 years, and only lost two match-play matches in the South East county league tournaments. He won the Kent Seniors Amateur Championship at Ashford, and then was able to enter the English and British championships. It should be pointed out that some of the players were former professionals who had returned to 'amateur' status after a break from the professional game. Dave played in the English and British championships, at the Royal Cinque Ports Club. He recalls: "I did well, I was in the top 10 in the English championship, and the top four English players in the British championship, which included a lot of American players."

As he was leaving the British Championship, Dave was approached by Richard Palmer, the England Amateur Seniors manager. Slightly surprised to be addressed as "Young Jessup", Palmer told Dave that his scores were impressive, and that he would keep an eye on Dave's progress. He also explained that the selectors picked the team based on performances in the Scottish, Irish and Welsh championships as well as the two tournaments that Dave had played. He also told Dave that he was good enough to be in the team.

Left: Dave with Lee Trevino, one of the best players in the history of the sport.

Left: Dave with the Celebrity Masters Trophy, which he won at Wentworth in 2004.
Right: Raising money for the Variety Club of Great Britain, with comedians Stan Boardman and Keith O'Keefe.

Above: The England Amateur Seniors Golf team at the 2010 European Championship:
Back: Chris Reynolds, Doug Arnold, Phil Slater, Andrew Carman; front: Dave, Richard Palmer (Manager), Alan Squires.

Left: Dave playing with Les Allison, the Managing Director of Kellands, who sponsored Dave during his time at King's Lynn.

Left: Dave winning the Henry Cooper Golf Classic and receiving the trophy from the famous boxer.

Above: Dave with the Henry Cooper Trophy.

Right: David Jessup with what his proud dad describes as a 'perfect swing'. David played golf professionally for a period.

Soon afterwards, Dave got a phone call telling him he had been selected for the England team: "It was wonderful, I was quite emotional. Then I took it seriously, I played every day and got down to scratch." BBC Radio Kent reported that he was to be the first person to represent England at speedway and golf. Dave told the station: "There aren't many people who do different sports and it's nice to be up there with the people who can play two sports for their country. When I'm on a golf course they still announce me as an ex-speedway rider; champion of this and that, but now they also say a county golfer and now there's the added bonus that they'll be able to say 'he represented his country' and that will please me quite a bit." On the BBC website, the report was included under 'motor sport' rather than golf.

The home internationals were in Tenby, playing against Wales, at the end of September 2008. Dave was not selected for the first morning foursomes, but played and won in the singles in the afternoon. He then played in the foursomes and singles matches against Scotland and Ireland for the next two days.

Dave played for England for around the next three years. He now played in the English, British, Irish, Scottish and Welsh championships regularly. In 2010, he was runner-up in the Scottish Championship by one shot, and finished tied third in the English Championship and fifth in the Welsh. After the Scottish Championship, he reflected on the Scottish Golf Union website that "I had a good chance last week at the Welsh Seniors but went on the attack too early. I was nice and patient out there today and knew that pars would be good. The eagle at 15 was great but not quite enough in the end, but I'm pleased to come all the way up to Scotland and get the Silver Medal."

That year, England was staging the European Championship at Fairhaven Golf Club in Lytham St Anne's. Dave recalls that: "There were 22 teams, and everyone played two rounds of medal (stroke) play all the scores counted to find each country's position. The worst score in each team was not counted, and I was nervous and shot an 82, which was our worst and led to some gentle banter over dinner. But the next day I was the leading scorer in the whole competition with a 71. Of our six players, only Chris Reynolds and I were not former professionals. Two played foursomes and the other four played singles. The tournament then split into three groups, and England qualified for the top eight. I played with Douglas Arnold in the foursomes and we were never beaten." Dave also remembers the European Championship for playing against Gustavo Larrazabal, whose son Pablo plays on the professional European tour. Gustavo is a 'very good golfer' in his own right.

Dave has played on all the major British courses, as well as in America and South Africa. There, he is a member of the East Rand Propietary Mines (ERPM) Golf Club. He has also played for the Ekurhuleni (formerly East Rand) Seniors team. He first played seniors golf in South Africa, and has even flown there specially for a few days to play in particular championships.

In Europe, Dave won a Mercedes tournament in Hardelow, near Boulogne, and finished third in the Mercedes world championship tournament in Berlin. He has also played for the Mercedes team, and in their tournaments, despite driving a much cared for vintage Porsche.

Another memorable tournament was when he was playing in a pro-celebrity tournament, and was sponsored by Dunlop Tyres. Dave rang them to see if he could get some new Dunlop gear for the event. He recalls: "An articulated lorry from Dunlop arrived at my house. They delivered a full set of clubs, a professional golf bag, two holdalls, four pairs of golf shoes, four cashmere jumpers, shirts and a gross (144) of golf balls. It was like Christmas had come early. I got to the tournament, and was unloading all this stuff when a chap came over. 'We supply all that', he said. I went to the Slazenger tent and got more! What was odd was the Slazenger and Dunlop were owned by the same company. Vicky also got some Slazenger clothes because she was going to be interviewed on television."

The question that is impossible to answer is how successful Dave could have been if he had focussed on golf from the beginning. He thinks, based on his achievements after he retired from speedway, that he probably could have played professionally, although he points out that the top professionals now play to six or seven under par. His son David did play professionally for two and a half years, but did not earn enough to stay on the circuit. Dave now thinks that maybe he started too young. Recently David has started playing again, now as an amateur. Dave says he is playing nicely and enjoying it.

Dave and Vicky's grandson Jensen will have a choice of sports, if he wants to take them up when he is older. Now aged four, he has a little motorbike which he rides enthusiastically round a local field. His proud grandmother has a video of him riding on her phone.

Dave and Vicky are now retired, enjoying both life in North Kent near their family and their holidays in South Africa. Dave still plays golf regularly, although his injured knee means that he uses a golf buggy to get round the course. He has had Gary Drake, the owner of Godden Engineering, make some very special parts for his buggy, along with some unavailable parts for his 911 Porsche. He is very proud of his achievements on the golf course, in a very different sport to speedway, and rightly so. He still follows speedway and attends the Kent Kings meetings every week.

Looking back, Dave was part of what now seems to be a golden age of British speedway. He was one of the best riders to come from the then newly established British League Second Division, and rode at the top level of the sport for 16 years.

He can reflect on a very successful speedway career, with six gold medals in the World Team Cup and World Best Pairs, the runners-up spot in the World Championship and wins in the British, Overseas and Commonwealth Finals. He represented England and Great Britain on 117 occasions. He won the Internationale, at the time the sport's most prestigious British meeting outside the World Championship, the Division Two Riders Championship (the youngest ever winner) and at least 25 other major individual meetings.

He rode for five top level clubs, including the famous Wembley Lions, and was the top scorer at four of them at least once. The exception was Wembley, where he was establishing himself as a First Division rider. But maybe importantly than his wins and trophies was that he was always a popular and sporting rider and gave value for money to the fans. And that really is the best achievement of all.

Appendix: Statistics and records

England and Great Britain record

World Team Cup

Date	Round	Opponents	Rides	Points	Result
15/9/1973	**Final**	**Sweden, Soviet Union, Poland**	0	0	**Won 37 points (reserve)**
11/8/1974	British	Australia, Scotland, New Zealand	4	10	Won 41 points
15/9/1974	**Final**	**Sweden, Poland, Soviet Union**	4	10	**Won 42 points**
14/7/1975	British	Australia, Scotland, New Zealand	4	10	Won 37 points
21/9/1975	**Final**	**Sweden, Poland, Soviet Union**	0	0	**Won 41 points (reserve)**
16/5/1976	British	Australia, Scotland, New Zealand	4	8	Second 35 points
19/6/1977	British	Australia, Scotland, New Zealand	4	12	Won 42 points (Max)
18/9/1977	**Final**	**Poland, Czechoslovakia, Sweden**	4	9	**Won 37 points**
21/5/1978	Round 1	Australia, USA, New Zealand	4	9	Won 43 points
18/6/1978	Intercontinental Final	Denmark, Sweden, Australia	1	0	Won 33 points
16/9/1978	Final	Denmark, Poland, Czechoslovakia	3	5	Runners-up 27 points
20/5/1979	Round A	Australia, USA, New Zealand	4	7	Third 22 points (reserve)
18/5/1980	Round 1	Australia, USA, New Zealand	4	11	Won 42 points
5/7/1980	Intercontinental Final	USA, Denmark, Sweden	4	12	Won 33 points (Max)
21/9/1980	**Final**	**USA, Poland, Czechoslovakia**	4	8	**Won 40 points**
17/5/1981	Round 1	Australia, USA, New Zealand	4	10	Won 36 points (capt)
28/6/1981	Intercontinental Final	Denmark, USA, Sweden	4	8	Second 30 points (capt)
16/8/1981	Final	Denmark, West Germany, Soviet Union	3	3	Runners-up 29 points (capt)
16/5/1982	Round 1	USA, Australia, New Zealand	4	11	Won 39 points (capt)
26/6/1982	Intercontinental Final	USA, Denmark, Sweden	4	4	Third 25 points

15/5/1983	Round 1	USA, New Zealand, Australia	1	0	Second 27 points (reserve)
26/6/1983	Intercontinental Final	Denmark, USA, Sweden	4	8	Third 26 points (reserve)
13/5/1984	Round 2	USA, Australia, New Zealand	1	1	Second 32 points (capt)
Totals	23 meetings		73	156	

23 meetings. Seven Finals: five wins, two runners-up. 73 rides, 156 points.

World Best Pairs

Date	Round	Partner	Rides	Points	Result
13/7/1974	Final	Peter Collins (12 points)	6	8	Fourth 20 points
8/6/1980	Semi-final 1	Peter Collins (10 points)	6	12	Joint second 22 points
22/6/1980	**Final**	**Peter Collins (14 points)**	**6**	**15**	**Won 29 points**
7/6/1981	Semi-final 1	Chris Morton (12 points)	6	11	Second 23 points
20/6/1981	Final	Chris Morton (10 points)	6	7	Sixth 17 points

5 meetings. Three finals: one win. 30 rides, 53 points

Young Britain and Young England

Date	Opposition	Venue	Result	Rides	Points	Bonus
16/8/1969 (YE)	Y Czechoslovakia	Canterbury	47–61	4	4	2
25/8/1969 (YE)	Y Czechoslovakia	Reading	51–57	1	1	0
10/9/1969 (YB)	Y Australasia	Crayford	62–46	6	11	1
21/9/1969 (YB)	Y Australasia	Eastbourne	69–38	6	14	2
23/7/1970 (YE)	Y Sweden	Middlesbrough	68–38	6	13	2
24/7/1970 (YE)	Y Sweden	Workington	75–32	5	8	3
25/7/1970 (YE)	Y Sweden	Berwick	54–54	1	0	0
27/7/1970 (YE)	Y Sweden	Reading	69–39	5	8	3
30/7/1970 (YE)	Y Sweden	Ipswich	71–37	6	12	3
6/8/1970 (YE)	Y Czechoslovakia	Romford	56–52	6	14	1
12/8/1970 (YE)	Y Czechoslovakia	King's Lynn	66–42	6	8	2
15/8/1970 (YE)	Y Czechoslovakia	Rayleigh	49–59	6	9	1
17/8/1970 (YE)	Y Czechoslovakia	Reading	53–55	5	12	0
27/8/1970 (YB)	Y Australasia	Middlesbrough	64–44	6	16	0
31/8/1970 (YB)	Y Australasia	Crewe	55–53	6	9	2
20/9/1970 (YB)	Y Australasia	Eastbourne	74–34	6	11	3

16 matches: Won: 11, Draw: 1, Lost: 4.
81 rides, 150 points, 25 bonus points

England and Great Britain

Date	Opposition	Venue	Result	Rides	Points	Bonus
20/7/1972	New Zealand	Wimbledon (IC)	51–26	3	6	0
14/9/1973 (a)	Scotland Select	Coatbridge	51–57	6	14	0
15/6/1974	Sweden	King's Lynn	71–37	6	15	1
19/6/1974	Sweden	Poole	66–42	6	13	1
21/6/1974	Sweden	Hackney	73–35	6	15	1
22/6/1974	Sweden	Coventry	71–37	6	15	2
12/7/1974	Poland	Hackney	88–19 (P Max)	6	14	4
14/7/1974	Poland	King's Lynn	78–30	6	9	2
15/7/1974	Poland	Exeter	73–35	6	11	3
17/7/1974	Poland	Hull	69–39	6	12	1
18/7/1974	Poland	Ipswich	78–30 (F Max)	6	18	0
20/7/1974	Poland	Halifax	65–42	5	7	2
23/7/1974	Poland	Leicester	76–32	6	9	6
27/7/1974	USSR	Swindon	66–41	6	16	0
9/8/1974	USSR	Newport (Ab)	17–19	2	3	1
7/6/1975	Poland	Bydgoszcz	37–71	6	8	0
8/6/1975	Poland	Gorzow	58–50	6	15	0
2/7/1975	Sweden	Poole	77–29	6	13	2
8/7/1975	Sweden	Leicester	66–42	6	10	2
11/7/1975	Sweden	Hackney	62–46	6	16	1
14/7/1975	Sweden	King's Lynn	70–38	6	14	0
15/7/1975	Sweden	Belle Vue	79–29	6	12	5
21/7/1975	Sweden (IT)	Sheffield	54–24	4	10	1
22/7/1975	Australia (IT)	Leicester	50–28	4	7	2
23/7/1975	Rest of World (IT)	Hull	41–37	4	6	2
2/10/1975	Rest of World (IT)	Ipswich	63–45	6	9	1
25/7/1976	Rest of World	Vojens	41–43	4	4	1
11/5/1977	Rest of World	White City	63–45	5	10	0
12/5/1977	Rest of World	Ipswich	51–57	6	14	0
21/5/1977	Rest of World	Coventry	48–59	6	10	3
23/5/1977	Rest of World	Reading	46–62	4	0	0
24/5/1977	Rest of World	Hull	55–53	4	8	0
10/8/1978	Australasia	Ipswich	51–57	2	0	0
18/8/1978	Australasia	Hackney	56–52	6	10	0
18/5/1979	Denmark	Vojens	37–40	2	0	0
12/7/1979	Australasia	Wimbledon	61–47	6	12	0
27/7/1979	Australasia	Swindon	67–41	6	15	1
2/8/1979	Australasia	Ipswich	60–48	6	11	1
22/8/1979	Australasia	Cradley H	72–36	6	16	1
3/5/1980	USA	Cradley H	62–46	6	17	0
14/5/1980	USA	Poole	44–63	6	13	1
24/5/1980	USA	Swindon	49–59	6	12	1
26/4/1981	USA	Belle Vue	60–48 (capt)	5	12	2
29/4/1981	USA	Poole	55–53 (capt)	5	11	1
2/5/1981	USA	Swindon	64–43 (capt)	6	13	1

Date	Opponent	Venue	Score			
7/5/1981	USA	Ipswich	44–52 (aban) (b) (capt)	5	11	0
10/5/1981	USA	Cradley H	69–38 (capt)	6	17	0
12/6/1981	Denmark	Hackney	62–46 (capt)	6	17	0
22/6/1981	Denmark	Reading	58–50 (capt)	6	12	3
26/6/1981	Denmark	Vojens	48–60	1	1	1
1/7/1981	Denmark	Coventry	46–62 (capt)	6	12	0
29/4/1982	USA	Wimbledon	63–45 (capt)	5	6	2
2/5/1982	USA	Swindon	47–60 (capt)	6	12	1
6/5/1982	USA	Ipswich	42–66 (capt)	6	8	0
9/5/1982	USA	Belle Vue	61–47 (capt)	3	2	2
19/5/1982	USA	Poole	39–69 (capt)	2	1	0
3/10/1982	USA, Denmark, Australasia	Eastbourne (4TT)	USA 46, Denmark 36, England 25 Australasia 1 (capt)	3	2	0
21/4/1983	USA	Wimbledon	43–64	5	4	0
24/4/1983	USA	Swindon	57–51	6	12	1
4/5/1983	USA	Poole	63–45	5	6	0
5/5/1983	USA	Ipswich	42–66	6	7	0
8/7/1983	Denmark	Hackney	65–43	6	10	2
12/9/1983	Rest of World, Denmark (3TT)	Cradley H	England 45, Rest of World 34, Denmark 29	4	4	1
14/9/1983	Rest of World, Denmark (3TT)	King's Lynn	Rest of World 39, Denmark 38, England 31	4	5	2
23/9/1983	Rest of World, Denmark (3TT)	Birmingham	Rest of World 41. England 37, Denmark 30	4	4	2
14/4/1984	USA	Swindon	50–58	6	12	1
29/4/1984	USA	Sheffield	58–50(capt)	6	10	1
5/5/1984	USA	Cradley H	49–59 (capt)	2	0	0
7/5/1984	USA	Ipswich	36–72 (capt)	4	3	1
4/6/1984	Denmark	Reading	54–54	6	11	1
7/6/1984	Denmark	Wimbledon	45–63	6	9	2
23/7/1985	Australasia	King's Lynn	71–37	6	15	0
5/9/1985	USA	Ipswich	50–58	6	12	2

69 matches: Won: 44, Draw: 1, Lost: 23, Abandoned: 1
1 Four team tournament: Third
3 Three team tournaments: Won: 1, Second: 1, Third: 1
376 rides, 710 points, 78 bonus points.

(a) England Select.
(b) Abandoned 16 heats result stood
IC: International Championship.
IT: International Tournament

England team manager

1998:
6 July	Wolverhampton	England 55 Australia 41
1 August	Eastbourne	England 56 Australia 40
2 August	King's Lynn	England 37 Australia 59

World Team Cup: England withdrew

1999:
11 June	Belle Vue	England 45 Australia 45
16 June	Hull	England 46 Australia 44
18 June	Oxford	England 60 Australia 30
18 September	Eastbourne	England 39 USA 51
18 October	Wolverhampton	England 48 USA 42

Third test at Ipswich versus USA was cancelled due to bad weather

World Team Cup
Semi-final: Poole 15 August Winner to final
England 53 Denmark 45 Germany 30 Hungary 16
Final: Pardubice, Czech Republic 2 October
Australia 51 Czech Republic 35 USA 29 England 29. USA won run-off for third place

2000:

World Team Cup
17 September Coventry
Sweden 40 England 40 USA 35 Australia 29. Sweden beat England in run-off for first place

Tests overall record:
Won: 5; Draw: 1; Lost: 2.

World Championship records

World Finals

Year	Venue	Points	Place
1974	Gothenburg	5	13th
1978	Wembley	11	4th
1979	Katowice	8	8th
1980	Gothenburg	12	2nd (after run-off)
1981	Wembley	7	8th
1982	Los Angeles	8	6th

Inter-Continental Finals

Year	Venue	Points	Place
1977	White City	7	9th
1979	White City	10	4th
1980	White City	9	7th
1981	Vojens	10	5th
1982	Vetlanda	8	7th

Commonwealth, Overseas and European Finals

Year	Venue	Points	Place
1974 (Euro)	Wembley	8	7th
1979 (Com)	White City	12	3rd
1980 (Com)	**Wimbledon**	**14**	**1st**
1981 (Over)	**White City**	**13**	**1st**
1982 (Over)	White City	13	1st
1984 (Over)	Belle Vue	3	14th

British-Nordic-American Final

Year	Venue	Points	Place
1974	Fredericia	10	6th

British Finals

Year	Venue	Points	Place
1972	Coventry	7	9th
1974	Coventry	11	3rd
1975	Coventry	6	9th
1976	Coventry	10	6th
1977	Coventry	13	2nd
1978	Coventry	12	2nd
1979	Coventry	12	3rd
1980	**Coventry**	**15 (Max)**	**1st**
1981	Coventry	9	6th
1982	Coventry	8	8th
1983	Coventry	6	10th
1984	Coventry	11	3rd
1985	Coventry	4	14th

13 British Finals: One win; two runner-up; two third place.

Major individual meetings

British League & National League Riders Championship

Year	Venue	Points	Place
1970 (Div 2)	**Hackney**	**14**	**1st**
1975	Belle Vue	8	9th
1976	Belle Vue	11	5th
1977	Belle Vue	5	11th
1978	Belle Vue	0	16th
1981	Belle Vue	9	5th
1982	Belle Vue	3	15th
1985	Belle Vue	3	13th
1986 (NL)	Coventry	4	13th
1987 (NL)	Coventry	8	8th

British Junior Championship

Year	Venue	Points	Place
1970	Swindon	14	2nd (run-off)
1971	Swindon	14	2nd

Internationale

Year	Venue	Points	Place
1974	Wimbledon	7	9th
1976	Wimbledon	11	3rd
1977	Wimbledon	9	5th
1978	Wimbledon	5	10th
1979	Wimbledon	4	14th
1980	**Wimbledon**	**15 (Max)**	**1st**
1981	Wimbledon	9	8th

Daily Express Spring Classic

Year	Venue	Points	Place
1974	Wimbledon	12	2nd (run-off)
1975	Wimbledon	8	8th
1976	**Wimbledon**	**13**	**1st**
1977	Wimbledon	13	3rd
1979	Wimbledon	11	3rd
1980	Wimbledon	12	2nd
1981	**Wimbledon**	**13**	**1st (joint with Ole Olsen)**

Wins in other major individual meetings

Year	Meeting	Venue	Points
1970	London Riders Championship (D2)	Romford	15 (Max)
1974	Midland Riders Championship	Coventry	14
1974	Laurels	Wimbledon	14
1974	Littlechild Trophy	King's Lynn	14
1975	London Riders Championship	Hackney	15 (Max)
1976	Yorkshire Television Trophy	Hull	15 (Max)
1976	Superama	Hackney	14
1976	Geoff Curtis Memorial Trophy	Reading	14
1976	Yorkshire Open	Sheffield	13
1977	Dews Trophy	Halifax	15 (Max)
1978	Bass Yorkshire Open	Sheffield	15 (Max)
1979	Traders' Trophy	Reading	15 (Max)
1979	Brandonapolis	Coventry	15 (Max)
1979	Duplex Litho Press Trophy	Swindon	14
1979	Pride of the East	King's Lynn	14
1980	Superama	Hackney	15 (Max)
1980	Littlechild Trophy	King's Lynn	15 (Max)
1980	Blue Riband	Poole	13
1980	Pride of the East	King's Lynn	15 (Max)
1981	Vic Harding memorial Trophy	Hackney	14
1983	WJ Cearns Memorial Shield	Wimbledon	10, won semi-final and final
1986	Champions Chase	Mildenhall	15 (Max)
1987	Central Riders Championship	Mildenhall	14

British club records

League, Knock Out Cup and League Cup meetings

Bold = ever present *Italic = top average in team* Maximums: F: Full P: Paid

Club trophies

Year	Team	Trophy
1970	Eastbourne	British League Division 2 runners-up
1972	Leicester	Midland Cup winners
1973	Leicester	Midland Cup runners-up
1974	Leicester	Midland Cup winners
1975	Leicester	Knock Out Cup runners-up
1977	Reading	Knock Out Cup runners-up
1977	Reading	Spring Gold Cup runners-up
1979	King's Lynn	Inter-League Knock Out Cup runners-up
1980	King's Lynn	Inter-League Knock Out Cup winners
1980	King's Lynn	Gauntlet Gold Cup winners
1983	Wimbledon	League Cup Semi-finalists
1983	Wimbledon	London Cup winners
1986	Mildenhall	Knock Out Cup runners-up
1987	Mildenhall	National League Best Pairs winners, National League Fours winners, Knock Out Cup runners-up, National League runners-up

Team averages League, Knock Out Cup and League Cup

Year	Team	Meetings	Rides	Points	Bonus	Average	Maximums
1969	**Eastbourne**	**31**	**136**	**201**	**24**	**6.62**	
	West Ham	3	12	4	1	1.67	
1970	*Eastbourne*	*30*	*123*	*285*	*12*	*9.66*	*5 F 2 P*
	Wembley	19	71	73.5	11	4.76	
1971	Wembley	28	120	202	21	7.43	
1972	Leicester	34	146	297	20	8.69	1 P
1973	Leicester	25	100	212	19	9.24	5 F 2 P
1974	*Leicester*	*32*	*142*	*336*	*7*	*9.66*	*6 F 1 P*
1975	*Leicester*	*38*	*166*	*431*	*1*	*10.41*	*14 F*
1976	**Reading**	**38**	**158**	**398**	**11**	**10.35**	**9 F 4 P**
1977	*Reading*	*45*	*193*	*489*	*9*	*10.32*	*21 F 3 P*
1978	*Reading*	*33*	*151*	*374*	*11*	*10.20*	*6 F 2 P*
1979	King's Lynn	33	137	325	8	9.72	8 F
1980	*King's Lynn*	*31*	*129*	*330*	*5*	*10.39*	*12 F 1 P*
1981	King's Lynn	44	216	496.5	20	9.57	9 F 2 P
1982	Wimbledon	35	141	297	12	8.77	3 F 1 P
1983	*Wimbledon*	*43*	*183*	*402*	*21*	*9.25*	*6 F 2 P*
1984	King's Lynn	50	200	342	29	7.42	2 F 1 P
1985	**King's Lynn**	**42**	**180**	**329**	**22**	**7.80**	

Year	Team						
1986	Mildenhall	44	193	509	7	10.69	16 F 3 P
1986	Swindon	3	12	15	2	5.67	
1987	Mildenhall	35	160	382	15	9.93	7 F 2 P
1988	Mildenhall	1	7	12	0	6.86	

Other team competitions averages

Year	Team	Competition	Meetings	Rides	Points	Bonus	Average	Maximums
1972	Leicester	Midland Cup	4	17	23	8	7.29	
1973	Leicester	Midland Cup	4	16	27	3	7.5	1 P
1974	Leicester	Midland Cup	4	17	43	2	10.59	1 F
1975	Leicester	Midland Cup	2	9	21	1	9.78	
1976	Reading	Spring Gold Cup	8	34	94	1	11.18	4 F 1 P
1977	Reading	Spring Gold Cup	7	33	92	0	11.15	2 F
1978	Reading	Spring Gold Cup	4	18	50	0	11.11	1 F
1979	King's Lynn	Gaunt Gold Cup	6	23	52	1	9.22	
1979	King's Lynn	Inter-League KO Cup	5	22	51	1	9.45	
1980	King's Lynn	Gaunt Gold Cup	6	25	70	1	11.36	3 F
1980	King's Lynn	Inter-League KO Cup	4	16	40	3	10.75	1 P
1983	Wimbledon	London Cup	2	8	17	1	9.00	

Longtrack

World Championship:

Semi-finals: 1977, 1978, 1979, 1981

Qualifying rounds: Won 1977 and 1979; third: 1978

Wimborne Whoppa: Won 1976

Lydden International: Second 1972 and 1974.

Bibliography

Books

Robert Bamford & Glynn Shailes *A History of the Speedway World Championship*, Tempus, 2002
Richard Bott & Ian Thomas *Speedway Grand Slam*, Studio Publications, 1981
Brian Burford *Kelly Moran – A Hell of a Life*, The History Press, 2014
Reg Fearman *Both sides of the fence,* The History Press, 2014
Chris Fenn & Barry Thomas *ThommoHawk – The Barry Thomas Story* Self-published, 2018
Peter Foster *A History of the Speedway Ashes*, Tempus, 2005
John Louis *A Life in Speedway*, Retro Speedway, 2015
Peter Lush & John Chaplin *When the Lions Roared*, London League Publications Ltd, 2016
Tony Macdonald *Michael Lee – Back from the Brink*, Retro Speedway 2010
Peter Oakes (Editor) *The complete history of the British League*, Front Page Books, 1991
Peter Oakes & Ivan Mauger MBE (Editors) *Who's Who of World Speedway*, Studio Publications, 1976
Martin Rogers *In my view*, Marlin Publications, 1988
Martin Rogers with Chris Hornby *Forty Years On*, Doonvilla, 2005
Len Silver *As Luck would have it*, Retro Speedway 2009
Malcolm Simmons with Tony McDonald *Simmo – The whole truth*, Retro Speedway 2006

Yearbooks

Speedway Yearbooks by Peter Oakes: 1978, 1979, 1980, 1981, 1982, 1986, 1990, 1991
The British Speedway Handbook 1969
Speedway Surveys Yearbook 1992 by Maurice Jones

Magazines

The Speedway Star 1969 to 2000
Backtrack (in particular issue 20)

Websites

Speedway Researcher
International Speedway
Speedway Archive
Grasstrack GB

THE JOHN SOMERVILLE
COLLECTION

The most extensive photographic history of speedway in the world
IS NOW AVAILABLE ONLINE AT

www.skidmarks1928.com

Browse and purchase iconic photos taken over many decades by the sport's best-known photographers, including Alf Weedon, Wright Wood, Mike Patrick, Trevor Meeks and many others.
From junior novices to world champions, portraits, action and team groups, etc, . . . there are thousands to evoke fond memories of days gone by.
All images on the website have been personally scanned by John himself from his base in Scotland. However, the quality of the original sources vary.

MY CRAZY SPEEDWAY WORLD

Bert HARKINS

"Here we are folks, after many months of being stuck to my computer keyboard, I finally finished my autobiography having bashed out every word, dot and comma along the way. It covers my early days growing up in Glasgow, to cycle speedway, road racing, speedway and life after I had hung up my white boots and tartan leathers. This is the story of a wandering Speedway Scotsman and I hope that you enjoy it."

Bert Harkins

Published in February 2018. Now available @ £16.95

Order direct from the publishers: London League Publications Ltd, for just £16.50 post free in the UK. Visit www.llpshop.co.uk for credit card orders or write to (cheques payable to London League Publications Ltd): PO Box 65784, London NW2 9NS. Also available on Amazon and Abe Books, and as an E-Book on Amazon for Kindle.
Or order from any bookshop. ISBN: 9781909885165. 252 pages with lots of photos.

Freddie Williams
DOUBLE WORLD SPEEDWAY CHAMPION

Peter Lush

Freddie Williams was the first British speedway rider to win the World Championship twice. He won the title at Wembley in 1950, aged just 24 and was the youngest ever World Champion at that time. He was in only his third season as a member of the Wembley Lions team. He was runner-up to Jack Young in 1952 before again winning the title in 1953.

His achievement was equalled by Peter Craven in 1962, but not surpassed until Tai Woffinden won his third title in 2018.

This authorised biography covers Freddie's life from his early days in Port Talbot, where he developed his skills riding grass track races. He signed for the Wembley Lions in 1946, and stayed with them for the rest of his career. He became a key member of the team that dominated the sport until 1954 and retired as a rider in 1956. With Wembley, he won the National League five times, the National Trophy twice and the London Cup five times. He rode for England 39 times.

He became manager of the Wembley Lions when the team returned to league racing in 1970 and 1971. He was President of the Veteran Speedway Riders Association in 1981, and became a member of the Welsh Sports Hall of Fame in 1998. He presented the trophies at the Speedway Grand Prix in Cardiff in August 2012 and did much else to support the sport. He died in January 2013 at the age of 86. The book also covers the sporting careers of his brothers Eric and Ian Williams, who were both distinguished speedway riders in their own right, and of Freddie's wife Pat, their children and grandchildren. A book that every speedway fan will enjoy!

Published in March 2019 @ £13.95. ISBN: 9781909885219
160 page paperback illustrated with over 100 photos.
Order direct from the publishers: London League Publications Ltd, for just £13.50 post free in the UK. Visit www.llpshop.co.uk for credit card orders or write to (cheques payable to London League Publications Ltd): PO Box 65784, London NW2 9NS. Also available on Amazon and Abe Books, and as an E-Book on Amazon for Kindle.

From 1929 to 1956, the Wembley Lions were the glamour team in British speedway. They won 10 League Championships, the National Trophy four times and the London Cup on nine occasions. Three Wembley riders won the World Championship: **Lionel Van Praag, Tommy Price and Freddie Williams.**

Part one looks at the Lions' fortunes from 1929 to 1939, when the team was launched by Sir Arthur Elvin and managed by the legendary Johnnie Hoskins and then Alec Jackson. From attendances of a couple of thousand, Wembley's support grew with crowds of 60,000 flocking to the Empire Stadium. This section is written by renowned speedway historian John Chaplin, who also recalls the exploits of Fay Taylour and other female riders and the story of the real Wembley Lions.

Part two looks at the 1946 to 1956 season-by-season. Huge crowds came to the Empire Stadium to see the Lions, who dominated the sport for nine years. Packed stadiums watched their away meetings.

But early in 1957, following the sudden death of Sir Arthur Elvin, Wembley Stadium's Chairman and Managing Director, and a great supporter of the sport, the Lions withdrew from British speedway. The book considers why speedway declined from the early 1950s, and the difficulties that Wembley had faced in making the sport viable in their huge stadium.

The third part of the book recalls the Lions' return to Wembley in 1970 for a two year spell under the direction of Trevor Redmond and Bernard Cottrell. Over 20,000 people came to their first home meeting. But the growth of football meant that the stadium was not available for a full league season in 1972, and the Lions withdrew from the league, never to return. The book includes a wide range of photos, profiles of the riders who rode for the Lions and comprehensive statistical records. With a foreword by former Wembley captain Bert Harkins, this is a book for every speedway fan.

Published in 2016 @ £14.95.

Order direct from the publishers: London League Publications Ltd, for just £14.50 post free in the UK. Visit www.llpshop.co.uk for credit card orders or write to (cheques payable to London League Publications Ltd): PO Box 65784, London NW2 9NS. Also available on Amazon and Abe Books, and as an E-Book on Amazon for Kindle.
264 page paperback. ISBN: 9781909885110

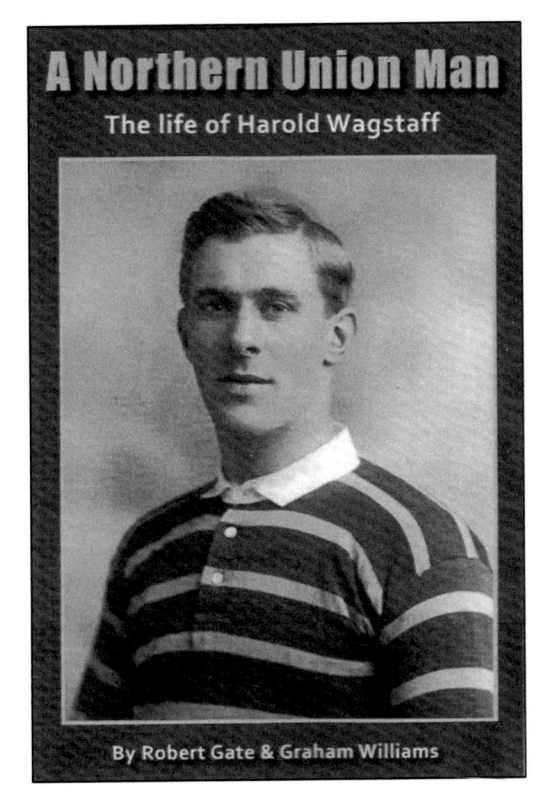

A Northern Union Man
The life of Harold Wagstaff
By Robert Gate & Graham Williams

Harold Wagstaff, known as the 'Prince of Centres', was one of the key players in the development of rugby league in the early twentieth century.

He made his debut for the Huddersfield first team in November 1906, at the age of 15, having previously played for Underbank. He joined the professional game at an important time for the sport. The number of players had been reduced to 13, and other rule changes made, including the introduction of play-the-ball after a tackle. This made Northern Union rugby a more open game, and Wagstaff and the Huddersfield team took full advantage of the changes.

He played for Yorkshire in 1908, and in January 1909 made his Great Britain debut against Australia, the first player aged under 18 to play for his country. He was made captain of Huddersfield in 1911, and under his direction the club won the Challenge Cup three times, the Northern Rugby League Championship three times, the Yorkshire League six times and the Yorkshire Cup five times. They won 'All Four Cups' in 1914–15, and were known as the 'Team of all the Talents'.

For Great Britain, Wagstaff captained the 1914 and 1920 Lions tours to Australia and New Zealand. This included the 1914 'Rorke's Drift' test, when a Great Britain team reduced to 10 men through injuries hung on to beat the Australians and win the Ashes.

However, it was not just his success that made him one of the sport's greatest players. It was the way he played the game, seeing the sport as a passing and handling game, rarely kicking the ball. He was made a founder member of the Rugby League Hall of Fame in 1988. This book, as well as contributions from the two authors, includes an autobiographical newspaper series that Wagstaff wrote in the 1930s, excerpts from an autobiographical series published in 1921 and contributions from other rugby league writers, including Tony Collins and Harry Edgar. It is a book that every rugby league and sports fan will enjoy.

Published in July 2019 @ £12.95. 170 page paperback. ISBN: 9781909885226

Order direct from the publishers: London League Publications Ltd, for just £12.50 post free in the UK. Visit www.llpshop.co.uk for credit card orders or write to (cheques payable to London League Publications Ltd): PO Box 65784, London NW2 9NS. Also available on Amazon and Abe Books, and as an E-Book on Amazon for Kindle.

For books on speedway, rugby league, football and other sports, visit www.llpshop.co.uk

All our books are available on Amazon and Abe Books and most are available as E-Books for Kindle.

Speedway fans: Look out for our forthcoming biography of Split Waterman. Due to be published in February 2021.